LEISURE TIME EDUCATION

LEISURE TIME

EDUCATION

A HANDBOOK OF CREATIVE
ACTIVITIES FOR TEACHERS
AND GROUP LEADERS

By ANNA MAY JONES

Educational and Vocational Counselor
New York City Public Schools

HARPER & BROTHERS

NEW YORK AND LONDON

LEISURE TIME EDUCATION

*To the many boys and girls who inspired
this handbook that others may learn to
select, pursue and enjoy worthy activities.*

❦ *Contents* ❧

Contents

~ *Preface* ~

This book was written because it seemed a natural result of years of service to boys and girls who needed assistance in the selection, pursuit, and enjoyment of their leisure time activities. The author wanted to pass on to others interested in youth some practical methods and materials that were found useful and that might help teachers and group leaders. There is a need for a handbook of this kind, according to the National Education Association and other major educational sources and libraries consulted.

The author first realized the need for leisure time education when working with boys and girls in East Side schools in New York in 1930 and 1931. Too many students were unaware of leisure time opportunities but they responded heartily to the schools' efforts to help them find and develop hobbies and talents. By 1939 the students in these schools seemed to be much more aware of what opportunities their neighborhood offered. After 1940 there was incorporated in group guidance programs for these schools a series of discussion lessons. These lessons were later distributed to all junior high schools in New York by the Department of Vocational and Educational Guidance of that city.

Included in this book are the findings of studies and demonstrations made in six junior high schools and one vocational high school in New York. The detailed reports and statistics are available. Illustrative stories are of real boys and girls whose names have been changed. Frequent references are also made to phases of leisure time education in many other sections of the country. These phases were reported by teachers, counselors, principals, and superintendents, in questionnaires which are on file. Treatises on phases of leisure time education programs particularly in connection with schools have been widely consulted. Any suggestions of outstanding efforts in leisure time education will be appreciated and used in the future revision of this book.

A few essential methods are discussed with teachers and group leaders who are interested in promoting leisure time opportunities. Some of the methods include:

Showing the avocational values of the curriculum
Discussing and demonstrating hobbies and talents
Presenting the afterschool program of activities
Co-ordinating school activities with outside activities
Guiding individuals into worthy use of leisure
Upholding high leadership standards for youth

Youth need specific information about community activities. They like information on what to do and where to go, summer activities, leisure time reading, radio programs and movies recommended, church activities, and what the afterschool program offers. Simple ways of procuring this information are here suggested.

A classified bibliography in the back of the book suggests references to meet individual needs and interests. It is arranged for quick reference by teachers, leaders, and youth. Many of the references are free or obtainable at small cost. Further sources of information are also indicated.

This book is designed for individual guidance as well as for groups. Perhaps only one interview is all that a student needs. Or a case study may be required, the student's interests may need to be looked into carefully, the parent may have to be sent for. One chapter shows how some schools work with these cases.

Chapter VII was written for the principal, group leader, or other administrators who may be organizing or training for leisure time education functions. It is the administrator who can select a liaison person to co-ordinate the leisure time education functions in the school and who can pass on to his staff a vital interest in the functions. With interest in the procedures teachers express the spark that kindles in the student satisfaction and joy that come from finding something he likes to do. Unless that interest is kindled the procedures will be merely academic or clerical with no benefit to the student.

The simple phases of leisure time education do not require an increase in the school staff or a change in the curriculum. Whatever may be the present setup in any school, the simple phases of leisure time education discussions, assemblies, and interviews can enrich that curriculum without additional personnel.

Teachers will have a much better time teaching students who like to do things, make things, go places, acquire new skills, pursue hobbies, display their interests, and develop their talents.

If this book helps teachers and group leaders to guide boys and girls in the selection, pursuit, and enjoyment of worthy leisure time activities, it will serve its full purpose.

A. M. J.

New York City
February 1, 1946

ᴄᴡᴀ Acknowledgments ᴀᴡᴄ

Acknowledgment is given the principals and teachers of these schools for the co-operation and encouragement given this study during the time the author worked there: Junior High Schools 43, 52, 81, 83, 159, 172, and former 184, and the Metropolitan Vocational High School, New York. Principals, teachers, and co-counselors contributed much in inspiration and encouragement toward helping students select, pursue and enjoy their leisure, long before a book was even thought of. Franklin J. Keller, Mary A. Hallinan, David Goldwasser, Anna E. Lawson, Abraham Wiener, Joseph O. Loretan, Leonard Covello, Morris Lapman, Elizabeth Wallace, and other school executives encouraged many phases of this leisure time education program in their schools.

Appreciation is expressed to Assistant Superintendents Rufus M. Hartill and Ellen A. G. Phillips[1] in whose districts many phases of leisure time education described here were tried out. They encouraged various district conferences and distributed findings of the study to their schools and community, from time to time. Others who gave helpful advice and encouragement are: Assistant Superintendents Mary A. Kennedy, Jacob Theobald, Benjamin Greenberg, Morris E. Siegel, Benjamin Veit,[1] and Associate Superintendents Elias Lieberman, Regina Burke, George Piggott, and Frank J. O'Brien.

Other leaders who by their knowledge of the author's work and of this manuscript have encouraged its publication are: Warren W. Knox, George E. Hutcherson, William G. Carr, John M. Brewer, George N. Shuster, and Frederic M. Thrasher. James E. Rogers and Weaver Pangburn of the National Recreation Association followed the study for ten years. Acknowledgment is extended to them and their office assistants for help in compiling and checking the bibliography and availing the author of the use of their extensive library on many occasions.

[1] Retired.

Rufus M. Hartill, Llewellyn C. Jones, Charles E. O'Toole and Charles M. Smith, reviewed at least parts of the manuscript in its various stages and offered valuable suggestions from their diverse expert viewpoints. Helen Carpenter of the Library Bureau assisted with the list of magazines for boys and girls. Elbert K. Fretwell and H. W. Hurt of the Boy Scouts of America gave suggestions which helped to direct the study.

Acknowledgment is also extended to Rho Chapter, Pi Lambda Theta, of New York University, for permission to use excerpts from articles in the *Rho Journal*, March, 1944. The public libraries of New York, Chicago, and Madison, Wisconsin, rendered outstanding helpful service in their reference and cataloguing rooms. The generous and enthusiastic permission given by many publishers for the use of excerpts is also gratefully acknowledged.

The following are a few organizations that co-operated through their sincere and unselfish efforts, or offered valuable ideas for the progress of the manuscript.

Association of Vocational and Educational Guidance
Boy Scouts of America
Boys Club Federation
Catholic Youth Organization
Children's Aid Society
East Harlem Council of Social Planning
Federation of Churches
Heckscher Foundation
Manhattan Council of Girl Scouts
Metropolitan Museum of Art
National Urban League
National Vocational Guidance Association
New York City Mission Society
New York Public Library
Russell Sage Foundation
United Neighborhood Houses
Welfare Council of New York City
West Harlem Council of Social Planning
Y.M.C.A., Y.W.C.A., Y.M.H.A., Y.W.H.A.

Acknowledgment is also given educators who furnished materials on efforts made in many schools throughout the country.

LEISURE TIME EDUCATION

Chapter 1

OUTLINES FOR DISCUSSION
AND PARTICIPATION IN ACTIVITIES

"To enjoy leisure is to enjoy freedom. . . .
We can no more afford to follow loose thinking in the sphere of leisure than in the sphere
of economics."

EDUARD C. LINDEMAN

THE main objective of a leisure time education plan is to habituate youth to the worthy use of their leisure. The discovery of students' special interests and the development of skills and attitudes for the enjoyment of their leisure hours are important steps toward that end. Another essential step is that of revealing opportunities for self-realization in the school and community. Adequate information about such opportunities aids in the selection and development of hobbies and talents suitable and appealing to each individual.

It is not the purpose of this book to direct the choices of youth but to develop self-direction through varied opportunities. Neither is it intended that there should be a sharp distinction between education for leisure and education for other purposes. Both are inter-related. Many teachers are so interested in the welfare of their students that they constantly help them solve their leisure time problems. This book may serve teachers and group leaders as a source of additional methods to supplement their present ones. Some organized efforts are needed if the school aims *to help students select, pursue, and enjoy their leisure*, and especially to help those individuals who do not get this training in the home.

At the present time some schools are making specific efforts in leisure time education through the curriculum. The harvest is ripe for those schools especially interested in the opportunity that leisure time education offers. This viewpoint is emphasized in Rogers' book in which he quotes Colonel Henry Breckenridge as follows:

> A vast amount is being done. A vast amount remains undone. The large task remaining is not a reason for pessimism. It is a challenge for action. The call is for a program that will guide the child into the abundant physical life of virility, courage, independence, self-reliance, initiative, the spirit of co-operation, fairness, loyalty, modesty, cheerfulness, chivalry and good citizenship.[1]

Those who feel this vital interest can help to make much more meaningful in the school curriculum one of the cardinal objectives of education: worthy use of leisure.

As schools instruct and guide boys and girls so that they will distinguish between the enjoyments that enrich and enlarge their lives and those that degrade and dissipate creative energies, and as the schools train in creative activities, so will youth develop more of their inner resources, aptitudes, interests, and enjoyment of life. Boredom is not likely to come to the discriminating student who has developed skills and a variety of hobbies.

It is apparent that the school has an unusual opportunity today to help students develop their interests and hobbies and to promote the use of the increasing community leisure time opportunities for youth. The community has much to offer youth if the school and individual agencies for leisure time activities work closely together. Youth's worthy activities can be praised more by the school and the community, and unworthy activities can gradually be replaced with those that develop youth.

By the emphasis of some of the functions described in the following pages students should develop more self-realization. The teacher who adapts and presents such ideas as are set forth here makes the ideas dynamic and vital. Ideas that are really sound, really dynamic, and really vital continue to live as guiding principles in the face of personal defeats. Students thus strengthen their guiding principles. They learn to rise above discouragement and to enjoy wholesome activities now and in adult life.

[1] James Edward Rogers, *The Child and Play*; based on reports of the White House conference on child health and protection, p. 189.

Subject teachers will find concrete suggestions for ready use in the outlines which correlate with subjects, home room, group guidance, the library, assemblies, shops, school clubs and activities.

What Is the Purpose?

The purpose of these outlines is to suggest ideas for discussion and participation in activities so that students may select, pursue, and enjoy worth-while activities, and develop some essential and interesting skills. Through these discussions may develop a spirit which to some extent will pervade hours of duties and give constant enjoyment in the little events of life.

John M. Brewer stressed leisure time education as follows:

> Mere exposure to high ideals for leisure is no longer to be relied upon; how then shall we make the thinking of students more effective for forming good habits? Obviously, by classroom discussion and individual counsel, in both of which we study the thinking of the student, and then observe him in his free time.[2]

What the student actually does in his free time is the test of the effectiveness of class discussions on the use of leisure time. Some of the questions for determining the degree to which the class discussions have helped students to improve their use of leisure are:

Has the student
   developed any of his interests and capabilities?
   developed an interest in a variety of activities to avoid boredom and to enjoy leisure?
   developed an interest in new activities?
   improved his selection of leisure time centers?
   acquired more skill in some worthy activity?
   improved and increased his experiences in his use of leisure?
   improved his selection of friends?
   improved his health?
   developed a sensible schedule of activities without overdoing them?
   cultivated rest, repose, and reflection which are as necessary as active play?

Although the suggestions that follow are not new, they may indicate where teachers and group leaders may need to place

---

[2] Brewer, *Education as Guidance*, p. 395.

more emphasis in order to help youth select, pursue and enjoy worthy activities.

Introduction to Leisure Time Education
Show students how to use their leisure healthfully, safely, and enjoyably.
Provide experience in pleasant social environment through school activities and clubs in which students may be intensely and profitably interested.
Make the school the center for creative and satisfying activities after 3 P.M.
Help students to develop interests, hobbies, special abilities and talents for the enjoyment of their free time.
Assist students of similar aptitudes to work together on projects outside of school.

Kinds of Leisure Time Activities
Introduce students to the wide range of leisure time interests: physical, social, cultural, intellectual.

Leisure Time Opportunities in the Community
Acquaint students with interesting places to go for worth-while activities.
Develop in youth the ability to recognize and demand good leadership in their activities.
Try to instill in them the desire to improve their community through their leisure time pursuits.

Hobbies
Encourage students to cultivate hobbies they can enjoy alone and hobbies they can enjoy with others.
Promote the following:
Familiarity with the best books and special magazines along the lines of students' interests; the study of biographies of famous men and women and their tastes and hobbies.
The use of the local public library for the development of wholesome reading appetites.
Appreciation of fine music and art; and skill in instrumental music, dancing, singing, and art.
Love of the outdoors; appreciation of flowers, landscape, sky and stars, animals, and birds.
Interest in creative art, collections, and making things.

Self-Improvement and Getting Along with Others
Develop sportsmanship, courage, personal habits, and social assets.

Encourage participation in games, sports, and hobbies which may be continued in later years.

Develop appreciations of lasting satisfactions in contrast to temporary diversions and unworthy activities.

Develop good health habits.

Planning the Use of Leisure

Help students to select and pursue worth-while and enjoyable leisure time activities.

Inspire students to so plan for leisure time activities that their activities may carry over and enrich their adult life.

Through such a plan as outlined above there can be leisure time education for health, home life, social living, citizenship, personality growth, and cultural enrichment.

Is the Approach Appealing?

The teacher's interest combined with individualized instruction help greatly toward successful discussions and the participation of all. Lecturing, on the other hand, is difficult to use successfully in the classroom.

The most vital approach to these discussions is through students' own leisure time interests and experiences like the following:

Favorite hobby
Membership in leisure time agencies
Favorite radio programs, motion pictures, books
Time devoted to radio, motion pictures, reading
Interesting sights seen, trips taken
Display of hobbies
Demonstration of a hobby or interest
Opportunities in local leisure time centers

Discussions should relate to life in the community: how to make use of community opportunities, and how to improve the community through creative living.

Students express their interests more freely when the teacher's attitude is without suggestion of "must," as these lines suggest:

In a cheerful room, eager children, busy, with an air of freedom, some whispering, but no disorder. Smiles come easily. Teachers cheerful, eager, informal, whose smiles also come easily.[3]

[3] *Education for the Recreational Use of Leisure through the Daily School Program,* National Recreational Assn., Bulletin 712, April, 1939.

Do the Students Participate?

Brewer encourages students' participation with these concrete suggestions:

> Suppose our class starts with a discussion of the value of leisure time, followed by a comprehensive study of available opportunities. All the common kinds of activities will be listed, set forth before the class, and their characteristics and relative values for various purposes discussed. Here courageous teaching is required, for the pupils will bring into the schoolroom actual newspapers, magazines, scenarios, and the like, and should be allowed freely to defend their own interests in the use of spare time, often of doubtful value. The questioning by the teacher and the interchange of opinions by the pupils should be so searching that evil practices and silly, harmful attempts at recreation cannot stand up against the criticism they receive. Of course the negative approach should not be common, and should never be the end, but cooperative negation—condemnation of evil by the group—should be encouraged when needed. The positive exposition should include descriptions of libraries, museums, concerts, lectures, crafts, nature, and other good things of leisure time. Some day it will be thought worth while to write textbooks to help teachers explain these things.[4]

Here are a few specific methods which may be helpful in leisure time education:

Pupil leadership in class discussions, with teacher guiding
Stimulation of pupil participation in all discussions
Individualized instruction
Pupil leadership for class pursuits
Projects for developing avocational skills: scrapbooks, exhibits, crafts, art illustrations
Demonstrations
Exhibit of hobbies, talents, interests: handwork, inventions, music, arts
Investigations of leisure time agencies
Visits
Committees for
    Surveys
    Visits
    Library investigations
    Exhibits
    Demonstrations
    Collections
    Assembly programs
    Other arrangements

[4] *Op. cit.*, p. 397.

Interviews with persons who have leisure time information
Reports of sightseeing observations, investigations
Use of a bibliography or other references
Home activities
Formation of hobby clubs to meet in homes under supervision of a parent
  capable of leading a group

The teacher's praise always improves participation in discussions, displays, committee work, or other efforts in the leisure time program. Many students who get no praise at home appreciate the teacher's kind praise even if it is no more than, "That's a good start. Now see if you can do a little better next time." Some students become so enthusiastic in discussing their interests that it may be necessary to guard against overstimulation sometimes.

Sample Outlines

Some of these topics may be unnecessary for certain situations, and additional suggestions will be necessary to meet other needs. The general succession in which the outlines are presented is recommended. For instance, in a junior high school the first ten could be generally adapted to the seventh grade, the next ten to the eighth, and the rest to the ninth grade.

The time to be allotted to any of these outlines may vary from one to four sessions according to students' leisure time problems and interests.

It is not expected that this outline will be followed precisely. Teachers and leaders will have questions, illustrations, and cases more interesting and valuable to the group at hand than some of the suggestions here. However, it is recommended that these broad subjects be considered:

Introduction to Leisure Time Education
Kinds of Leisure Time Activities
Leisure Time Opportunities in the Community
Hobbies
Self-improvement and Getting Along with Others
Plans for the Use of Leisure

These broad subjects are developed in detailed outlines under the 44 following topics:

Outlines for Group Discussions on Leisure Time

INTRODUCTION TO LEISURE TIME EDUCATION

1. Significance of Leisure
2. The Leisure Time Value of School Subjects
3. Hobbies and School Clubs
4. Display of Hobby Activities
5. Safety in Play

KINDS OF LEISURE TIME ACTIVITIES

6. Sports
7. Social Activities
8. Passive Activities
9. Dramatics, Radio, Motion Pictures
10. Enjoyment of Home Activities
11. Travel
12. Reports on Leisure Time Literature
13. How to Select Leisure Time Activities

LEISURE TIME OPPORTUNITIES IN THE COMMUNITY

14. Extracurricular Activities and Leisure Time Agencies
15. Municipal Opportunities for Leisure Time
16. Scouting
17. The Importance of Good Leadership
18. Improving the Community through Our Leisure
19. Planning Summer Activities
20. Sightseeing Opportunities
21. Museums and Art Galleries
22. The Use of Leisure in Other Lands

HOBBIES

23. Collections
24. Pets
25. Nature
26. Making Things (Including Crafts and Shopwork)
27. Kinds of Art (Including Photography)
28. Fine Arts
29. Music Appreciation
30. Reading—Magazines and Newspapers
31. Reading—Books and Libraries
32. Assembly Program on Hobbies

SELF-IMPROVEMENT AND GETTING ALONG WITH OTHERS

33. Sportsmanship in Our Leisure Time Activities
34. Personal Habits Worth Developing in Our Leisure
35. The Art of Conversation as a Leisure Time Asset
36. Cultural Habits Worth Developing in Our Leisure
37. Friendship—Its Relation to Enjoyment of Leisure
38. The Relation of Avocations to Vocations

PLANNING THE USE OF LEISURE

39. Planning Time for Study
40. Planning Time for Various Activities
41. Leisure Time Activities for a Well-rounded Life
42. My Leisure Time Activities
43. Shorter Working Days and Leisure
44. The Carry-over of Our Leisure Time Interests into Life

SERIES ON INTRODUCTION TO LEISURE TIME EDUCATION
Outlines 1-5

Outline 1

Significance of Leisure

How one chooses to use his leisure is at least as important as
how one earns a living.

Aim: To show students how leisure is increasing and to encourage discussion
on interesting ways of using leisure.

Suggestions for students' discussion:

1. What is the meaning of leisure? Discuss:
    Time free from work, study, and responsibility.
    Time in which there may be recreation, self-improvement, services
    to others and to the community.
2. Why is there increasing interest in the United States in the use of
    leisure?
3. Discuss the increase in machinery in relation to leisure.
    (If the joy of creation cannot be found in work it can be found in
    leisure activities.)
4. What is meant by the increase of leisure in the United States?
    Have working days become longer or shorter in the past 50 years?
    Weavers in 1844 worked 84 hours a week. Shoemakers in 1855
    worked 72 hours a week.
    Farmers used to labor from sunup to sundown. The result was
    great physical fatigue. Between 1890 and 1913 the average work-

ing hours per week were shortened from 58 to 53. By 1926 the standard hours of work in manufacturing industries came down to 50 a week, as a rule. Today, many plants operate only five days a week or a total of about 40 hours, except for government emergencies.

5. What are some of the values of leisure time activities? Discuss:
New interests which give joy, happiness, health.
Outlet for creative abilities.
Relief from monotony and boredom.
A chance to refresh one for study and work.
Development of talents.
Expression of the imagination and skills.
Development of self-sufficiency.
Sense of satisfaction through self-realization.
Development of interests which may lead to vocations.

6. Discuss the meaning of:
A hobby acts as an outlet for pent-up energies and a diversion from the routine of daily tasks.

7. What meaning do you find in the following statements?
To build a playground is to destroy a jail.
To provide a swimming pool is to empty a hospital.
To open a park is to close an asylum.

Suggested activities:

Ask your grandparents how many hours a day they worked when they were young. Compare with the present normal working hours in the same kind of work to see the increase in leisure time of workers.

Visit some industry to discover how machines save labor and time, and report your findings to your class.

Gather a few points on the topic, "Why students should learn in school how to use their leisure time." Discuss these points in class.

Reference:

Community Life; A suggested Unit Organization for the Seventh Grade Program in Social Studies. Bulletin III-7, Division of Secondary Education, New York State Dept. of Education, Albany, N. Y., October 15, 1941.

Outline 2

The Leisure Time Value of School Subjects

"And this our life exempt from public haunt
Finds tongues in trees, books in running brooks,
Sermons in stones and good in everything."
—From *As You Like It*, by SHAKESPEARE

Outlines for Discussion

Aim: To suggest leisure time use of school subjects.

Suggestions for students' discussion:

1. Leisure time value of school subjects

   What are some of the school subjects that lead to the enjoyment of leisure? How?

   Which subjects give you an opportunity to develop skills that you can enjoy now and later?

   Which subjects help you to beautify the home?

   Name other leisure time values of school subjects.

2. Value of extracurricular activities

   What are extracurricular activities?

   (Extracurricular activities are those afterschool activities in which the students themselves assume responsibilities, make decisions, and direct activity, with teacher leadership.)

   Name the extracurricular activities in this school.

   Discuss: dramatics, orchestra, band, school newspaper, clubs, and athletics.

   What are some of the social values of our extracurricular activities?

   Discuss: new friends, wise use of leisure, school spirit, social adjustments.

Suggested activities:

Write briefly about how you are using any school subject or extracurricular activity in your spare time.

These brief reports may be discussed in the next session.

References:

George A. Boyce and Willard W. Beatty, *Mathematics of Everyday Life*; Leisure Unit, The Economics of Leisure Activities.

Archie Frederick Collins, *Inventing for Fun and Profit*.

Education for the Recreational Use of Leisure through the Daily School Program, National Recreation Assn., New York.

Good Reading, The National Council of Teachers of English, 211 W. 68th Street, Chicago.

Helen Halter, *Society in Action*.

J. R. Hildebrand, "The Geography of Games," *National Geographic Magazine*, August, 1919.

"Lively Games That Are Played All Over the World," *Compton's Pictured Encyclopedia*, pp. 247-50.

Laura K. Martin, *A Selected List of Magazines for High School Libraries*. Tennessee Book Co., Nashville, Tenn.

Bertha M. Parker, *Beyond the Solar System*.

Popular Science Magazine.

Radio News Magazine.

Outline 3

Hobbies and School Clubs

"The hours that make us happy, make us wise."
—JOHN MASEFIELD

Aim: To acquaint students with school clubs and to encourage hobbies through club participation.

Suggestions for students' discussion:

1. Why do we have clubs in this school?
   Why is it desirable to have many different clubs?
2. Which of our school clubs are for the following?
   Entertainment
   Development of skill: of hand, voice, body
   Development of special abilities: imagination, creative ability
   Improvement of knowledge and other purposes
3. How can the school help you to develop your hobby?
   What is your hobby?
   Do you have more than one hobby?
   Can you give an exhibition of your hobby some day?
   If you have no hobby do you wish the school to give you suggestions?

Suggested activities:

Write on a slip of paper your name and class,
   the school club which interests you most,
      (you may name from one to five if you wish)
   your hobby,
      then indicate whether you wish the school to give you suggestions about developing your hobbies.

References:
   Ernest Elmo Calkins, *Care and Feeding of Hobby Horses.*
   Ruth Lampland, *Hobbies for Everyone.*

Outline 4

Display of Hobby Activities

To make, to show, to tell.

Aim: To show students how school subjects may offer leisure time enjoyment.

Suggestions for students' discussion:

1. How has the school helped you to develop leisure time activities through clubs? through various school subjects?

2. What does the class think about displaying their hobbies which have been encouraged by the school clubs and school subjects?
3. How shall we prepare? Discuss committees of students for the following purposes:
> To list the kinds of activities and hobbies to be displayed by each member of the class
>
> To arrange ways of presenting the activities and hobbies
>
> To decide on an outline or on questions which displayers may follow in general in presenting their activity to the group
4. Questions suggested for discussion during the display are:
> How did you become interested in this activity?
>
> To what school subject is the activity related?
>
> Where one may go to learn more about this hobby or activity?
>
> What is one reading reference about this activity?
>
> How has this activity affected your attitude toward the school subject?
>
> Does the class wish to show the exhibits to other classes?

Further activities suggested:
> Other displays of home hobbies may be arranged.

Outline 5

Safety in Play

Each activity carries its own safety rules.

Aim: To teach students to observe safety rules in play and to understand the purpose of the rules.

Preparation: Reports may be prepared on safety rules of certain leisure time activities and the significance of the rules. Some students may wish to report on the references suggested at the end of this outline.

Suggestions for students' discussion:

1. What are some safety rules and their significance, pertaining to the following activities?
> Bicycling
>
> Motoring
>
> Playing in this community
>
> Experiments
>
> Hiking
> > (Carrying your own water
> >
> > First-aid equipment
> >
> > Dangers of hitchhiking)
>
> Making fires

Swimming
Woodworking and other shopwork
Playgrounds (safer than streets or empty buildings to play in)
Playing on the farm

2. What kind of accidents can be avoided in the home by observing rules of safety? Discuss safe work and play in the home.
3. Discuss the dangers of hitchhiking on autos, trucks, streetcars and trains.
4. In what play situation is it necessary to give attention to the care of the eyes?
5. Relate an experience in which you avoided an accident by following a rule of safety.

References:

Boy Scout Handbook, pp. 173-181.
Eleanor Boykin, *This Way, Please*, pp. 280-281.
The Center for Safety Education, New York University, New York, has helpful materials.
Thomas F. Dougherty and Paul W. Kearney, *Fire.*
Girl Scout Handbook, pp. 210, 232, 564, 610-637.
A. Jenkins, "Drive Right!" *Reader's Digest*, August, 1934.
Munro Leaf, *Safety Can Be Fun.*
The National Safety Council, 20 North Wacker Drive, Chicago, furnishes posters and lessons on safety at a small charge.
Travelers Insurance Company, Hartford, Conn., also sends materials.

SERIES ON KINDS OF LEISURE TIME ACTIVITIES
Outlines 6-13.

Outline 6

Sports

To enjoy is more important than
excelling in activities.

Aim: To introduce students to various kinds of active interests and games in which they may wish to engage.

Suggestions for students' discussion:

1. What kinds of active games, sports, and hobbies do boys and girls your age enjoy?
    (Note to teacher: Games and sports are the natural starting point for education in recreation.)
2. What are some of the benefits from athletics? Discuss:
    Bodily development: respiration, digestion, circulation aided
    Social development: rules of the game, co-operation with others, respect for ability of the team and opponents

Character development: fair play, self-control, good sportsmanship

3. Name some physical activities like running and jumping which are used in games. Discussion of lifting, throwing, climbing, swimming, reaching, kicking.

4. How may skill in any of these activities help you in dangerous situations?

5. Name some competitive activities.
   (athletics, baseball, basketball, bowling, checkers, football, group games, hockey, ping-pong, tennis)

6. What are some noncompetitive activities? Discuss:

* Camping	* Folk dancing	* Playground activities
* Clubs	Gardening	* Plays
Coasting	* Group singing	* Puppets
Crafts	* Hiking	Reading
* Day camping	Hobbies	Sightseeing
* Discussions	Nature study	Skating
* Dramatics	* Orchestras	* Social dancing
Experimenting	* Parties	Swimming
Exploring woods, fields, etc.	* Picnics	Trips and travel

7. Which of these noncompetitive activities are especially co-operative? (See those starred * for suggestions.)
   Discuss what is meant by co-operative activities.

8. Discuss this statement:
   More co-operative activities and less of the competitive ones are necessary in this country. Competitive activities have been carried somewhat to excess.

9. Is it best to specialize highly in one activity? Discuss.

10. How do co-operative activities help you socially?
    Show the social value of planning a picnic, for instance.
    May competitive activities be co-operative also? Illustrate.

11. How can competitive games between schools develop school spirit instead of mob spirit?

12. Discuss the comparative value of "excellence" and "enjoyment in activities."

13. Tell about the contests of various kinds in which you have participated: city-wide, department store, magazine, newspaper, radio, school, and other contests.

14. To avoid boresomeness a person should play outdoor and indoor games. Name those you play, or those you plan to learn soon.

References:

J. J. Boniface, *Riding.*
Capt. Paul A. Curtis, *Guns and Gunning.*

Roland C. Geist, *Bicycling as a Hobby*.
Frank Graham, *McGraw of the Giants*.
Sonja Henie, *Wings on My Feet*.
Jennie Holliman, *American Sports, 1785-1835*.
B. S. Mason and E. D. Mitchell, *Active Games and Contests*.
Outdoors Indoors, National Recreation Assn., New York.
Friedl Pfeifer, ed., *The Sun Valley Ski Book*.
John R. Tunis, *Sports for the Fun of It*.

Outline 7

Social Activities

"He that will make a good use of any part of his life, must allow a large portion of it to recreation."

—Locke

Aim: To show students that social activities are as beneficial to the individual as solitary activities.

Suggestions for students' discussion:

1. What is meant by a social activity? Discuss:

Checkers	Folk dancing	Shuffleboard
Chess	Letter-writing	Social games
Clubs	Parlor games	Stunts
Dancing	Parties	Visiting
Entertaining	Picnics	

2. In what ways are school teams and athletics social?
   Are competitive sports between schools a good thing?
   What is the difference between developing school spirit and mob spirit toward competitive activities?
3. How are preparing and presenting a play social activities?
4. How does a Scout jamboree promote good feeling between groups and communities?
5. What are the benefits from learning to play together?
   Discuss: co-operation, understanding between boys and girls, and natural acquaintance between boys and girls.
6. Discuss enjoyment of mealtime as a social occasion and an opportunity for comradeship. In the home eating should be something of an enjoyable ceremony and not a hurried chore.
7. Name games of a social nature which are becoming more popular. Discuss softball, badminton, and other games.
8. Geraldine told the class that she competes with herself in her hobbies. What did she mean? How do you compete with yourself?
9. Jack daydreams too much. He is not content to be alone.

How may he become a better companion to himself?
Why should Jack break his habit of daydreaming now?
How do you avoid getting into Jack's attitude of mind?

10. What is the value of good skill in dancing? Discuss: skill, grace, beauty, sociability, appreciation of good music.
11. Name some solitary activities which you can recommend to students your age.
12. What are some of the advantages of solitary activities? Discuss: independence, personal development, concentration.

Suggested activities:

Make a plan for the next week of the ways you intend to spend your leisure.
Keep a daily schedule of how you actually spend your time, every day next week.
Discuss and criticize the schedule in class after one week.

References:

Mary J. Breen, *For the Storyteller*.
L. Dudley, "Can You Entertain Yourself?" N. E. A. *Journal*, November, 1943.
Henry and Mrs. Ford, *Good Morning*.
An Index to Folk Dances and Singing Games, American Library Association, Chicago.
Joseph Leeming, *Magic for Everybody*.
Parties A to Z, National Recreation Association.
Teen Parties, Woman's Home Companion Service Bureau, New York.
Blanche Wheeler, *Party Plans*.
Lee Wulff, *Let's Go Fishing*.

Outline 8

Passive Activities

Have you spectatoritis or sititis?

Aim: To help students to learn that passive enjoyment is important but that one needs to participate in some activities and not always merely look on.

Suggestions for students' discussion:

1. What do we mean by passive uses of leisure?
   Discuss: watching games, theater programs including motion pictures, concerts, circuses, listening to others, listening to the radio, looking at art and other collections, and other entertainment without much activity.

The following may be included in passive activities: reading, thinking, resting, sleeping, sitting on the porch or in the park.

2. What work of experts have you seen or heard recently which inspired you?

3. Why should a person participate in activities in addition to enjoying them passively?

Is there too much active use or too much passive use of leisure in America?

Which allows for more self-expression, the active or passive activities? Are both necessary?

What do you think is meant by "spectatoritis" and "sititis"?

4. Give the meaning of these lines in your own words:

"We should not quarrel about participation versus observation, but should seek to encourage both. The right balance of these two types of activity varies with the individual, but for the average person each activity supports and enriches the other."[5]

". . . We may learn to enjoy taking part in amateur theatricals and through such activities reap a richer harvest in watching the performance of professional actors."[6]

5. Name some inexpensive passive activities.

6. What passive activities do you enjoy now or plan to enjoy later?

Outline 9

Dramatics, Radio, Motion Pictures

"It might not be too much to say that the commercialized amusements are as influential a force for education as we have, not excepting the public schools."

—WHITE HOUSE CONFERENCE

Aim: To assist students to use the drama, radio, and motion pictures to the best advantage and to encourage them to co-operate with community efforts for improvement.

Preparation suggested:

Committees may be appointed two weeks in advance to report in an interesting way on recommended programs.

It is suggested that a broadcast be visited by several students.

Materials such as radio programs may be sent for by an interested student.

[5] *The Purpose of Education in American Democracy*, The Educational Policies Commission, N. E. A., p. 65.
[6] *Ibid.*

Suggestions for students' discussion:

1. Drama

   There are many kinds of activities connected with the drama. In which have you participated? Discuss:

Stage setting	Costuming	Pantomime
Lighting	Make-up	Pageantry
Storytelling	Circuses	Parades
Making scenery	Puppetry	

   Some students like to make believe. Name some activities in which they can make believe.

   If you have ever written a play will you tell the class about it or bring it to the next discussion?

2. Radio

   What radio program can you recommend to the class? Discuss:

Amateur programs	Quizzes
Music	Educational programs
Plays	Classes: cooking, music, and other subjects
News	Humor
Sports	

   How do you avoid spending too much time listening to the radio?
   How may we consider the rights of others in our use of the radio?

3. Motion pictures

   Why did you see the last motion picture which you saw?
   Because you did not know what else to do?
   Because you planned to see that definite picture for a certain reason? Other reasons?

   How does too frequent attendance at motion pictures interfere with: enjoyment of pictures? scholarship? health? wise use of leisure?

   Which pictures have added to your knowledge of foreign lands, current events, science, literature?

   What would you consider in judging the worth of a motion picture? Discuss: the stars, direction, acting, story, photography, educational value, enjoyment it gives, and character fitness.

   Which museums and recreational centers have good motion pictures? Are any scheduled now?

   How can our local motion pictures be made more satisfying to boys and girls? How can we help in the improvement of local motion pictures? Whom shall we contact now?

4. Do you think that commercialized amusements influence people as much as schools do?

   (Note to teacher or leader: The idea may be left with the students that the drama, radio, and motion pictures are our good friends and companions if we select them properly. We can look forward to seeing and hearing programs which we plan ahead to enjoy.)

Suggested activities:

A committee may be organized to contact a parents' organization and other civic groups, for the purpose of promoting the improvement of motion pictures in the community. Results of such efforts may be discussed in the class.

Pupils may keep an account of the amount of time they listen to the radio in the next three days. When the teacher determines their favorite programs he will see the opportunity to encourage and guide individuals.

References:

Everybody's Radio Manual, Popular Science Pub. Co.
Fred A. Hacker and Prescott W. Eames, *How to Put On an Amateur Circus.*
Alice Keith, *How to Speak and Write for Radio.*
Olive McCormick, *Water Pageants—Games and Stunts.*
Radio News Magazine.
Milton Smith, *Guide to Play Selection.*

Outline 10

Enjoyment of Home Activities

The home is the center of leisure time enjoyment.

Aim: To help students to enjoy a variety of activities with the family members and also alone, and to emphasize family co-operation.

Suggestions for student's discussion:

1. What are some of the leisure time activities which you may enjoy in your home? Discuss:

Collections	Making things
Drawing	Millinery
Dressmaking	Music
Experiments	Poetry
Interior decorating	Reading: fiction, current events
Lace and fancy work	Shop work
Letter-writing to friends	Upholstery

2. What do you like to do that requires only a little space at home?
3. Since it is well to have one hobby which can be fitted into small fragments of time, name such hobbies which you prefer.
4. What can you make at home for use in playing games?
5. Discuss family co-operation and participation.
   Which hobbies of your parents do you enjoy with them?
   Name other ways in which all members of a family may enjoy each other better: in the home, when away from the home together, on holidays.

Discuss: games, stories, reading aloud, music, making things, sight-seeing, picnicking, entertainments, concerts, and other means of family enjoyment.

How do you think families spent their leisure together 50 years ago, in comparison with the present day?

6. What school training have you had which helps you to contribute comforts and beauty to the home?

Discuss:

Shop contributes to comfort in home furnishings: woodwork, electrical repair, handy work, painting, upholstery.

Sewing, crocheting, embroidery work, knitting, and weaving contribute beauty to home decorations: draperies, cushions, towels, curtains, mending, fancy work.

Cooking contributes to the family's enjoyment and to entertainment.

How many such skills for home enjoyment do you have? What are they?

7. Discuss what you think are good attitudes to practice in the home:
Rights of others; privacy, taking turns, respect, courtesy
Caring for home and property
Caring for younger children
Showing love, sympathy, loyalty

8. Discuss the cultivation of rest habits and reflection which are as necessary as active play.

9. Mary started to help her mother clear the table and wash the supper dishes but soon put on her hat and said to her mother, "I'm going to see some of the girls before we go to the Mother's Helper Club." The mother had to do the work after she put the baby to sleep. How would you have handled the situation?

Suggested activity:

Hobby groups may be formed to meet in homes of students with the co-operation and supervision of parents who are able leaders.

References:

Giant Home Workshop Manual, Popular Science Pub. Co.
Landscaping the Farmstead, Bulletin 189, Government Printing Office.
Arthur Lawson, *Fun in the Backyard.*
Eleanor Lee, *Practical Home Decorating.*
Joseph Leeming, *Games to Make and Play at Home.*
Jerome S. Meyer, *Fun for the Family.*
Julian Starr, *50 Things to Make for the Home.*
Fred N. Vanderwalker, *Interior Wall Decoration.*
Lucina Wakefield, *101 Home Furnishings and How to Make Them.*
Arthur Wakeling, ed., *Things to Make in Your Home Workshop.*

Outline 11

Travel

Travel corrects impressions of places and
people, and heightens our appreciations.

Aim: To introduce students to enjoyable sights, near and far, and to develop appreciation of nature and people.

Preparation suggested:

Various members of the class may wish to send for pictures and posters
relating to national park scenes. Railroad companies frequently have
such materials.

Compton's *Pictured Encyclopedia*, Volume 10, may be consulted for a full
list and description of national parks and monuments.

The park departments at the various state capitols furnish information on
free camp and picnic sites in the state parks and forests.

The National Park Service, Washington, D. C., Department of the Interior, furnishes information on new national parks now being opened
to the public.

Talks may be prepared by students on such natural wonders as Bryce
Canyon, Yellowstone, or the Great Smokies.

Suggestions for students' discussion:

1. The reports on materials gathered may be presented.
2. Auto or bus trips:
   What did you see or do on some long trip?
   Where, within 50 miles of your home, would you like to go in an
   auto to see and do things with your family?
   Do all people who motor enjoy nature? Why or why not?
   Discuss how speed may prevent full enjoyment of nature.
3. What are the names of some of our national parks?
   Where are they located?
   What may one see there in the way of geological formations, forests,
   plants, animals?
   What may people do there? Discuss: camping, fishing, mountain-
   climbing, horseback riding, hiking, swimming, skating, skiing.
4. Name the national and state parks and other large recreational areas in
   your state. Discuss how people may enjoy these areas.
5. What has the government done to make our national and state forests
   more suitable for recreational purposes? Discuss: trails, construction
   of camps, dams, picnic sites.
6. Why should forests be conserved? How do some people destroy them?
7. Bicycle trips:
   What did you see and do on one of your bicycle trips?

What other places around here do you recommend for a day's trip for some members of this class?

What provisions are necessary to take?

Suggested activities:

A few students may wish to plan a bicycle trip of a few miles and keep the class informed of their arrangements and achievements.

The class may wish to plan a class picnic in a county or state park. A city park may be substituted if necessary.

Students interested in youth hostels may write to: American Youth Hostels, Inc., Northfield, Mass.

References:

Know Your Community, National Recreation Association.

National Geographic Magazine.

Weaver Weddell Pangburn, *Adventures in Recreation*, pp. 114-117.

Outline 12

Reports on Leisure Time Literature

"Books are the treasured wealth of the world,
the fit inheritance of generations and nations." —THOREAU

Aim: To inspire students to increase their knowledge of and skills in hobbies through reading.

Preparation suggested:

An assignment may be made three weeks in advance so that students may be prepared to report on the reading they have done relative to their hobbies.

Special emphasis may be given to biographies of famous men and women and their tastes and hobbies.

Reports may be briefly written but verbally presented to the class in about five minutes.

Points to include in the report are suggested below:

Name of the reference on favorite hobby.

Author's name and his authority for writing on that hobby.

Brief review of the contents.

Essential help which the reference gives to an amateur.

Fitness of the reference for boys and girls of certain ages and interests.

Part found to be of special interest.

Display of the reference before the class.

Procedures suggested:

Two sessions, at least, may be devoted exclusively to these reports. The teacher may wish to have some reports given as soon as a few students are ready.

References reported upon may be posted on the class bulletin board. Headings suggested for the bulletin board report are:

Hobby described

Name of book, magazine, article, or other reference

Author

Publisher and year

Name of student reporting

Date of report

When all of the reports have been given, the class may wish to vote which students presented their reports most interestingly.

References for students' reading are suggested in the bibliography at the back of the book.

Outline 13

How to Select Leisure Time Activities

"To the art of working well, a civilized race
would add the art of playing well."

—GEORGE SANTAYANA

Aim: To assist students in the selection of leisure time activities fitting to their needs and interests.

Preparation suggested:

The class may wish to collect and mount pictures of leisure time activities which appeal to them individually. These may be posted with the student's name. Some students may prefer to draw pictures.

Suggestions for students' discussion:

1. Why is it necessary to select leisure time activities in which we have definite interests?

2. Is it sometimes necessary to select leisure time activities according to our needs? Discuss selection of recreation which uses some of the energies and powers not used in one's regular duties.

    What general activities can you suggest for:

    An engineer who sits at a desk all day making fine drawings of bridges?

    A dressmaker who works long hours at fine sewing?

    A gymnasium teacher?

    A traveling salesman?

    A telephone operator?

    A doctor?

3. Discuss taking advantage of the seasonal activities of interest to boys and girls, including activities such as the following:

    Fall activities: hiking, football

Winter activities: skating, coasting
Spring activities: nature walks, marbles
Summer activities: camping, fishing, swimming

4. What advice can you give these students?

A student inquired for a list of leisure time activities which he (or she) could enjoy at home without spending much money. Can you suggest a list of ten hobbies which are inexpensive?

William complained that he had no money to buy a pair of ice skates but he attended the motion pictures twice each week. How many motion pictures may William omit to save enough money for each of the following?

Ice skates	Football	Tennis racket
Wood-carving set	Sled	Checkers
Paints	Violin	Trumpet

5. Name some hobbies or other activities which you plan to enjoy all of your life.

Discuss life hobbies such as:

Church activities	Music
Collections	Nature study
Concerts	Reading
Conversation	Shuffleboard
Dramatics	Swimming
Folk dancing	Table games
Golf	Theater
Horseshoe pitching	Travel

Why should one develop skill in lifelong activities instead of skill merely in sports?

Think of six middle-aged people you know. How many of them have some leisure time skill? How many of them have two or more leisure time skills? Do leisure time skills help the personality of the middle-aged people you know? How do your leisure time skills help you?

6. Do you agree with this statement? Discuss:

Skill and enjoyment in all play are more important than expertness.

(Note to teacher or leader: If necessary, discuss topics such as the following on the misuse of leisure:

Waste through laziness

Wrong kind of pleasures which waste one's time, energy, and opportunities

Too much attention to one activity

Lack of outdoor activities, reading, or hobbies

Lack of balance in activities

Each person should have at least one active hobby, and home activities.)

7. What can we do about any inferior amusements in our community?
   (Note to teacher or leader: Since many students live in communities where there are some inferior amusements it is necessary to develop in students the ability to select and to enjoy the worth-while amusements. The problem of inferior community motion pictures, for instance, is one which can be discussed in the classroom by teachers who have a firsthand knowledge of current local amusements.)

8. What are some of the points which you think should be considered when you are selecting leisure time activities? Discuss:
   A natural interest
   A talent
   Activities which meet our needs
   Season activities which interest us
   Activities which we can afford
   A lifelong activity
   Worthwhile activities
   Moderate activities and not excessive, with time for reflection
   Social needs
   Safety
   Development of mind and skill
   Promotion of high standards of character
   Opportunities to make good friends
   Activities which do not interfere with our religion or home life
   Must every leisure time activity cover all of these?
   Show how an activity may fit one person but be undesirable to another.
   May one good hobby be sufficient for some people? Illustrate.

9. What is meant by development of our talents?
   Do you think any member of this class has shown a talent for doing something? What talents are they?

Suggested activities:
Answer these questions, briefly, on a slip of paper:
   1. Which of these values can you enjoy from your favorite hobby?
      Good times
      Health
      Friends
      Culture
      Personal development
      Education
      Home co-operation
      Skill
   2. Where can you go to enjoy the activities you desire or how may you start them?

3. Indicate your plan for the use of your leisure next week. Estimate the amount of time you may devote to each kind of leisure time activity in which you will engage.

(Note to teacher or leader: Topics for further discussions may include: appreciation of opportunities for activities at little or no cost, and fun with the family.)

References:

Modern Recreation Series, Chicago Park District, Administration Building, Burnham Park, Chicago.

Margaret Powers, *A Book of Little Crafts*.

Emanuele Stieri, *The Book of Indoor Hobbies*.

SERIES ON LEISURE TIME OPPORTUNITIES IN THE COMMUNITY
Outlines 14-22.

Outline 14

Extracurricular Activities and Leisure Time Agencies

"Melancholy visits the empty mind and settles there; the mind full of interesting or exciting ideas cannot be invaded by depression."

—WILLIAM LYON PHELPS

Aim: To assist students to participate in the variety of leisure time opportunities within the school and in the community.

Preparation suggested:

It is advisable to prepare to center the discussion around a list of leisure time opportunities in the school and in the community. Films and slides of the activities are recommended. Well supervised activities of high standards should be stressed.

Suggestions for students' discussion:

1. Extracurricular Activities
    What activities are offered in our school after 3 P.M.?
    What are some of the advantages of activities in the school building?
    What schools in this area are open after 3 P.M. for play of any kind?
2. Leisure Time Agencies
    (Note to teacher or leader: These questions may be discussed by a panel of students who belong to some outside clubs and activities in the community.)
    Where may students find sports and games in this community?

Where may a student find music or art taught free or at little cost?
Where do the Scouts meet? What activities do they offer? (One out of every four boys and girls of Scout age becomes a Scout.)
What activities are offered by various religious organizations in this community?
Discuss the kind of activities available in:
Libraries
Museums and exhibitions
Places of historic interest
Other places of interest: radio stations, ocean liners, large establishments, natural beauty
Discuss places and habits to avoid, such as:
Pool parlors of a questionable reputation
Private clubrooms without proper leadership
Cheap dance halls
Street corners where groups hang around
Bad company
Loafing
Too little social contact
Too much responsibility which leaves no time for fun
Spending too much time with the opposite sex
How can you tell the difference between worthless and worth-while books and motion pictures?

3. What do you think of the boy in this story?

Max was good in art work. His parents could not afford to pay for art lessons. The school arranged with an art center for him to receive a scholarship in art for six months. This scholarship would cover his tuition for Saturday classes. He was advised to take the letter which the school gave him to the art class teacher the following Saturday. He seemed willing to do this but not very enthusiastic. Two weeks later his teacher in school asked him how he liked the art class. Max answered, "I didn't go. It was raining." The teacher asked, "Did you go the second Saturday?" "No, I forgot. Maybe I'll go next Saturday."

What do you think of Max's attitude?
What kind of boys and girls are deserving of free scholarships?
What places near this community offer free classes or scholarships for art, music, or other interests?

4. Which extra-curricular activities, and which community activities, do you attend?

Suggested activities:
1. Write on a slip of paper which activities you attend:
1) extracurricular activities
2) community activities

2. State whether you are satisfied or dissatisfied with the activities so that the school may help you if necessary.

References:

B. S. Mason and E. D. Mitchell, *Active Games and Contests.*
——, *Social Games for Recreation.*
Starting and Maintaining a Community Orchestra, National Recreation Assn.

Outline 15

Municipal Opportunities for Leisure Time

At our door lie more interesting recreational opportunities than we can utilize.

Aim: To assist students to enjoy municipal opportunities in their leisure.

Suggestions for students' discussion:
1. Name some of the playgrounds which have activities for boys and girls in your community.
   What are the activities offered?
   What are the interesting park activities?
2. Where can you get opportunities in music, art, drama, and reading?
3. How does public recreation help to make this community a better place in which to live?
   The National Recreation Association claims that the total park and recreation acreage within city limits should be one acre to each 100 of the total local population; and that boys and girls should not have to walk more than a quarter of a mile to a play area.
   Does this community have sufficient acreage devoted to municipal recreation?
   Where is the nearest play center to your home?
4. What civic organizations in this community are promoting playgrounds, swimming pools, or community centers?
   How may students show their interest in such civic organizations in order to help promote adequate recreation and leisure time opportunities?
5. Why do some boys and girls act unladylike or ungentlemanly in parks or on the street when there is no supervision?
   Do you think they realize how they impress others?
6. Name some of the nearest museums and exhibits and tell why they interest you.
7. What other sights can you recommend?
   Discuss: places of historic and other interest, radio stations, natural beauties, zoos, ocean liners, and large establishments.

Suggested activities:

1. Make a map of the streets in this vicinity, showing some of the places
   of interest within walking distance of your home: libraries, community
   houses, churches with activities, parks, playgrounds, and other places.
2. Visit a playground, a park, or any municipal recreational center and
   give a report on it to your class. Notice the recreational facilities,
   activities, and things worth reporting upon.
3. Talk to your parents and receive their consent before you visit any
   play centers discussed today.

(Note to teacher or leader: It is advisable to follow up on students who
joined outside activities as a result of these discussions, so that they may
be assisted further if necessary.)

References:

Community Life; A Suggested Unit Organization for the Seventh Grade
Program in Social Studies. Bulletin III-7, New York State Dept. of Edu-
cation, Albany, N. Y.
Berta and Elmer Hader, *Little Town.*
Weaver Weddell Pangburn, *Adventures in Recreation.*

Outline 16

Scouting

"A Scout is trustworthy, loyal, helpful, friendly, courteous and
kind. A Scout is obedient, cheerful, thrifty, brave, clean, and
reverent."

—BOY SCOUT HANDBOOK

Aim: To stimulate an interest in Scouting and to encourage membership in
the local troops.

Preparation suggested:

Information about Scouting may be brought to class by interested students,
preferably Scouts. *Boy Scout Handbook* and *Girl Scout Handbook* are
recommended as sources of information on standards, activities, and
other information about Scouting.
Arrangements may be made for a local Scout leader to address the group
or the assembly.
Information such as the following should be obtained ready for the
discussion.

Boy Scouting

1. Scouting is a program of interesting, useful things for boys to do in
   their leisure time.

2. Scouting is chartered by the U.S. Congress, and the President of the U. S. is its honorary president.
3. The Scoutmasters are chosen local men who give their time without pay because of their interest in the boys of America.
4. Scouting includes the mystery of woodcraft, first aid, outdoor cooking and camping, swimming and lifesaving, signaling, map making, hiking, athletics, and citizenship.
5. Scouting gives boys a chance to serve their community and fellow men.
    Scouts are prepared to meet community emergencies.
    Scouts are always in readiness to serve.
6. Scouting is neither military nor antimilitary.
7. Scouting knows no race, creed, or class.
8. Scouting helps a boy "find himself" and to "be prepared."
9. Scouts value time and use it thriftily and with purpose.

A Scout! What fun he finds in hiking into the woods! He tells North from South, by the moss on the trees, or East from West by the shadows. He can talk to a brother Scout across a river by signaling. He knows the principal trees and birds and animals that he meets, he knows which are poisonous weeds or reptiles, he can find his way by the stars as did the Indians and pioneers before him.

If matches are forgotten, he laughs and proceeds to kindle fire by rubbing sticks together or by striking steel on flint. The fire once started, what good things he can cook out there in the open! He keeps himself physically fit, he avoids poisons of alcohol or tobacco; he guards his tongue from loose speech or boasting or sacrilege. When he speaks of anyone, he tries to speak well of him.

Girl Scouting

Girl Scouting gives you a chance to do more of the things in which you are already interested and to plan good times with other girls and older friends. Girl Scouting is the sort of fun that will last because it can help you to be an interesting and useful person, with ideals and a code that girls the world over try to follow.

Do you ever wonder what to do with your free time? Girl Scouts hike, camp, and cook a meal in the outdoors. They may sing, dance, and plan a party. They learn to use their hands—fashion a bowl, carve wood, use a needle effectively, and create their own designs. They find things in nature and in their community to interest them. They play games and develop skill in different sports. From all of the things to do in the Girl Scout program, you will surely find many that you will enjoy all the year round.

The Girl Scout Laws are:
1. A Girl Scout's honor is to be trusted.
2. A Girl Scout is loyal.
3. A Girl Scout's duty is to be useful and to help others.
4. A Girl Scout is a friend to all and a sister to every other Girl Scout.
5. A Girl Scout is courteous.
6. A Girl Scout is a friend to animals.
7. A Girl Scout obeys orders.
8. A Girl Scout is cheerful.
9. A Girl Scout is thrifty.
10. A Girl Scout is clean in thought, word, and deed.

The Girl Scout Motto is: "Be Prepared."
The Girl Scout Slogan is: "Do a Good Turn Daily."

Suggestions for students' discussion:
1. Can you review some of the standards and activities reported on Scouting?
2. Where do some of the local troops meet?
   Place, day, hour? Leaders' names? (The main offices of the Scouts will furnish this information.)
3. Do you wish to become a Scout or to visit a troop?

Suggested activities:

Indicate on a slip of paper whether you are now a Scout, or whether you wish to become one if your parent consents. If you prefer to visit a troop first, say so on your slip so that a visit can be arranged for you by some Scout.

References:

The American Girl Magazine.
Boy Scout Handbook.
Boys' Life Magazine.
Girl Scout Handbook.

Outline 17

The Importance of Good Leadership

To choose our leaders is our right.

Aim: To help students to discriminate between worthy and inferior leadership in community activities and to seek good leadership.

Suggestions for students' discussion:
1. When you selected your class officers what were some of the qualities you looked for in each officer? How do these qualities compare with

those you look for in persons engaged in civic government such as a mayor?

2. Why is it important to seek good leadership in our play centers? What are the advantages of trained leadership in play activities? Discuss: standards for games, fair play, civil play, wholesome atmosphere, and educational training.

3. Summarize (and discuss further if necessary) the qualities which help to make good leadership.
    (Emphasis may be placed on such qualities as:
        Knowledge of play activities
        Use of high standards in all activities
        Setting a worthy example before youth
        A liking for youth
        Enthusiasm
        Regular attendance in duties in order to hold the group
        Sense of humor
        Good temper in words, voice, and actions
        Fair-mindedness)

4. How does this school help you to develop leadership ability? (Discuss experience through school clubs, teams, committees, activities, and classes.)

References:

Henry M. Busch, *Leadership in Group Work*.
Floyd L. Ruch and Gordon N. Mackenzie, *People Are Important*.
Standards of Training, Experience and Compensation in Community Recreation Work, National Recreation Association.

Outline 18

Improving the Community through Our Leisure

Service to others.

Aim: To encourage students to try to help improve some of the community's surroundings and facilities.

Preparation suggested:

Activities such as the following may be arranged by committees:

1. Visit a high class real estate development and notice any features relating to leisure time facilities.
2. Visit a part of your city or town where there is a lack of play facilities in the community and observe conditions such as: amount of facilities, leadership, congestion, activities for boys and girls, and apparent needs.

3. Find out whether any river banks in your area are given over to dumps, recreation facilities, or beauty spots.
4. Write to a community organization such as the parents' association to find out how the class may help them improve the appearance of this community, or to ask their opinion on some service which the class is willing to render.

Suggestions for students' discussion:

1. Discuss the presentation of reports on visits and contacts made by students.
2. How does the pursuit of wealth in a city sometimes destroy the beauty of a community?
3. How can boys and girls co-operate with the city in keeping trees, grass, flowers, and bushes in good condition in the parks and on the streets?
4. How may we show community pride in caring for the general appearance of the community?
   Discuss: care of vacant lots, proper disposal of waste, and proper play habits.
5. Discuss some dangers in play, for instance, in throwing stones where there would be danger.

References:

Helen Halter, *Society in Action.*
Junior Red Cross Journal.

Outline 19

Planning Summer Activities

A friend, a book and a walk.

Aim: To inform students of summer opportunities and to assist them in planning for enjoyable activities.

Preparation suggested:

A list of summer leisure time opportunities for the group should accompany this discussion.

Suggestions for students' discussion:

1. Charles (or Mary) plans to have fun this summer in various activities. He knows where he can play games, swim, or make things. Once a week he expects to go to a day camp. When he feels like reading he knows where to go to read books and magazines on many topics which he likes.

   What are some of the play centers not far from here where Charles may go this summer? Discuss:

Neighborhood houses
Y's
Churches
Libraries
Play streets
School play yards
Parks
Pools

2. What is a day camp?
   How may a student arrange to go to a day camp?
3. What kind of books or magazines do you think are available for summer reading in our local library? Where is the library located?
4. What churches in this neighborhood will have summer programs?
5. Where may students go to swim?
6. Where may students go for art? music?
7. To what radio programs will you listen?
8. Name some sightseeing opportunities for summer.
   Discuss: museums, historical places of interest, nature trips.
9. What are your plans for the summer? Where may you obtain the activities you wish?
   John H. Finley, who was a leading educator, advised students to *have a good friend*, *read a good book*, and *take a long walk*, to enjoy a vacation.

Suggested activities:

1. Students may discuss library references which others in the class may wish for summer reading.
2. Each student may write his plan for the summer and ask for any necessary information or help. Another discussion is suggested on the results of the written work in order to help students further. Some students will need individual interviews.
3. Plans may be discussed concerning a display of students' hobbies which should be arranged before the summer vacation.

References:

Dan Beard, *Do It Yourself.*
L. Dudley, "Can You Entertain Yourself?" N. E. A. *Journal*, November, 1943.
Fishing Facts, Outdoor Life, New York.
Roland C. Geist, *Bicycling as a Hobby.*
Frank Graham, *McGraw of the Giants.*
Fred A. Hacker and Prescott W. Eames, *How to Put On an Amateur Circus.*
Eleanor King, *Make Your Own Movies.*

Arthur Lawson, *Fun in the Backyard*.
Wheeler McMillen, *The Young Collector*.
Martha Parkhill and Dorothy Spaeth, *It's Fun to Make Things*.
Betty Price, *Adventuring in Nature*.
Mrs. Mary H. Thomas, *Mary Thomas's Knitting Book*.

Outline 20

Sightseeing Opportunities

"Afoot and light-hearted I take to the open road,
    Healthy, free, the world before me,
    The long brown path before me leading wherever I choose."
                                                    —Walt Whitman

Aim: To call students' attention to the local sightseeing opportunities and
    to encourage them to visit interesting places.

Preparation suggested:
    Films and slides are useful in this discussion.
    Committees may be formed to arrange trips of various kinds to see:
        Historical places
            Old sections of the city or town
            Homes of noted people
            Historical buildings, statues, memorials
        Exhibits
            Zoos
            Botanical gardens
            Radio exhibits
            Art, music
        Nature
            Day camping, hiking, nature study, picnics, parks
        Public buildings
            Libraries
            Railroad stations
            Large stores
            Colleges
        Places of structural interest
            Bridges, housing projects
        Places of vocational interest
            Industries
            Stores
            Municipal buildings
            Agricultural centers
            Vocational guidance bureaus

Suggestions for students' discussion:

1. The verbal reports by the committee members may be presented on what they saw, what they liked the best and why, and the educational and enjoyment values of their trips.

2. What place of interest would you like to visit?
    Discuss: how to get there, time it takes to get there, and what to do or see, cost.

Suggested activities:

The students may draw a map showing the places they have visited within 25 miles of their homes. These maps may be discussed later for the purpose of helping students to broaden their knowledge of their environment.

References:

A local guidebook for sightseeing may be useful. For instance, *The Red Book Information Guide to Manhattan*, sold at news stands.

(Note to teacher or leader: It is advisable to get the parents' consent and co-operation for any sightseeing trip planned for a few students or a group.)

Outline 21

Museums and Art Galleries

Museums offer opportunity for recreation, for study, for pleasure, and for greater understanding of the world in which we live.

Aim: To interest students in various museums and art galleries for students' cultural development and enjoyment.

Preparation suggested:

One committee of students may consult newspapers and guidebooks for information about museums and art galleries: location, visiting hours, fees, kinds of exhibits.

Another committee may visit several museums and art galleries and give a verbal report to the group.

Suggestions for students' discussion:

1. Committee reports may be presented on information gathered about museums and art galleries.
    Location, visiting hours, fees, kinds of exhibits.
    How the exhibits relate to school work.
    Exhibits of special interest.

2. How can you enjoy museums to the best advantage?
    Why do some people rush through a museum?
3. Discussion of lists of museums and art galleries.

References:

Anna Curtis Chandler, *Story Lives of Master Artists.*
Arthur Zaidenberg, *Drawing the Human Figure.*

Outline 22

The Use of Leisure in Other Lands

"How full and rich a world
Theirs to inhabit is."

—ZANGWILL

Aim: To impart appreciation of the culture of boys and girls in other lands, as expressed through the use of leisure.

Preparation suggested:

A committee of students may wish to plan for the following:
    A demonstration of some leisure time activity of another land. Students who have come from other lands may bring in samples of handwork, or perform on a musical instrument or present a folk dance.
    Reports may be prepared on library reading or an interview on the use of leisure in some other land.

Suggestions for students' discussion:

1. Discussion of committee reports and demonstrations.
2. What are some of the pastimes of people in other lands? Discuss:
    Scandinavians ski and do folk dancing.
    Hawaiians sing and play ukuleles, and play in the surf.
    Australians enjoy games and water sports.
    Young men in Greenland wrestle and swim.
    Czechs often play the violin.
    English people like outdoor life and sports.
3. What were some of the leisure time activities of early American Indians? Discuss dances, games, songs, arts and crafts.
4. What leisure time activities are suggested through excavations of archeologists in Egypt and Mexico?
    Discuss: wrestling, carvings, paintings, seesaws, gardening, dancing, ball games, music.

References:

Elizabeth Burchenal, *Folk Dances and Singing Games.*
Rachel Davis Du Bois, *Get Together Americans.*

Lively Games That Are Played All Over the World.
Weaver W. Pangburn, *Adventures in Recreation*, pp. 7 and 8.

SERIES ON HOBBIES
Outlines 23-32.

Outline 23

Collections

One who collects is seldom bored.

Aim: To help students to realize the variety of collections boys and girls make and to assist them if they wish to start a collection.

Preparation suggested:
  Interested students may be asked to bring to class samples of their collections of various things.
  A visit may be arranged to see some collections.

Suggestions for students' discussion:
  1. What is a philatelist?
      Discuss: old and new stamps, stamp book, familiarity with stamps of other countries.
  2. Discuss coin collecting:
      Places where coins are exhibited
      How to add to your collection
      Books on the subject
      How to spell "numismatology" and "numismatologist"
  3. How does science offer a chance for collecting objects?
      Discuss: minerals, stones, insects, butterflies, leaves, shells, plants, pictures of birds and flowers.
      How may other people enjoy your collections?
  4. What do you collect?
      How did you get started?
      What satisfactions do you get out of this hobby?
          (include enjoyment of the home)
  5. What other collections do boys and girls make?
      Discuss: autographs, pictures, slogans, recipes, books, poetry, puzzles.

References:
  Walter Brooks, "The Shoestring Book Collector," *Reader's Digest*, June, 1932.
  Wheeler McMillen, *The Young Collector*.
  Bertha Parker, *Fishes*.

Outline 24

Pets

Shelter, food, and kindness are all they ask.

Aim: To help students cultivate an understanding and enjoyment of animals.

Preparation suggested:

Arrangements may be made for an exhibition of a few pets belonging to members of the group.

It may interest the group to visit the nearest branch of the Society for the Prevention of Cruelty to Animals to determine:

Purpose of that Society
Principles governing the care of pets
Animals cared for by the Society
Content of literature from the Society

A visit to the zoo may be considered also.

Suggestions for students' discussion:

1. Discuss the kinds of pets in this community: usual, unusual.
2. Exhibition of students' pets. Discuss their care and training.
3. Report visits made to such places as the Society for the Prevention of Cruelty to Animals, and the zoo.
   Name the animals seen.
   Describe the care and training given them.
4. What have you learned about the needs and care of a certain animal? Discuss the three main needs: proper shelter, proper feeding, and kindness.

Outline 25

Nature

"There is no more fundamental approach to the future wise use of leisure than through the proper teaching of what is commonly called nature study."
—*The Challenge of Leisure*, by Arthur Newton Park

Aim: To arouse students' interest in the beauty and enjoyment of nature, and the importance of getting enough outdoor air and sunshine.

Preparation suggested:

Samples of scoutcraft and nature lore may be brought to class by the students, for discussion.

Suggestions for students' discussion:

1. How has the school helped you to enjoy nature?
2. Discuss any displays of scoutcraft and nature lore brought in by students.
3. Why do city people, especially, need to develop an interest in nature?
4. Mary is a young girl who works in an office. Her work requires close concentration and this is often a strain on her eyes and nerves.

     What kind of activities can you suggest for Mary to consider?

     What kind should she generally avoid in order to gain the maximum relaxation?

     Would playing bridge, exercising outdoors, or knitting be better for her? Why?
5. Charles likes plants and wants to have a little garden but does not see how this is possible while he lives in a city apartment.

     What suggestions can you offer?

     Discuss: gardening in the back yard, in vacant lots, in window boxes, in water.
6. How may a student satisfy a desire for natural beauty?

     Discuss: seeing sunsets, scenery, colors in the woods, sky effects; appreciations through nature study, hiking, photography, camping, and picnics.
7. Suppose two students in this class wish us to have a hike into the country. How may this be arranged? Where shall we go? What shall we take? How long will we be gone?
8. What do Scouts do on hikes?

     What do they do in scoutcraft?

Suggested activities:

1. The nature class in the school may be emphasized.
2. Students may wish to have a talk with teachers about how they became interested in their hobby and what it has meant to them. A verbal report may be made at the next session.
3. The Children's Flower Mission, 5700 Detroit Ave., Cleveland, Ohio, sells penny packets of seeds through teachers or group leaders. Free catalogue.
4. Further discussion may interest the students on nature hobbies such as: picnicking, outdoor cooking, camping, fishing, hiking, walking, gardening; and the study of ferns, butterflies, flowers, shells, minerals, and tree culture.

References:

Dan Beard, *Do It Yourself.*
The Junior Natural History Magazine.
Janette May Lucas, *Where Did Your Garden Grow?*
Margaret McKenny, *A Book of Garden Flowers.*

National Geographic Magazine.
Nature Magazine.
Bertha M. Parker, *Living Things.*
Betty Price, *Adventuring in Nature.*

Outline 26

Making Things (Including Crafts and Shopwork)

"Not what I have but what I do
is my kingdom."

—THOMAS CARLYLE

Aim: To arouse more interest in making things of beauty, form, or color
  and to enjoy what others do in art, crafts, and other forms of
  expression.

Preparation suggested:

  A committee of students may try to get the class to bring samples of
  things they have made.

Suggestions for students' discussion:

  1. What things may boys and girls make outside of school? Discuss:
    Aquarium
    Airplane and boat models
    Dollhouse
    Radio cabinet
    Sewed articles: clothes, cushions, home decorations
    Experiments: microscopic, electrical, chemical
    Carvings
    Pictures
    Rugs
    Candy and desserts
    Toys

  2. What materials may be used to make different things? Discuss:

Wood	Leather	Wax
Cloth	Clay	Paper
Thread	Paint	Rope
Yarn	Beads	Braids
Soap	Metals	Food
Tools, paste, scissors		Chemicals

  3. What articles can you make out of materials that are commonly
    thrown away? What are these materials?
    Discuss: boxes, tires, stockings, crating.
      What can you make that you can show the class?

4. How can you illustrate some of your school subjects?

> Janet liked history and also liked to carve soap. She made Cleopatra's Needle from a bar of soap.

> John liked to study geography. He made a pair of Chinese sandals when he was studying about China.

5. Discuss things that students would like to learn to make: materials required, cost, necessary plans.

Suggested activities:

> The class may wish to make something together such as an aquarium. Their plans may include:

>> materials necessary; clean sand, aquatic plants, water snails, glass aquarium, tropical fish, fish food, waterproofing of the aquarium, care of the aquarium, and care of the fish.

References:

Katharine Britton, *What Makes It Tick?*

H. Burket, "We Plan Alterations: Game Room for the Keenans' Basement," *Woman's Home Companion*, January, 1945.

William F. Crosby, *Amateur Boat Building.*

Robert E. Dodds, *Handicrafts as a Hobby.*

Herbert W. Faulkner, *Woodcarving as a Hobby.*

Ruth E. Finley, *Old Patchwork Quilts and the Women Who Made Them.*

F. P. Graham and R. M. Cleveland, editors, *The Model Plane Annual.*

Amanda W. Hellum and Franklin H. Gottshall, *You Can Whittle and Carve.*

Ben Hunt, *Ben Hunt's Whittling Book.*

Bernard S. Mason, *Woodcraft.*

E. Mochrie and I. P. Roseaman, *Felt Toys.*

Model Airplane News.

Model Railways, Popular Science Pub. Co.

Edith Moody, *Dressed Soft Toys.*

Evadna Kraus Perry, *Art Adventures with Discarded Materials.*

Mary Brooks Picken, *Sewing for Everybody.*

Edna Plimpton, *How to Make Toys.*

Popular Mechanics Magazine.

Vee W. Powell, *How to Make and Trim Your Own Hats.*

Square-knot Book, P. C. Herweg Co., New York.

Mrs. Mary H. Thomas: *Mary Thomas's Knitting Book.*

John and Enid Wells, *You Can Fix It.*

"A Whittler's Kit," for beginners is available at the Popular Science Pub. Co., 383 Fourth Ave., New York. Five objects for carving are included.

You Can Make It Series, Government Printing Office.

Harry Zarchy, *Let's Make Something.*

Outline 27

Kinds of Art (Including Photography)

Everyone can learn to express art
in some form.

Aim: To encourage students to try themselves out in some kinds of art.

Preparation suggested:

Samples of students' art work, especially that done at home, may be
brought to the class, displayed, and discussed. Kodak pictures taken or
finished by the students may be of interest to the class.

Suggestions for students' discussion:

1. Discussion of art pieces brought in by students.
2. What kinds of art do you think interest boys and girls? Discuss:

Block printing
Book binding
Carving: wood, soap
Clay modeling
Collecting art objects
Crafts
Dramatics: scenery, costuming
Gardening
Linoleum cuts

Make-believe play: dolls, drama-
tics, circuses
Painting
Photography
Portrait work
Pottery
Sculpturing
Sewing
Sketching

3. What evidences have you observed of art in industry and business?
What are the buildings, not far from here, that stand out for their
beauty?
4. What skills and appreciations are developed in photography? Discuss:
Observation
Appreciation of beauty, nature
Skill in mixing chemicals and developing films
Skill in mounting
Skill in tinting
Appreciation of comradeship
5. What skills and appreciations are developed in the art that you prefer?
6. Discuss the value of art in personality development. Emphasize:
Art brings comfort, serenity, joy, and mental balance.
Art offers a way to develop your personality and to find the satisfac-
tion and pleasure of belonging intimately in another world—a world
outside your school and work, where your mind is free to explore
the many possibilities that have had no chance in your daily life.
More people than ever before are now enjoying some form of art.

Art is used more now to improve the appearance of the home, to improve sales, to improve architecture.

More people are attending our museums than ever before.

Some form of art is the hobby of many boys, girls, and adults.

7. What form of art appeals to you?

What plans do you have for pursuing your interest in art?

Suggested activities:

An art group may be formed for the purpose of taking a few local photographs or sketching. The results may be displayed and discussed.

References:

Joseph Alger, *Get in There and Paint!* National Recreation Assn.

Charlotte D. Bone, *Linoleum Block Printing for Amateurs.*

Charles X. Carlson, *The Essentials of Pastel Painting.*

Anna Curtis Chandler, *A Voyage to Treasure Land.*

Jacob Deschin, *Tabletop Photography.*

Ruth E. Finley, *Old Patchwork Quilts and the Women Who Made Them.*

David Greenhood, *Down to Earth Mapping for Everybody.*

How to Make Your Own Photographic Equipment, Popular Science Pub. Co.

Eleanor King, *Make Your Own Movies.*

J. H. McFarland, R. M. Hatton, and D. J. Foley, *Garden Bulbs in Color.*

Chuck Thorndike, *The Secrets of Cartooning*

Outline 28

Fine Arts

"Recreation includes all the beautiful skills, crafts and hobbies that human beings can practice, on and up to the finest of the fine arts. I call this the higher recreation."

—L. P. JACKS

Aim: To give students opportunities for the development of appreciation of fine art.

Preparation suggested:

One committee may list the reproductions of well-known paintings which are found in the school building.

Another committee may report on two pictures painted by artists mentioned below, or by other artists well known.

Suggestions for students' discussed:

1. Discuss the meaning of fine art.
2. Reports may be presented on some of the reproductions found in the school.

Name of the picture
Painter's name
When painted
Meaning of the picture
Information about the painter and the picture

3. Discussion of some famous painters such as the following:

Breughel	Matisse
Cezanne	Monet
Daumier	Picasso
Dürer	Raphael
El Greco	Renoir
Gainsborough	Rousseau
Gauguin	Rubens
Goya	Van Gogh
Manet	Velasquez

References:

Anna Curtis Chandler, *Dragons on Guard.*
————, *Story Lives of Master Artists.*
The Studio Publications, Inc., 381 Fourth Ave., New York.
Arthur Zaidenberg, *Drawing the Human Figure.*

Outline 29

Music Appreciation

A common language of the world—music.

Aim: To help students enjoy good music and to find opportunities for participation.

Preparation suggested:

One student may exhibit his musical ability before the group through some selection agreeable to the teacher.
A victrola and records are helpful aids for this discussion.
Radio programs may also be worked into the discussion.

Suggestions for students' discussion:

1. A student may render some musical number and discuss the selection: name of composer, name of selection, and other information of interest. Victrola records may also be played and discussed.
   (Note to teacher or leader: It is suggested that students learn to recognize the selections and to name the composers after hearing the music played from time to time. The selections should be played completely through before students are asked to name them.

2. If a student shows natural rhythm, what are some leisure time activities in which this student can express rhythm? Discuss:
>   Singing alone
>   Chorus singing, or around the piano at home
>   Church choir
>   Playing some musical instrument
>   Orchestra
>   Band
>   Family orchestra
>   School orchestra

>   Can one enjoy rhythm in other ways besides through music? How?
>   In what ways do you enjoy rhythm?
>   Do you have a natural appreciation of rhythm?

3. What radio programs do you think offer good musical selections for the coming week?
4. What songs with good music can you sing whenever you feel like it? (The class may aim to learn a few such songs together.)

Suggested activities:

An assignment such as one of the following may help students to profit further from this discussion:

1. Write a brief biography of a famous musician and tell why this one appeals to you. Consult the encyclopedia and other books in your library.
2. Write a short story on some musical program you enjoyed. Name some selections you liked.
3. Try to compose a few measures of music and present it to the group next week.

References:

Fred B. Barton, *Music as a Hobby*.
G. S. Mytinger, "Trying for Records," *Reader's Digest*, November, 1935.
Cary Randolph, *The Cary Randolph Quick Method of Note Reading*.
Sigmund Gottfried Spaeth, *Music for Fun*.

Outline 30

Reading—Magazines and Newspapers

"Reading is to the mind, what exercise is to the body."
—ADDISON

Aim: To motivate interest in worth-while magazines and newspapers, for pleasurable enjoyment.

Preparation suggested:

One committee may find out from the group which magazines they prefer and contact the local library for suggestions of magazines for boys and girls.

A student may be willing to tell one story which he has read in a magazine such as those recommended by the public library.

Another committee may do the same regarding newspapers. The better newspapers may also be displayed and discussed for their various values.

Suggestions for students' discussion:

1. Present and discuss the committee reports on magazines and newspapers, in relation to:

Unbiased and accurate news
Quality of illustrations
Kind of advertisements
Degree of sensationalism
Arrangement
Enjoyment value
Educational value
Quality of articles
Comics: kinds (good and grotesque); danger of reading comics to the exclusion of other literature.

2. Present a story to the group from some magazine such as those mentioned below.

References:

The American Girl Magazine
Aviation
Boys' Life
Child Life
Flying
Horn Book
The Junior Natural History Magazine
Junior Red Cross Journal
Model Airplane News
National Geographic Magazine
Natural History
Nature Magazine
The Open Road for Boys
Popular Mechanics Magazine
Popular Science Magazine
Radio-Craft and Popular Electronics
Radio News Magazine
Science News Letter

Senior Scholastic
Seventeen
Story Parade
Young America

Outline 31

Reading—Books and Libraries

"Reading for fun is no unworthy occupation, nor is it one that can be followed without some preliminary training."
—THE EDUCATIONAL POLICIES COMMISSION

Aim: To help students cultivate a taste for good books and a readiness to use the libraries.

Preparation suggested:

1. It is advisable to give the group a choice of reading materials suitable to their personal enjoyment. The bibliography at the back of the book is classified for ready use in guiding students' reading.
2. These excerpts may be helpful to teachers and leaders:

"Reading for fun is no unworthy occupation, nor is it one that can be followed without some preliminary training. Children should come to know books as a means of acquaintanceship with other boys and girls, as a way of learning about animals and birds and plants and stones, of finding out how people live in the country and in the city, and of enjoying fairy tales, nonsense rhymes, and stories of wonderland. From these beginnings emerge the continuing life interests in recreational reading pursued during adult life to escape temporarily from reality, to relive common everyday experiences, to learn of immediate current happenings or of those far from one's own environment, and to pursue a hobby. . . .

Fiction, travel, biography, history, or even scientific and technical materials, may serve these ends depending upon the interest and purpose of the reader."[7]

Suggestions for students' discussion:

1. Name five benefits from the habit of good reading.
2. What is meant by the following: A good book can be an inspiration to us for many years after we read it.
3. What kinds of books does your local library have for boys and girls?

[7] *The Purpose of Education in American Democracy*, The Educational Policies Commission, N. E. A., Washington, D. C., 1938, p. 66.

Discuss the general classification:

Adventure	History	Poetry
Animal stories	Hobbies	Romance
Biographies	Human interest	Travel
Detective stories	Humorous stories	Vocations
Essays	Plays	

4. If you think that a person may be judged by the kind of books, magazines, and newspapers he reads, explain your opinion.
5. Why do people miss much who read only magazines and newspapers, and never read a book?
6. What kinds of books do boys like? What kinds do girls like?
7. What is one of your favorite books? Can you give an account of it to the class? (A brief report may be given to the class and a few excerpts read.)
8. Why is it a good plan to keep a list of the books we read, with names of authors?
9. Discuss any original poetry of class members.
10. Discuss how to read:
    What is meant by thoughtful reading?
    Should one always read rapidly? Why or why not?
    Explain the saying, "Some books need only to be tasted, others to be swallowed and a few to be chewed and digested."
    When may a book be an especially good friend to you?
    Discuss: when you are alone, when you are tired, when you are recovering from illness.
11. How does this school help you to read for meaning, for main ideas, and for enjoyment?

Suggested activities:

1. Reading aloud stories, poetry, and plays may be done by one or two students, with explanations.
2. The bibliography in the back of the book may help students to select a book to read on a favorite hobby, or a new one.
3. Original poetry of students may be read to the group and posted.

References:

The bibliography in the back of the book offers a classified list of books on hobbies for boys and girls.

Outline 32

Assembly Program on Hobbies

To see one's own handiwork brings creative satisfaction.

Aim: To stimulate students to creative activity by the display of their hobbies.

Preparation suggested:

1. The students in the group may indicate on paper what hobby they can display in the assembly. Some may be able to entertain with music and other talents.
2. A committee of students may plan the assembly display of hobbies.
3. A representative of a local leisure time agency may be asked to speak for about ten minutes, or to give some interesting demonstration of an activity in that agency.

Suggestions for students' discussion:

1. What pleasure does your hobby give you?
2. What is its cultural value? its utility value?
3. What materials are necessary and what is the cost?
4. How long does it take to develop skill in your hobby?
5. What personal qualities does the hobby develop in one who enjoys that hobby?
6. What famous characters enjoyed that hobby?

Suggested activities:

For further discussion students may wish to contact persons proficient in some hobby and to report the interview to the group.

Visits may be arranged to places where hobbies are exhibited.

Reference:

Auditorium Activities: Elementary and Junior High School Grades, Austin Public Schools, Austin, Texas.

SERIES ON SELF-IMPROVEMENT AND GETTING ALONG WITH OTHERS
Outlines 33-38.

Outline 33

Sportsmanship in Our Leisure Time Activities

". . . the Chicago playgrounds are experimenting with a scoring system for games: 60 points for sportsmanship, 10 for reliability, and 30 for winning."

—JOHN M. BREWER

Aim: To assist students to cultivate high standards of sportsmanship.

Suggestions for students' discussion:

1. What do you mean by good sportsmanship in play?
   Discuss:
     The Golden Rule

Good loser
Modest winner

2. Name other qualities pertaining to sportsmanship.
Discuss:
Determination
Courage
Fairness
Modesty
Courtesy
Dependability
Self-control
Earnest play
Not giving an alibi when losing
Meeting roughness without resentment

3. Can you suggest some principles of sportsmanship in these or any other situations?
When picnicking
At the beach
Listening to the radio at home
When you play a visiting team
When you lose a game
When you do not feel like doing what others wish
When someone asks you to do something which is contrary to your own principles
When your parents wish you to join the family in a walk in the park when you thought of calling on a friend
When you saw a child damaging property

4. Discuss constructive and destructive play, and the meaning of vandalism.

(Note to teacher or leader: This quotation may be of interest):
"In some way we must make virtue attractive and profitable, unless recreation is to be governed by pessimism. Reward for good performance is logical and right, and we need never fail in any honest attempt to teach young people that there are a number of things worse than losing."[8]

Suggested activity:

Students may write a short account from their own experiences on such a topic as "Examples of good Sportsmanship." These accounts may be discussed in the next session.

[8] John M. Brewer, *Education as Guidance*, p. 405.

References:

The American Girl Magazine.
Eleanor Boykin, *This Way, Please*, p. 236.
Boys' Life Magazine.

Outline 34

Personal Habits Worth Developing in Our Leisure

"Who does not delight in fine manner? Their charm cannot be predicted or overstated. . . . It is even true that grace is more beautiful than beauty."
—From "Social Aims," by RALPH WALDO EMERSON

Aim: To work closely with students in their effort to solve their personal problems especially relating to personal habits.

Preparation suggested:

It is suggested that a few students prepare verbal reports on some topic taken from such references as those given at the end of this discussion.

Suggestions for students' discussion:

1. Discuss the importance of good health habits.
   Emphasize a sound body as well as a sound mind.
2. Personal appearance. Discuss according to the needs of the group:
   Weekly and daily routine
   Clothes
     wise planning
     shopping for clothes, selection
     practical outfits
     care of clothes
   Posture
   Manners
     being natural
     willing service
     moderate disposition
     privacy for make-up
     consideration for others
   Voice and diction
   Health habits
     exercises which you find benefit your health
3. Discuss the personal value of shared experiences.
   Formerly people planned parties, shared experiences, and made their own entertainment. Now people do not plan as much for simple parties but go to be amused in movies and ball games. What oppor-

tunities are there for participation? What plans have you made or wish to make for social participation?

4. Discussion of the following suggestions from the Paul Junior High School, Washington, D. C.

1) Remember that at all school functions teachers and principals are more or less held responsible for your conduct.

2) See to it that chaperons are properly treated. Greet them when you arrive; do your part to see that they are entertained; refrain from making embarrassing requests about late hours and the like; protect your reputation and theirs.

3) Never forget that at such parties you are either a host or a guest and that in either case you have social duties.

4) Perhaps yours is one of those intense romances that decrees dancing with one person all evening. Too bad to take the joy out of life, but all the etiquette books rule thumbs down on that. Everyone is there for a good time, so help out by scattering yourself around a bit.

5) Boys, when a dance is concluded, don't leave a girl standing in the middle of the floor. If you must escape, escort her to a seat. Bettter still, entertain her until the next dance.

6) It is almost impossible for a girl to refuse a dance, especially at a school dance. A girl should never refuse one person and then dance off with another. This is just a little too pointed to be in good taste.

7) Good posture is a part of good dancing. Stand erect, not on the bias. Keep your distance. How can any boy expect a girl to do her best if he clutches her in a vise-like grip and uses her as a sort of bumper! No girl should twine her arm all the way around her escort's neck or lean too heavily on his manly chest. Don't go in for acrobatics, strangle holds, or sink-or-swim attitudes. Try not to bounce or prance. Be smooth.

8) Wait to see how refreshments are to be served before taking matters into your own hands. In case paper cups and plates are used, don't leave them strewn about the floor when you have finished. Pick them up and put them in containers.

9) At a school dance (or any dance), chewing gum, whistling or humming are not done by people of good breeding.

10) There is undoubtedly more display of actual bad manners at school assemblies and at school parties than there is at almost any other school activity. In large groups we do things that as individuals we may refrain from doing. The members of our higher grades should certainly set the example for the other students in our school.

Other topics suggested for future discussions:
  The first impression
  Manners on excursions
  Getting along with people

References:

  B. and M. Allen, *Behave Yourself!*
  Ray Stannard Baker, *Under My Elm.*
  Margaret E. Bennett and H. C. Hand, *Designs for Personality.*
  Ruth Fedder, *A Girl Grows Up.*
  Nell Giles, *Susan Be Smooth.*
  Harry C. McKown and Marion Le Bron, *A Boy Grows Up.*
  Floyd L. Ruch and Gordon N. Mackenzie, *People Are Important.*
  Mildred Ryan, *Cues for You.*

Outline 35

The Art of Conversation as a Leisure Time Asset

To listen with interest is an art worth cultivating

Aim: To inspire students to give thought to self-improvement in conversation as a social asset which brings satisfaction.

Preparation suggested:

  Several students may tell the group about some experience which they think will interest the others.

Suggestions for students' discussion:

  1. Dolores desired to become a good conversationalist but she did not know what to talk about. When she was in a group she felt shy. It seemed to her that everyone had something interesting to say except her.
      How do you think Dolores can begin to develop the art of good conversation?
      Discuss: observation, experiences, reading.
  2. What did you see recently which may be of interest to others? (The class may criticize constructively each other's conversation.)
  3. Why are some people easier to talk to than others?
  4. Name some of the traits of a good conversationalist. Discuss:
      Good speech: clear voice, pronunciation, grammar
      Being natural
      Moderate tone
      Getting others to talk
      Listening with interest
      Consideration of others
      Friendly attitude

5. What should be avoided if one is to become a good conversationalist? Discuss:
    Interrupting
    Arguing
    Correcting or contradicting
    Bragging
    Useless expressions
    Talking too much or too little
6. James gave Robert confidential information which Robert promised not to tell anyone. A friend of Robert wished to know the information. Should Robert tell him? why?

Suggested activity:

Make a brief list of the ways in which you wish to improve your conversation abilities, so that the school may help you in your regular classes.

References:

Eleanor Boykin, *This Way, Please*, p. 89.
H. Fisher, *Riddle-de-Quiz.*
Frederic J. Haskin, *The American Quiz and Answer Book.*
Senior Scholastic Magazine.
Seventeen, magazine.
Story Parade, magazine.

Outline 36

Cultural Habits Worth Developing in Our Leisure

"Man needs knowledge; not merely as a means of livelihood, but as a means of life."

—Sir John Lubbock

Aim: To inspire students to develop cultural enjoyments.

Suggestions for students' discussion:

1. Discuss cultural habits.
    What do you think the author meant by these lines?
    "Some folks in looks take so much pride,
    They don't think much of what's inside."

—John Kendrick Bangs

    What lectures or talks interested you most? Why?
    Discuss: travel, exploration, adventure, nature, fashion, personality development, vocations, as general topics for lectures, drama, or pictures.

Where can you go for interesting lectures or stories?
  What day and hour?
  Discuss opportunities in museums, art galleries, department stores, neighborhood centers.
  If students develop the habit of attending good lectures, how are they preparing for enjoyment when they are older?
  Compare the cultural values of these activities:
    Boxing, and reading Emerson's poems.
    Watching a ball game, and visiting the museum.
  Show how cultural leisure activities may result from the spirit of curiosity.
  How can you include in your leisure the enjoyment of beauty? Why is this enjoyment necessary?
2. Discuss service to others.
  What opportunities for service to others may be found in our school?
    Discuss: coaching other pupils who need help, collecting and distributing clothing for the needy, making toys for needy or sick children.
    Can you name some great people who performed services to others?
    How do you render service to members of your family?
3. Discuss meditation and the need for it as much as for activity.
  Sitting quietly and enjoying scenery
  Quietly thinking through a problem
  Resting quietly after continuous work or strain
  Looking back on what you accomplished and making plans for the next day and the future

References:

Ralph Waldo Emerson, *Essays.*
Sydney Greenbie, *Leisure for Living.*
May Van Arsdale and Mary Lingenfelter, *Manners Now and Then.*

Outline 37

Friendship—Its Relation to Enjoyment of Leisure

"A friend is a person with whom I may be sincere. Before him I may think aloud."

—RALPH WALDO EMERSON

Aim: To assist students with their problem of selecting their friends.

Suggestions for students' discussion:
  1. Give your own definition of a friend.
    Do you agree with Emerson?

2. What are some of the qualities you have found in people who have kindled your sense of friendliness? Discuss:
> Attentiveness
> Interest in people for their qualities
> Happiness at the success of others
> Cheerfulness
> Good humor, but not at expense of others
> Patience with others
> Praise of others
> Cleanliness
> Cordiality
> Co-operation
> Modesty about possessions or success
> Generosity
> Adaptation
> Loyalty
3. Why does it take a long time to build up a true friendship?
4. Why do some people not respond to our friendliness?
5. What should be considered when choosing friends of the opposite sex? Discuss:
> Intellectual and temperamental factors: interests, hobbies, aims, tastes, habits
> Consent of parents
6. Discuss these comments:
> 1) Your friends show what kind of person you are.
> 2) If you look for the best in people you bring out their best.
>> "Be noble! and the nobleness that lies
>> In other men, sleeping, but never dead,
>> Will rise in majesty to meet thine own."
>> —JAMES RUSSELL LOWELL
> 3) An ancient saying reflects the true meaning of friendship: "Kindness, a language the dumb can speak and the deaf can understand."
> 4) Discuss a few ways of getting along with people.
> 5) "Half the world is on the wrong scent in the pursuit of happiness. They think it consists in having and getting, and in being served by others. It consists in giving and in serving others."
>> —HENRY DRUMMOND
7. How can one meet congenial friends? Where should one go? Discuss giving parties and attending community clubs.
8. How does this discussion relate to world peace?

Suggested activity:

Students who wish to meet friends of their interests may indicate this on a slip of paper. The school has information about interest groups in the community.

References:

Ralph Waldo Emerson, *Essays*, especially one on "Friendship."
B. S. Mason and E. D. Mitchell, *Social Games for Recreation.*
Parties A to Z, National Recreation Association.

Outline 38

The Relation of Avocations to Vocations

". . . we must plan to educate man for leisure as well as for livelihood. . . ."

—ARTHUR NEWTON PACK

Aim: To reveal to students the opportunities which avocations hold for vocational pursuits, and to encourage hobbies allied to their vocational interests.

Preparation suggested:

Students who have hobbies which relate to their vocational choices may read about vocational requirements: training, education, ability, and personality. The avocational and vocational choices and reports may be presented to the group.

Teachers and leaders may be interested in what Pack says:

"If we wish to keep from falling hopelessly behind in what Wells calls 'the race between education and catastrophe' we must plan from now on to educate the whole man, to educate him for leisure as well as for livelihood, by teaching him to exercise his own resourcefulness and adaptability, to develop such specialized skills as he may need on his own initiative and through his own efforts, and to attain a mutual adjustment with his mental and physical environment."[9]

Suggestions for students' activities:

1. What is the differerence between avocations and vocations?
   Discuss:
   Activity which one engages in for mere interest is an avocation.
   Activity which one engages in for a living is a vocation.
2. Can you give examples of how avocations became vocations?
   Example:
   Clarence W. White, of North Bennington, Vermont, made a vehicle for his small son, Freddy, which gained such praise in his neighborhood that this vehicle finally became our Kiddie-Kar.
3. How can your hobby become your life's work?
   Discuss reports of students who looked up vocational information.

[9] Arthur Newton Pack, *The Challenge of Leisure*, pp. 227-228.

4. Do skills need to be thought of merely as vocational skills?
   Remarks of Charles M. Smith:[10]
      "We need not think of skills as leading us only toward a vocation.
      "The community profits by our participation in social hobbies in
      our own communities.
      "A statistician might be interested in music and turn to his musical
      abilities for his avocation.
      "It is important to develop general abilities. Thus we develop
      adaptability."
5. When Charles Evans Hughes was Chief Justice of the United States
   Supreme Court he managed to find time to write helpful articles which
   interested thousands of people. He arose earlier to do this, declined
   many social engagements, and was always punctual about his appointments.
      Do you believe that it is the "busy people that get things done"?
      How did Edison, Curie, Rockefeller, and others spend most of their
   leisure, do you think?

(Note to teacher or leader: It may be emphasized that work and leisure are
two interdependent parts of one and the same thing, which is an interesting and a useful life. He who does not work loses one of the greatest of
life's enjoyments, and he who has no adequate leisure and no knowledge
of how to use that leisure is deprived of life's greatest satisfaction.)

References:

Aviation, magazine.
George A. Boyce and Willard W. Beatty, *Mathematics of Everyday Life*,
   Leisure Unit.
C. F. Brooks, *Why the Weather?*
A. Frederick Collins, *Inventing for Fun and Profit*.
The Condensed Butterick Sewing and Dressmaking Book.
Flying, magazine.
F. Foshag, *Minerals from Earth and Sky*.
Sonja Henie, *Wings of My Feet*.
Alfred C. Hottes, *Plant Propagation*.
How to Make Good Pictures, Eastman Kodak Co., Rochester, N. Y.
How Planes Ffy, Aviation Research Associates, Harper & Brothers.
Alice Keith, *How to Speak and Write for Radio*.
Alice Keliher, ed., *Farm Workers*.
———, *Household Workers*. (See the series on vocations.)
Joseph Leeming, *Magic for Everybody*.
Model Airplane News, magazine.
H. P. Oldham, *How to Fly a Plane*.
Radio-Craft and Popular Electronics, magazine.

[10] Former Director of Vocational and Educational Guidance, New York City Schools.

Grantland Rice and Harford Powel, *The Omnibus of Sport.*
Fred N. Vanderwalker, *Interior Wall Decoration.*
Raymond Francis Yates, *Science Calls to Youth.*
You Can Make It for Profit, from the *You Can Make It Series*, Government Printing Office.
Herbert S. Zim, *Air Navigation.*

SERIES OF PLANNING THE USE OF LEISURE
Outlines 39-44.

Outline 39

Planning Time for Study

"For the price of one ticket to an ephemeral entertainment, you can secure a book that will give strength and leisure to your mind all your life."

—WILLIAM LYON PHELPS

Aim: To encourage students to so plan their leisure activities that they will arrange a regular time for study.

Suggestions for students' discussion:

1. Fred does not do his daily homework. He says he will study hard a day or two before tests and he thinks he can pass the tests that way.
    What do you think of Fred's study habits?
    Why is daily effort necessary in homework?
2. Margaret says she would study more but she does not like to refuse her girl friends when they ask her to go places after school and in the evenings. Her friends do not do good work in school. Margaret wants to improve her work.
    What advice can you give Margaret?
3. Name a few principles which may help you to plan time for study. Discuss:
    The habit of studying at the same time daily. What hours are best?
    Quiet environment. You can get family co-operation so that you can have the maximum quiet when you are studying.
    Control of the radio certain hours.
4. What advantages will good study habits give you by next term? by graduation time? by the end of high school?
5. Discuss budgeting time for your various activities outside of school:
    Home study
    Library
    Educational pursuits

Suggested activity:

Students may bring in an account of the time they spend on daily study, in libraries, and in other educational pursuits. These accounts may be discussed in the next session.

References:

Horn Book, magazine.
Natural History, magazine.
The Open Road for Boys, magazine.
Senior Scholastic, magazine.

Outline 40

Planning Time for Various Activities

They who make the best use of their leisure have none to spare.

Aim: To assist students in planning for various activities without confusion.

Suggestions for students' discussion:

1. Which is more necessary for an interesting and useful life, work or enjoyable leisure? Discuss.
2. Discuss Dr. Richard Cabot's book, *What Men Live By.*
   What is meant by a balanced life?
   Why are work, play, love, and worship necessary for everyone?
   Discuss service to others.
3. Marge has a good job in a store but complains because she cannot express her interest in music in her job.
   If jobs do not give full opportunity for the expression of all of one's interests, what should a person like Marge do?
4. Jim belongs to the Scouts, the neighborhood play center, and a local baseball team. He likes to make things in his home in the evenings. He enjoys a good motion picture, and takes saxophone lessons twice a week.
   About how much time do you think Jim should allow for his club activities, music, and motion pictures, each week?
   About how much time should he devote to studying?
   What general advice can you give Jim about arranging his time?
5. How can you tell the difference between good and inferior leisure time activities?
   Discuss values such as the following which may result from the worthy use of leisure:
   Improved health
   Friends
   Culture
   Education

Skill
Wholesome attitudes
Esthetic development
Good times
Adventure
Clean thoughts
Self-realization

Note to teacher or leader: The following viewpoint may be of interest:

"Advice that may appropriately grow out of the slow process of classroom work, without preaching, may include such points as: 1) balance your time; 2) plan your time; 3) earn the fun you take; 4) choose the kinds that best meet your needs; 5) play hard, do not fool; 6) use good taste and be discriminating; and 7) do not let your play interfere with other duties but use it to make you more efficient in all you do."[11]

Suggested activities:

1. Make out a daily time schedule for a week's period showing how you spend your waking hours in leisure time activities, study, eating, home duties. Include weekdays after school, Saturday and Sunday.
2. Make out another schedule showing how you intend to arrange your time for a better balance of activities. These plans may be discussed in class.

References:

Richard Cabot, *What Men Live By*.
Weaver Weddell Pangburn, *Adventures in Recreation*.
E. De Alton Partridge and Catherine Mooney, *Time Out for Living*.
H. Atwood Reynolds, *Low-cost Crafts for Everyone*.

Outline 41

Leisure Time Activities for a Well-rounded Life

". . . it is to be doubted whether any elements of the 'regular' curriculum are more truly educative than the activities associated with recreation."

—THE EDUCATIONAL POLICIES COMMISSION

Aim: To help students develop inner resources of enjoyment for their present and future life.

Preparation suggested:

The class may collect, mount and display pictures of leisure time activities which appeal to them. Some students may wish to draw pictures illustrating their choices.

[11] John M. Brewer, *Education as Guidance*, p. 397.

Suggestions for students' discussion:

1. What do you mean by a "well-rounded life"?
   Review the reference to a balanced life in Outline 40.
   Discuss civic, patriotic, religious, and personal service.

2. Illustrate how you select your leisure time activities.
   Discuss the importance of having real interests and of expressing them.

3. What kind of activities might you select if you were:
   An artist who makes fine drawings of buildings all day
   A storekeeper who is on his feet from early morning until 6 P.M.
   A subway cashier
   A forest ranger
   A laboratory technician

4. Discuss some of the values you enjoy from your own leisure time activity, such as:
   Skill
   Health
   Good times
   Freedom
   Friendships
   Patriotic value
   Education
   Personal satisfaction

5. What opportunities will you find in your next school or your next year here, for developing your natural interests? If you plan to leave school to go to work next year where can you go to develop your interests?

References:

Ray Stannard Baker, *Under My Elm.*
Ernest Elmo Calkins, *Care and Feeding of Hobby Horses.*
Sydney Greenbie, *Leisure for Living.*
Emanuele Stieri, *The Book of Indoor Hobbies.*

Outline 42

My Leisure Time Activities

"There is no problem before the world today more important than the training for the right use of leisure."

—ELIHU ROOT

Aim: To determine the actual benefits which students have received from the class discussions and activities.

Suggestions for students' discussion:

1. How important do you think is leisure time planning?

   Dorothy Canfield Fisher has said:

   "Leisure is no longer the privilege of the few but the possession of the majority, and planning for its wise use is as important a function of education as is preparation for vocational life."

2. Discuss and fill in such a form as the following:

Questionnaire

1) What active activity do you enjoy with others?_____
2) What hobby do you pursue by yourself?_____
3) In what way have your leisure time activities helped the community? _____
4) Name any lifelong activity which you have started.
5) How many hours a week do you spend on the following?
   Studying_____
   Reading for pleasure_____
   Listening to the radio_____
   Doing things with one or more members of the family_____
6) Do you have one good friend with whom you play?
   Yes_____   No_____
7) How have the class discussions helped you most?_____
8) Tell whether the class discussions and activities helped you in these or other ways:

	Yes	How?	No
Conversation	____	_____	____
Sportsmanship	____	_____	____
Personal habits	____	_____	____
Cultural habits	____	_____	____
Other ways	_____		

9) What do you require of your leaders in your activities?_____
10) Name the community centers where students of your age may attend. _____

11) Can you continue your hobbies without further help from this school? _____

Outline 43

Shorter Working Days and Leisure

"Every hour of human life freed from enforced toil by the machine is a potential treasure for the race."

—DOROTHY CANFIELD FISHER

Aim: To remind students of the modern trends in leisure and to encourage them to plan for wise use of leisure.

Suggestions for students' discussion:

1. Review the main topics in Outline 1 on Significance of Leisure
2. Discuss students' vocational plans in light of the amount of leisure they will have. Use the questionnaires made out last session.

(Note to teacher or leader: Some students will need individual guidance for leisure time and vocational planning.)

Outline 44

The Carry-over of Our Leisure Time Interests into Life

"Men and women are the products of their leisure time."

—THEODORE ROOSEVELT

Aim: To assist students to develop interests which will carry over into their adult life.

Note to teacher or leader: These excerpts may furnish helpful suggestions for discussion.

"Examination of the leisure time pursuits of these pupils indicates that many of the constructive activities begun in school are left off as soon as the pupils leave school. It is apparent that neither the school not the adult organizations in local communities make any systematic effort to encourage out-of-school youth to continue activities begun in school.

"It is also apparent that many pupils do not have, at the time they leave school, sufficient resources to guide them into constructive leisure time activities without the help of adults."[12]

"While there are some healthy signs of achievement in the field of leisure time education, as illustrated by the number of active musicians and the number reading worthwhile magazines, most of the information provided by the interviews would indicate that the leisure time interests of these former pupils do not reflect the best kind of training that might have been given."[13]

Specific ways of continuing hobbies and interests started in school should be discussed so that students may see how one may grow through his avocational interests. Some students may need individual help.

It may be emphasized that how one chooses to use his leisure is at least as important as how he earns his living.

[12] Ruth E. Eckert and Thomas O. Marshall, *Report of the Regents' Inquiry*: *When Youth Leave School*, p. 300.
[13] *Ibid.*, p. 301.

Suggestions for students' discussion:

1. Discuss how hobbies started in school may continue to be interesting after one leaves school. Discuss your own hobbies and the future opportunities they offer for enjoyment. Example:

   John became interested in fish when he was in the elementary school. He was a member of a committee that kept the aquarium clean and the fish fed. When he reached junior high school he became interested in fishing and often discussed this interest in his class. His teacher suggested a reference book which he looked up in the public library. This book made him realise how many kinds of poles and bait there were and how important it was to fish according to fresh water, salt water, streams, or weather. When John graduated from high school he fixed up a shop in his basement and started to make fish poles out of bamboo by splitting and glueing parts together in such a way that the poles would bend correctly. A bait company gave him helpful booklets but warned him that it would take a long time before he could make a satisfactory pole. John did not mind the time. He just wanted to make some good poles. He is now a man and an authority in his community on fishing, poles, and tackle.

2. Discuss the practical meaning of these statements:

   1) The educated person is participant and spectator in many sports and other pastimes.
   2) The educated person finds no end to his hobby but enjoys new adventure.

3. What are the possibilities for this group arranging one or more home clubs for the pursuit of some common interests of a few students? How can we get parents' co-operation? What plans do you suggest?

Reference:

Harry A. Overstreet, *A Guide to Civilised Leisure.*

BIBLIOGRAPHY

"Creating Vocational Interests," *Occupations*, May, 1942.
FORRESTER, GERTRUDE. *Methods of Vocational Guidance*, Chap. X, "Broadening Occupational Horizons Through Avocational Pursuits."
HURT, HUBER W. *The Influencing of Character.*
PANGBURN, WEAVER WEDDELL. *Adventures in Recreation.*
PARTRIDGE, E. DE ALTON, AND MOONEY, CATHERINE. *Time Out for Living.*
MEARNS, HUGHES. *Creative Youth.*

Chapter II

LEISURE TIME EDUCATION
THROUGH THE CURRICULUM

"It would be a far more difficult task of civilization to teach men to use leisure rightly than to instruct them how to labor efficiently."
—JOHN H. FINLEY

A MAN of long ago said, "Tell me the way in which a people uses its leisure and I will tell you the quality of its civilization."

No approach to a school subject is more appealing to boys and girls than one relating to their hobbies, interests, or the things they do just because they want to. Such an approach can be made to all school subjects and activities.

A well-rounded curriculum relates to all phases of living. More emphasis, however, needs to be placed on the avocational value of all school subjects such as English, social science, music, art, library, health education, shop, crafts, and home economics. School authorities agree that students should learn to do a number of things well before graduating; for instance, speaking, drawing, swimming, and handwork. Some students are encouraged by the school to develop skill in several activities, and their lives are the richer for it. Interest in art, weaving, homemaking, music, speech, and shop can be carried over in a definite way into the home and community. Dramatics, orchestra, crafts, school paper, and the service squads offer a wealth of avocational enjoyment which may carry over into the home and community life. Regardless of the subject there can be a pleasurable carry-over into the out-of-school hours in the home and community.

When subjects are related to leisure time opportunities in the community they take on a vital meaning. For instance, the student who can be encouraged by his history or geography teacher to go and see the group of Alaskan natives, huts, dogs, and equipment in the museum will certainly show some class co-operation in the lesson on Alaska. The teacher sees his school subject grow and blossom into the afterschool activities which he suggested.

A student interested in his subject as something to enjoy is likely to be a better student than if he considers it just another subject. There is the student who is inspired through his science class to make a collection of minerals illustrating his subject with sketches and other art work, joining a club at the Planetarium, or taking a sightseeing trip just to find out something for himself, often at the gentle suggestion of the teacher.

Where home supervision is adequate, the school's influence and interest may carry over into that span of eighteen hours a day outside the classroom. Where home direction and provision are inadequate, the school finds it necessary to exert much more conscious influence through a carefully planned curriculum aimed to fit the social needs of all students.

Schools may not have an elaborate program for leisure time education but they may be doing much that contributes to the worthy use of leisure. Schools do not usually make a sharp distinction between education for leisure and education for other purposes because both are inter-related in the program of education.

A. School Subjects

English

The English teacher heightens and develops appreciations for many interests including poetry, Shakespeare, drama, creative writing, fiction, and hobby books, by interesting presentation, demonstration, and correlation with cultural opportunities in the community.

The Russell School, Lexington, Kentucky, makes these statements:

> We encourage students to spend some leisure time in reading for their own pleasure, reading to those unable to read and reporting results to class. The students are thus entertained on certain days by the reports of their reading activities. This is school work correlated with leisure time.

In Junior High School 172, Manhattan, students of the ninth grade gave verbal reviews of books and articles pertaining to their hobbies. A brief digest of these reports was then written for the school paper. Trips to leisure time centers and sightseeing trips were also reported and prepared for the school paper.

Students may write compositions on such a topic as "My Hobby" in their English class, with an outline similar to this one:

> How I became interested in my hobby
> Benefits I enjoy from my hobby
> How I may enjoy my hobby
> at home
> in neighborhood centers
> other places
> Advice or help needed

The teacher or the grade adviser may be interested to see the compositions and to arrange for any necessary individual guidance.

Quotations on the worthy use of leisure may be discussed and used in the composition. Here is one on appreciation of reading, by William Ellery Channing:

> In the best books, great men talk to us, give us their most precious thoughts, and pour their souls into ours.

The following are lines by Eduard C. Lindeman:

> To enjoy leisure is to enjoy freedom. . . . We can no more afford to follow loose thinking in the sphere of leisure than in the sphere of economics. . . . The ends of leisure are fulfillment, growth and enjoyment. These are the important ends of life itself.

Other quotations are suggested in the various discussion lessons in Chapter I.

Some students in the Elijah D. Clark Junior High School in the Bronx, New York, made models of Roman bridges, chariots, and dog sleds, and brought them to their English classes for illustrations in their literature.

Original one-act plays may be written and produced along the lines of students' hobbies, and presented in the assembly. In one such play two English class students, a boy and a girl, complained that their community offered them no recreation. As their friends came upon the scene each told what he liked to do and where he went to enjoy his interest. Soon the original two students were impressed with the fact that eight recreational centers were available to them for all the activities they liked.

The outlines in Chapter I which may be incorporated in English are: 12, 30, 31, and 35. Additional suggestions may be found in the bibliography in the back of the book.

Social Science

The civics, geography, history, or social science students may be encouraged to visit leisure time agencies in the community and to prepare information on opportunities for class use. Handwork, collections, experimentations, and scrapbooks may be used to emphasize individual skills. One student made a pair of Chinese sandals for his geography class when China was discussed. Another carved Cleopatra's Needle out of soap for her history class. Many schools have interesting class projects that are invaluable for discovering skills and developing social attitudes which are essential aims in social science.

Social science classes may encourage membership in certain clubs which offer training in community living. For example, in the Woodrow Wilson Junior High School, Terre Haute, Indiana, "The Hi-Y Club, Girl Reserve, Boy and Girl Scout Troops, Junior Red Cross, and Student Council provide experience in community responsibilities for students." Social science teachers may be interested in determining and using local resources for developing social attitudes such as co-operation among students.

The following paragraphs may furnish ideas for discussion on the significance of leisure:

Leisure is a precious possession, especially if it has some relation to toil. A whole life of leisure would be a boresome state to endure from day to day and throughout the years. But after work, leisure has some tang to it, and we appreciate it.

It is simply not conceivable that the idle rich nor, indeed, the wholly unemployed can find salty relish in their do-nothing mode of living. On the other hand, too much labor and too little free time do not make a good balance either. Men who worked from sun-up to sun-down in days of yore had little opportunity to live the good life promised by our code of democracy. They led a grinding, spiritless existence. . . .

Leisure Increased This is not the situation today. If anything, it is the other way round. Automatic machinery hitched to electric power, together with highly efficient management, have led to the creation of more and more free time for the mass of industrial toilers and, as a by-product, for office workers also. Then, in addition, humane considerations based upon the dictum that "man does not live by bread alone" have had their effect in bringing about what we see today. Furthermore, to the housewife, all those modern labor-saving gadgets have given a world of release from drudgery and opened opportunities for new uses of time.

The eight-hour day and five-day week have come to be regarded as normal work periods in the business world. However, great numbers of people work even less than this forty hours per week—some as little as thirty-five. But the wizards of electrical engineering tell us that we have not yet seen the end of this tendency to shorten work periods, and even Henry Ford, as long ago as 1926, declared that "the five-day week is not the ultimate, and neither is the eight-hour day."

In addition to free time released by curtailed working hours, we must remember that there are more holidays than formerly, and that vacations—even with pay—are more freely granted by employers. Can we not readily agree, then, with the conclusion of others who have dug deeply into this subject that "no generation has had as much leisure to deal with as has the present generation . . ."?

Significance of Leisure History reveals that, for ages, men have been yearning, struggling for free time—time they could call their own; time free from intolerable yokes; time in which to be more and do more to satisfy inner cravings; time to "invite their souls." And now it is theirs, for them to do with as they please. In a large sense, we have in this situation a social revolution. And the question is pertinent: Will the larger leisure mean benefit or destruction for the masses of people who possess it? Will it be accepted in a big way, and consciously, as a glorious opportunity to enrich our democratic way of life?

Leisure Is Choose Time Why is it that people use their gift of free time so differently—some in worth-while ways, others in wasteful or downright harmful ways; some always sitting to look on while others perform, others enjoying active participation in sports, music, dramatics, crafts, and similar things; so many indulging in trashy, obscene reading when a world of delightful literature is theirs for the asking at the public library? Of course, the answer goes back to what is in people and then, too, what is outside of them. On the one hand, there are the interests and tastes built up by home, church, school, and community influences. On the other hand, there are all those calls in the environment, more numerous than ever before, beckoning people to come hither and partake of this and that during their leisure time.

The interaction of these two forces, the impelling desires of the individual and the influences from without, will determine what will be done with that time. Choices must be made, and leisure is time for choosing. If the majority of people in any community choose wisely, they and their community will benefit; if they choose unwisely, they and their community and their country will suffer.[1]

The outlines in Chapter I that may be used in social sciences are: 14-22, and 33-44. Other discussions on group living in the immediate community and also the larger community may be included.

Helen Halter, author of *Society in Action*, discusses fifty vital units for the student or teacher to use in social science.

Music

Community organizations welcome school music on their programs. In Woodrow Wilson Junior High School, previously mentioned, opportunities are made for music students in these ways: Members of the band, orchestra, and boys' and girls' glee clubs are invited with their instructor to appear on the programs for a number of civic organization meetings during the school year. Three talent shows with students and local professional entertainers are promoted each year by the school. The funds raised in this way provide free auditorium programs for students during the year.

One junior high school orchestra plays in some of the neighborhood elementary schools. Each term the guidance counselor visits these elementary schools to consult with the sixth grade teachers about incoming students, their special abilities and their problems, so that the junior high school may give early attention to them. On these occasions she sometimes takes a few musicians with her, such as a trumpeter, pianist and accordionist. The elementary school children show an interest in the music, and in the school's music clubs and orchestra which are described to them. One music teacher said, "Teach a student to blow a horn and he will never blow a safe."

The tonetta band is used in some elementary schools from the

[1] Eugene T. Lies, *How You Can Make Democracy Work*, pp. 73-75 and 77.

third to the eighth grades as a successful means for developing musical interests among young children.

The school co-ordinates its music with community activities in many ways. In the Monticello Junior High School, Cleveland Heights, Ohio, "Young People's Concerts are arranged with the co-operation of the Cleveland Orchestra. The school also arranges a music memory contest."

Another effort is reported by Miss Anna E. Lawson, Principal, Junior High School 81, New York:

For over ten years we conducted the Moton Choir, a group of some 35 girls who showed ability in music. They met weekly for rehearsals. They gave concerts, sang in churches, over the radio, as well as in the school. It was a practical example of a leisure time program. When started, it was the first movement of its kind in the community. Later other groups started similar choirs.

The director of the Music Department of the Board of Education in Gloversville, New York, Miss Emma E. Devendorf, keeps the love of music alive in the hearts of her students. She says:

Requests come to the schools from many directions—service clubs, patriotic organizations, church groups, parent-teacher associations—for assistance in carrying out their varied programs.

The school bands are popular for the parades, celebrating the national days and local service drives. Their colorful uniforms are striking to the eye, and their martial music is pleasing to the ear.

School choirs and orchestras are large groups, and need auditoriums of considerable size when asked to help. In most of our smaller cities, a civic auditorium is fast becoming a necessity.

The schools encourage membership in the local church choirs and the students are an asset to these choirs because of their music training in the schools.

. . . These are the heralds of a brighter day. They feel confident that some day the whole world will sing, and that there will be, Everywhere! Everywhere! Music.[2]

A representative of an interesting music project, Dr. Julia C. Harney, Assistant Superintendent of Schools, Jersey City, New Jersey, reports:

In recent years there has been a brave effort on the part of a comparatively small, music-loving group in the community to establish and maintain a

[2] *Rho Journal,* March, 1944, Pi Lambda Theta, New York University, p. 40.

symphony orchestra. This is never an easy objective to realize, but means much work and sacrifice by those holding such an ideal. For the past two seasons the municipal government has subsidized symphony concerts by this orchestra for high school students and pupils in the upper elementary grades. The conductor is very successful in arranging suitable programs, is an interesting commentator, and has, on occasion, included a familiar song to be sung by the audience of children accompanied by the orchestra. At one of the concerts some of the better instrumentalists of the high schools were allowed to join the orchestra in the playing of a selection and the high school teachers of instrumental music were permitted to conduct portions of a number.

This year the Jersey City Teachers Association, unable to sponsor the series of concerts that had been offered for several seasons, is collaborating with the Jersey City Philharmonic Symphony Society in what promises to be a successful series of concerts. Surely this type of school and community collaboration is the finest kind of morale building in these days of stress.[3]

Many outlines in Chapter I may be useful to the music teacher. Some of the outlines are: 2, 9, 10, 14, 29, 31, 32, 36, 38, 40, 41, and 44.

Music teachers have an opportunity for making contacts for students to develop their musical ability and interest in music through all the available community resources.

Art

The student who enjoys art may need to be shown how to develop his interest in community centers that have art classes. The nearest schools for art and the charge for lessons can be explained to students.

Art and crafts are common outlets for emotional energy for all students. The Garland Street Junior High School of Bangor, Maine, placed special emphasis on art work for the purpose of self-adjustment of certain students. Some schools organize a group for special therapy through art work and crafts. About ten should be the maximum for a group of this kind needing therapy.

Students generally like to make posters on their own particular hobby. Posters on students' hobbies or about local activity centers may be made in the art class and used in discussions. In one school the posters were tacked on sticks and used effectively as banners in an assembly skit on hobbies when students told about

[3] *Ibid.*, p. 39.

their hobby, how they got interested in it, and where they went to pursue it.

Some schools and the local museums work together in these ways: arrange for museum exhibits in the school, plan trips for students to the museum, arrange for the use of visual aids from museums, and conduct illustrated lectures related to the curriculum. In Van Nuys High School, Van Nuys, California, "A group of junior high school pupils go to the museum every Saturday morning to attend classes and laboratory experiments in nature study, botany, and zoology. They also see collections, some of which are by students."

The outlines in Chapter I which relate to art are: 2, 10, 15, 21, 26, 27, 28, 29, 31, 36, 38, 41, and 44.

The art teacher is in a position to give information to groups and individuals about community opportunities for art work and appreciation.

Library

Attractive and illustrated books, magazines, and pamphlets on students' interests and hobbies may be displayed and discussed in the school library each term.

In Junior High School 83, Manhattan, a list of magazines was compiled for the school districts 10 and 11, Manhattan, with the approval of Miss Helen Carpenter, the acting superintendent of libraries of the Board of Education. This list appears in the bibliography under "Magazines for Boys and Girls." It is only a sample of the many magazines available. The magazines made a colorful and interesting display at a principals' conference in Supt. Rufus M. Hartill's office and in one of the schools where students saw the list and the magazines. The local public libraries can make additional suggestions for magazines for boys and girls.

The community library is glad to have the English or library teachers send students there to explore materials on avocations. Librarians prepare displays of materials for students to see and to discuss with the readers' assistant.

In Terre Haute, Indiana, the students of Woodrow Wilson Junior High School may go to the library for recreational reading each day before class in the morning, at noon, and after school.

To get students to go to the local library is a problem in many schools. The distractions that students experience today make it necessary for the school to try many different methods to get them into the local library or otherwise to make them take advantage of the reading opportunities. Students have been known to flock to the library to see posters which they and their friends made in school. Posters showing students' hobbies or vocational choices, English compositions on choices, or a display of students' hobbies may at least get the students inside the local library. Then the library will have reading material related to their hobbies and other interests ready for them to peruse.

For instance, there was Horace, who cared for nothing but pigeons. He heard his teacher tell about the book on the care and training of pigeons and decided to study about the different kinds of pigeons and the food they required. Horace became conversant with pigeons from what he read. The librarian in the Aguilar Branch Library, New York, who gave him the book said that the pigeon books showed signs of much use and popularity and that it required an eagle eye to keep them from disappearing for days at a time.

A teacher in Keyport, New York, Miss Mildred Lackey, stimulated first and second graders in reading and buying books of their own. The Parent-Teachers Association assisted by giving the proceeds from a cake sale for an exhibit of inexpensive but modern books. The teacher related that:

> After examining the books we discussed twenty books a day. When we set up the exhibit we allowed each child to plan on a fifteen-cent purchase. It was interesting to see them choose their book at five cents, ten cents, or fifteen cents each. Then we invited their parents, with the result that the children made further purchases. Interest in reading increased. The beginning of the following term every child owned at least one book. Bookcases were built to keep the children's books in the schoolroom until school closed.

A similar account comes from Miss Margaret M. Grandfield, Assistant to Principal, Public School 24, Brooklyn, New York:

For nearly a year one sixth grade class in our school, under the direction of their teacher, Mrs. Louise Bausch, has been working on a Little Folks' Library. This class needed remedial work in reading but lacked reading material on their interest level. By encouraging the pupils to organize a library for children much younger than themselves they were "exposed" to many books which they were able to read easily, but which would not have interested them otherwise because of the content.

We turned over a room to them and told them they could have entire charge of it. The class visited the public library for information on the organization and conduct of a library. They visited museums to find out what and how to plan for exhibits. Members of the class canvassed neighborhood stores and then discussed the merits of the goods offered for sale in relation to the prices asked. Comparative studies of "values received" were made.

Books on different peoples of the earth gave the teacher an opportunity to discuss national backgrounds of literature, geography, art, and history. All of these, with planned story hours by story tellers in costume (from other classes), have made this project a means of leisure time education and given children ideas for decoration, purchasing, budgeting and figuring.

More than 1000 books have been read, classified, indexed, catalogued and annotated. Book lists for children of various ages have been made for parents who wish guidance in the selection of books for gifts.

As a supervisor, I feel that Mrs. Bausch has worked out one of the few real units of work that "has everything"—a real life motive within the comprehension of the children, integration of all subjects without "artificiality," community service, and concrete realization of plans.[4]

The school librarian is the main source of guidance on interesting reading materials in the school and in the local libraries. Many individual students are inspired by the school librarian to read about their leisure time interests and to look up certain references in the local libraries.

The public libraries print annotated lists of references on interesting hobbies and other topics. Two useful sources which develop reading horizons of individual students are: *The Choice of a Hobby*, by Anne Carroll Moore, and *Reading for Fun*, by Eloise Ramsey. These are interesting classified bibliographies of interest to boys and girls.

The outlines in Chapter I which may suggest discussions or projects for the library class are: 30, 31, 39, and 44. Some of the references in the classified bibliography at the end of the book

[4] *Rho Journal*, March, 1944, p. 44.

should also be stimulating to students who wish to read about their special interests.

Home Room Sessions

The home room offers an exceptionally good opportunity for discussions on leisure time. The follow-up of students' choices resulting from the group discussions should be informal and friendly without giving students the sense of being directed or told what to do. A minimum of three periods each term may be devoted to the exclusive discussion of leisure time. More time is needed for demonstrations and other activities. If students can actually do things, make things, discuss, and tell about their leisure time experiences, the home room period will be more appealing than lectures.

In some schools the home room teacher is the only one equipped to give current information about all the leisure time opportunities in the community, such as are discussed in Chapter III.

The bibliography at the end of the book has been prepared with the home room teacher in mind. Leisure time hobbies and other interests are listed so that references may be offered any student without delay. The bibliography may also be consulted by the student. When a fitting reference cannot be found for an inquiring student, it may be obtained through the general sources listed.

Health Education

The health education teacher sees the need of each individual student for physical activity as well as for avocational pursuits. There was Louis, one of the brightest students in high school but thin and undernourished. His hobby was reading when he was not working in the freight office. He was not in the habit of participating in activities until he was in his senior year, when a new director of athletics was assigned. When the new director heard about this honor student, he immediately observed his need for physical development and stimulated the boy to desire a strong body. With chest up and clenched fists Louis told the director,

"From now on I'm developing my body. Nobody ever made me realize my need like you have. I want to learn the games, every game. What are marks in the nineties with a weak body!"

It is the health education teacher who is in one of the best positions for teaching the importance of good health, sportsmanship, courage, honesty, and loyalty, through actual situations. The following show methods used by some health education teachers:

Additional recreational opportunities are provided such as a well organized and supervised square dance program. The school works closely with the parent-teachers association, coordinating council, Y.M.C.A. and service clubs in this work.

Van Nuys High School, Van Nuys, California

We have co-recreational activities in physical education and swimming classes.

Morey Junior High School, Denver, Col.

The school conducts a series of sports tournaments for girls in the sixth, seventh and eighth grades and for boys of the seventh and eighth grades. Each child is given an opportunity to participate in one team sport each season such as softball in the spring, basketball in the winter. A round robin tournament is conducted so that each team plays every other team. Each sport is usually carried on for about six weeks. Individual tournaments are conducted and refereed by the children of the seventh and eighth grades in boxball and handball (single and double).

Bellerose School, Floral Park, N.Y.

Who is in a better position to give opportunities for folk games and dances than the health education teacher? A Spanish student who knows Spanish dances from seeing her parents entertain with dancing in the home may be asked to dance in Spanish costume, and even to teach other students. In one school many Italian parents came to a school fiesta to see their children participate in dances such as the parents themselves used to dance.

The health education teacher who knows where a student may go for folk dancing, sports, tournaments, baseball, and other activities which the school has introduced to them can be of great service to all students under his direction.

Two authors make the following points on the development of attitudes:

... If our schools, by means of play, hope to develop in the child attitudes of the honesty or loyalty type, the play teacher must call attention to these points whenever opportunities are presented in the games. A child probably will not gain a respect for sportsmanship from his play if the teacher does not stress its importance, and especially not, if no move is made to bring reproof to the offender through the condemnation of activities that are unsportsmanlike.[5]

Right habits of living were emphasized by another authority:

A problem of physical education is to establish right habits of living. These right habits are not just a matter of the training of muscles, big or little; they have to do fundamentally with the emotions and the mental processes quite as well as with physical efficiency. In respect to this physical, emotional, and mental health, the individual must become increasingly self-directive. . . . Sane athletics is worthwhile here and now, but much is lost if athletics does not carry over into behavior, emotional, mental, and physical, in later life.[6]

The following paragraphs by Lies furnish some interesting suggestions for further discussion:

Too many people use their leisure in sitting; they fail to participate in pursuits that nourish growth. Some years ago, Stuart Chase compiled a list showing the enormous number of people who go in for sitting. Here is what he presented: newspapers and tabloids, 35,000,000 readers a day; radio, 30,000,000 listeners a night; phonographs and player pianos, 15,000,000 players a night; moving pictures, 50,000,000 admissions a week; theaters, concerts, shows, popular lectures, and revivals, 5,000,000 admissions a week; popular magazines, 15,000,000 readers a month; professional baseball, 40,-000,000 admissions a year; football, 20,000,000 admissions a year; horse racing, 10,000,000 admissions a year, prizefights, 10,000,000 admissions a year.

This is certainly a formidable list, and should give us pause. One supposes that Mr. Chase would not contend that all these forms of leisure-time expenditure are necessarily harmful and none "up-building" in nature. He is simply making the point that so many Americans do indulge themselves in *merely seeing and listening to others perform, in perusing the thoughts of others*; that *too few take part*, try themselves out, explore, associate themselves with others in group activities, or create, and so lose much in satisfaction and in growth. We would agree with these observations and criticism.

It is possible to have *more fun for less money*. The types of free-time indulgence cited by Mr. Chase are all commercial, be it remembered. At this present time of emergency, the nation grievously needs well-developed

[5] Elmer D. Mitchell and Bernard S. Mason, *The Theory of Play*, p. 276.
[6] Elbert K. Fretwell, *Extra-curricular Activities in Secondary Schools*, p. 414.

bodies and balanced nerves. Participation in physical activities and joyful games can materially help to develop these.[7]

Shop, Crafts, Home Economics

Where shop, crafts, or home economics is offered, there is one of the best opportunities for students to express themselves, to show their aptitudes, to see results of their own efforts, and to experience real satisfaction by doing.

These avenues can relate directly to leisure time activities in the home and community and can carry over into the student's life experiences now and later.

Shop teachers are in a key position to discuss topics such as are represented in these outlines in Chapter I: 4, 5, 10, 26, 38, 40, and 44.

The crafts teachers and club leaders will find that these outlines may be adapted to the group: 2, 3, 4, 10, 26, 27, and 38.

From East Orange, New Jersey, Mrs. Stella Hope Page sends these suggestions for the home economics teacher:

It is commonly accepted that any town or city can be judged by the amount and kind of attention paid to the welfare and problems of its children. Some of these problems of youths can be answered through home economics which deals with "head, heart, hand, and home." The war-created Junior Canteen is a social center for high school boys and girls where they may meet to dance, play games, and share a bottle of pop, all with the help of a responsible educator who may very well be a home economist. This teacher, as an adviser in hospitality, can help both sexes in their quest for poise and freedom from that awkwardness which harasses adolescents. Thus the Junior Canteen can more effectively coordinate the activities of the home economist with the younger elements of the community.[8]

Home economics teachers may find that outlines 5, 7, 10, 26, 38, and 41 emphasize the leisure time value of their subject.

B. ACTIVITIES AND VISUAL AIDS

School Clubs and Activities

The many kinds of school clubs and activities are too numerous to mention. The most common ones pertain to art, crafts, drama-

[7] Eugene T. Lies, *How You Can Make Democracy Work*, p. 73.
[8] *Rho Journal*, March, 1944, p. 34.

tics, games, and school subjects. It has been found that teachers' hobbies and skills frequently determine what clubs a school will offer. For instance, one teacher enjoyed carving small models of airplanes, boats, and locomotives out of wood, soap, or clay, and volunteered to conduct a club for modeling. The club was in such demand that several clubs were organized for boys and girls to model a variety of articles.

Here are suggestions for teachers who have been assigned a club or activity but who do not know what to choose:

Adventure
Agriculture
Airplane building
Animals
Aptitudes
Art:
   Cartooning
   Commercial
   Junior artists
   Marionettes
   Metal
   Modeling
   Painting
   Posters and signs
   Sketching
   Stagecraft
Athletics:
   Baseball
   Basketball
   Handball
   Swimming
   Tournament
   Track
Autograph
Auto repair
Aviation
Badminton
Basketmaking
Bees
Bicycling
Birds
Blueprinting
Boat building

Boating
Book
Bookbinding
Boxing
Boy Scouts
Brush
Buttons
Camp Fire Girls
Camping
Canoe
Careers
Carving
Church choir
Circus
Coins
Cokes and snacks
Collecting
Community
Crafts:
   Art weaving
   Block printing
   Bookmaking
   Cork
   Crocheting
   Embroidery
   Knitting
   Knotting
   Lacemaking
   Leather
   Metal and foil
   Needlecraft
   Papercraft
   Party favors

Passe partout
Pottery
Spattering
Woodcraft
Current events
Dancing:
  Folk
  Social
  Tap
Debating
Dolls
Dramatics:
  Costuming
  Lighting
  Make-up
  Screen making
  Script writing
  Speech
  Stage directing
  Stage setting
Electrical
English to foreigners
Excursions
Experiments
Farm
First aid
Fishes
Fishing
Fix-it
Flowers
Foreign language
Friendship
Fun from books
Fun from games
Fun in manners
Fun from songs
Games:
  Backgammon
  Checkers
  Chess
  Table tennis
  Word games
Gardening:
  Bulbs

Flowers
Herbs
Plant propagation
Vegetables
Water garden
Window garden
Girl Reserves
Girl Scouts
Golf
Gourds
Health
Hiking
Hi-Y
Hobby
Home decorating
Home hobbies
Homemaking
Horseback riding
Horsemen
Indian craft
Industrial
Information Please
Interior decorating
Interracial
Ju-jutsu
Journalism:
  Newspaper
  Reporters
  Writers
Knitting
Knotting
Know your city
Landscape gardening
Leadership
Literature:
  Library
  Literary Guild
  Negro culture
  Reading
  Story hour
Magazine
Magic
Marionettes
Metal crafts

Minerals
Model building:
  Airplane
  Miniatures
  Railroad
  Ship
Music:
  Current Programs
  Drum and bugle
  Glee club
  Harmonica
  Orchestra
  Piano
  Singing
  Trumpet
Nature:
  Birds
  Garden
  Hiking
  Indoor gardening
  Outdoor fun
  Walking
  Wild flowers
Opera
Outdoor
Painting
Parliamentary law
Parties
Patchwork quilts
Patrol
Personality
Pets
Photography and motion pictures
Ping-pong
Planetarium
Plants
Poetry
Pottery
Puppet •
Puzzles and quizzes
Quill
Quizz
Radio
Reading

Red Cross
Reptiles
School management:
  G. O.
  Gym leaders
  Officers
  Patrol
  Projection crew
  Publicity
  Safety
  Service league
  Stage crew
  Traffic
Science clubs:
  Astronomy
  Botany
  Chemistry
  Experimental
  Radio
  Science collections
  Science trips
  Television
  Weather
Scouts
Scrapbook
Scribblers
Scribes
Service clubs:
  Community service
  School service
Sewing clubs:
  Colonial sampler
  Costume designing
  Dressmaking
  Embroidery
  Fancy needlework
  Millinery
  Needle-point
  Remodeling
  Thrift
Shopwork
Sightseeing
Singing
Soap carving

Social
Social attitudes
Speech
Sports:
  Boxing
  Football
  Handball
  Hockey
  Skating
  Skiing
  Soccer
  Softball
  Swimming and diving
  Tennis
  Volley ball
  Water sports
  Winter sports
  Wrestling
Stamps
Stars
Story and story-telling:
  Adventure
  Biography
  Classics
  Detective stories
  Exploration
  Fiction
  Hobbies
Peoples of other lands
Personality
Poetry
Romance
Vocations
Study
Stunt
Summer clubs including home
  clubs and activities
Swimming
Table decorations
Tatting
Tennis
Tool hobbies
Toymaking
Travel
Trees
Tricks
Trips and excursions
Typewriting
Ventriloquism
Vocational guidance
Weaving
Whittling
Winter sports
Woodworking
Writing

How some schools throughout the country carry on activities is indicated in a few situations described here:

Our archery clubs and Junior Maine Guide clubs make their own equipment and use it—bows and arrows, flies, camp kits and other articles, giving youth training for lifelong hobbies and leisure time activities. The Guides take actual field trips and specialists in different fields visit and demonstrate skills in fly tying, casting, and reflector oven cooking.

> Dorothy E. Babcock, Guidance Director,
> Garland Street Junior High School, Bangor, Maine.

A dramatic club holds regular meetings and produces two shows each year for assembly.

> Madge Polk Tousley,
> Woodrow Wilson Junior High School, Terre Haute, Indiana

The Junior Literary Guild in our school has studied the making of a book. They have been featured in *Young Wings* for a number of years. They have a large library purchased with money earned by the Guild.

Letitia J. Jones, Columbia School, Hammond, Indiana

Besides having school clubs, one of our schools has opportunity groups organized to train for future civic activities.

Director of Research and Guidance,
Kalamazoo Public Schools, Michigan

Our assembly program in the Fall is related to the summer activities. A large book, its pages turned by animated book ends, reveals the number of books read in the summer. Then there is a long procession of craftsmen, each group distinguished by its own banner bearing such names as Painters, Gardeners, and others. Each of these children carries something she has made which gives some idea of the creative activities of the vacation period.

Gertrude S. Schloss,
Junior High School 159, New York, N.Y.

Miss Effie A. Selvig, Enderlin Public Schools, Enderlin, North Dakota, offers these comments:

In our Young Citizens League I teach the mechanism of conducting and taking part in business meetings in the seventh grade so that when they come into the eighth grade they can feel it is truly their organization.

I think the best way a boy or girl can use leisure time is in service for the benefit of all. . . . Students have done exceptionally well in patriotic drives. Their minute man flag is on display.

It is apparent that schools are using diversified ways for the development of students' interests and skills. Some schools have enriched programs with special classes. The Childs Park School of St. Petersburg, Florida, for instance, now conducts hobby classes. In Lewiston Junior High School, Lewiston, Idaho, a Visual Education Operators' Club is in process. Development of special aptitudes was the purpose of one club organized in Leland Junior High School, Chevy Chase, Maryland.

All students should be given an opportunity to see and hear the many interesting results of the clubs in their school through assemblies and displays of their work. The results represent their hobbies, talents, and their creative interests of intrinsic value. The enjoyment which students feel in the clubs can carry over into school subjects and be further encouraged by subject teachers. Articles made or skills developed in a club may be illustrative of a school subject. The student who belonged to the photography club took photos of community play centers showing good and inadequate facilities. His civics teacher heard about the photos and asked him to show them to the class and to discuss community recreational facilities and needs.

The exploratory nature of school clubs makes them an excellent means for training youth in the worthy use of their leisure. The teachers' vital interest makes these clubs a real opportunity for students' self-realization. The clubs are the students' own free choices. They do not feel urged to join any particular club.

The National Audubon Society assists with exploratory clubs such as the Audubon Junior Club in the school or community. Students find it is fun to study bird habits. Every member of the Club receives a membership tag bearing the inscription, "Protector of American Wildlife," and a set of six illustrated, four-page leaflets describing the year-round activities of birds and other wildlife. Every club receives copies of *News on the Wing*, the junior club paper published four times a year, and a copy of *Audubon Teachers' Guide*, a 96-page booklet with suggestions for organization, club activities, field trips, and other information. For further details about forming a bird club in the school or community, one may write to that Society, 1006 Fifth Avenue, New York.

Teachers, too, have hobbies! When teachers conduct clubs in their own hobbies their spontaneous interest is likely to create that essential spirit of spontaneity among their club members. In this connection, one author says:

"Just for fun" should receive greater attention in our aim to help pupils in all forms of recreation. Now that club periods and play are becoming a required part of the curriculum, care must be taken to keep the idea of spontaneity in the foreground. This idea should be extended to work, of course, but it should never be lost in what we call play.[9]

Teachers may tell students where they may continue their club interests in community activities. The club activity can thus carry

[9] John M. Brewer, *Education as Guidance*, p. 401.

over into the future life of the individual. Dr. E. George Payne, former Dean of the School of Education, New York University, stressed the importance of this carry-over into community living. Thus, a student's interest in school clubs finds continued satisfaction in constructive and well-directed activities outside the school.

Club leaders will find that certain outlines in Chapter I pertain to their club. Leaders of nature clubs may find these outlines helpful: 4, 11, 16, 20, 23, 24, 25, 30, and 44.

Collection clubs may use outlines 3, 4, 10, 21, 23, 25, 30 32, 38, and 40.

Personality clubs may wish to look over the suggestions in outlines 7, 10, 17, 33, 34, 35, 36, 37, 41, and 44.

Crafts, which are the bases for many interesting clubs, are discussed in outlines 3, 4, 26, 27, 30, and 38.

Community service clubs may find some hints in outlines 5, 9-11, 14, 15, 17, 18, 20, 21, 33, and 43.

Clubs for understanding others may discuss such themes as those presented in outlines 9, 11, 22, 34, 35, and 37.

Content for a variety of other clubs may be gathered from the bibliography in the outlines and also from the classified bibliography in the back of the book.

The club activity will not end within the school walls if leaders will try to see that those interests and skills awakened and nurtured in school clubs are carried over into the student's home life and community life.

Each club leader is an important guide in adjusting students in community activities relating to their club or activity. That leader is an important source of information.

Noon Activities

What a few schools are doing about noon activities is indicated in these brief reports:

In cold weather noon table games, supervised by a teacher, are played in the cafeteria after everyone has finished eating. A popular song program sponsored by a faculty committee is held one day each week during the noon hour. Class picnics are held in the spring with teachers and parents as sponsors.

Woodrow Wilson Junior High School, Terre Haute, Indiana

We planned an interesting noon hour activity program which solved the confusion for pupils who stay in school from 8:15 A.M. to 3 P.M.

Edna May Smithies, Assistant Principal,
University of Chicago High School

Other schools with large enrollment and double lunch period, require movies. We do not. But to keep restless adolescents occupied after lunch, the assistant principal has this year developed a series of spectator activities about twice a week; ping-pong or badminton, one-reel pictures, cheering rallies in the auditorium, two soft-ball games outside. Very effective. Almost the whole school attends. Teachers, pupils, custodians participate.

Monticello Junior High School,
Cleveland Heights, Ohio

Noon-hour singing is conducted at Central High School in Flint, Michigan. Another noon activity is a milk bar operated by the student council in Haverford Senior High School, Upper Darby, Pennsylvania.

Where the local library is near the school, a session of reading may be enjoyed for a half-hour at noon. A Finnish boy, whose father told him stories about his experiences on the high seas years ago, frequented the local library at noon to read about Viking ships, the life of a sailor, and the merchant marine. The librarian knew him and his interests and served him quickly and well. One noon his counselor saw him there absorbed in a story such as his father used to tell. After a half-hour he ran back to his school around the corner. Later his counselor interviewed him about his educational and vocational plans. This boy's hobby was reading about maritime work, which is likely to be his vocation. At noontime in the quiet atmosphere of the local friendly library a boy pursues his natural interest intently. The counselor carried that picture in her mind, wondering whether more students could be guided to read about their interests. Perhaps they need help in finding some absorbing interest. The awakening of an absorbing interest is no doubt the heart of leisure time education as well as vocational success.

Dramatics and Speech

Dramatic sketches may be presented by students with only a few suggestions from teachers. Some of the community opportunities can be most interestingly related through a playlet. One teacher says, "The teacher or a student can read a story and let students act the parts." Panel discussions and a resemblance of a radio broadcast have been successful means of conveying information about community opportunities.

In a class where children represented seven nationalities, an ingenious teacher developed an exceptionally friendly class spirit through a playlet. Dances, songs, and costumes showed activities of boys and girls of other lands. The students saw the possibilities of the dramatic sketch in which their speech was carefully coached, and their understanding of other peoples was enlightened.

The following is an account of an important event that may interest teachers of dramatics. This was written by Miss Augusta Droesch and Miss Barbara Warwick, teachers in the Floral Park-Bellerose School, Floral Park, New York.

The pageant entitled "Free Men," a musical dramatization of the Educational Policies Commission report, "The Education of Free Men in American Democracy," was presented jointly by the schools, churches, veterans' organizations, parent-teachers' association, civic and social organizations, of this school district.

The Floral Park-Bellerose School acted as the center of co-ordination. Through the school the activities of the other agencies were interwoven into a complete production. The principal of the Floral Park-Bellerose School acted as chairman of the production committee, with three music directors of the schools acting as co-ordinators of the fifteen unit directors. Through excellent co-operation of these core leaders, greater community co-operation with its resultant pageant was made possible.

The properties needed in producing this demonstration were gathered from all corners of the community such as the Talmud used in the Jewish episode, the chalice, chancel rail and candles used in the Roman Catholic scene, and the pennants of the various states used in the citizens' scene which were made by the art classes of the Floral Park-Bellerose School. The make-up group had their work so efficiently planned and timed that all members of the cast were ready at their appointed times with the minimum amount of confusion. The unit directors, pressed for time, called upon the mothers of the community to sew many of the costumes. Here again was an excellent example of working co-operation.

The pageant was presented on two successive evenings during the first part of June at the Floral Park-Bellerose School. The audience numbered approximately 2000 and the price of admission was the price of a War Stamp or Bond. . . .

Those of us who helped in this co-operative enterprise, felt that the time was well spent toward the achievement of this ultimate goal—"This pledge your school can and does give you. Whatever happens in the future, whatever hardships or good fortune may come our way, in peace or war, this school, these teachers, these young people will never cease to teach and to learn the knowledge, the loyalties, and the discipline of "Free Men."[10]

The dramatics teacher in Oceanside High School, New York, Mrs. Frances Weaver Heinley, carries over her subject into the community life, as the following paragraphs indicate:

Since my specialty is dramatics and speech, I am astounded at times by the talks my pupils make on a wide variety of subjects. In order to provide real speech situations, and at the same time to present high school students at their best, I wrote letters to all the organizations in the community telling them that we have available a number of students who can provide entertainment in the form of dramatic readings, panel discussions, and talks on topics of public interest. We have had invitations from the American Legion, Northeast Civic Association, Sea Scouts, an elementary school parent-teachers' association, an elementary school faculty group, the Public Library Association and a young people's church group.

Our most popular program has been a series of talks on the history of the community. Because there is no recorded history, the pupils need to do considerable research. This pleases the older residents, and has contributed to a better understanding between the school and the "old timers" who have resented the rapid growth of the village and the consequent tax rise.

All in all I believe that the community offers a laboratory, a workshop, that the school cannot afford to disregard. It provides a proving ground for the ways of world understanding and citizenship. Co-ordination of school and community may eventually bring about the general acceptance of necessary virtues now championed mainly by teachers and preachers.[11]

Some of the outlines in Chapter I which may be adapted by dramatics or speech teachers are 15, 17, 19, 35, 38, and 41. These teachers are guides in directing students to community opportunities in dramatics and related activities.

Assemblies

The regular school assembly can be used to awaken an active interest in various activities and to display students' hobbies, talents, and skills. Today the student assembly has new and varied

---

[10] *Rho Journal*, March, 1944, p. 48.
[11] *Ibid.*, p. 47.

uses. It takes care of demonstrations, hobby exhibits, recitals, panel discussions, lectures, and various other school and community social, cultural, and recreational activities. Museum, theater, radio, and recreational programs recommended by the school may be announced in these assemblies.

It is important that assemblies on leisure time be arranged early in students' experience in secondary schools, to habituate them to the worthy use of their leisure.

Fretwell comments on pupil participation as follows:

If the school exists to educate the pupils, it is wise to enable the pupils to share in the educative experience of developing and presenting assembly programs.[12]

Students' talents and skills are commonly displayed in assemblies through all school activities which may include:

> Music
> Dramatics
> Dancing, including folk dancing
> Art
> Sculpture
> Clay modeling
> Woodcarving
> Marionettes

Displays of interest of many kinds are excellent means for inspiring creative activity. Playlets which have the same end results may be originated to emphasize community information, talents, or skills—always in a happy vein. School clubs furnish excellent programs for promoting interest in leisure time activities.

Further suggestions may be found in outlines 4 and 32 of Chapter I.

Speakers

When outside speakers are invited to the assemblies, they should be carefully selected for leisure time assembly programs. It is best to omit speakers unless they qualify in these minimum essentials:

[12] Fretwell, *Extra-curricular Activities in the Secondary Schools*, p. 250.

Ability to adapt the talk to the group

Ability to keep within the time limit (otherwise, restlessness and disinterest may occur)

Clarity of voice and diction

Enough enthusiasm to interest the group

The New York Vocational Guidance Association (Speakers' Committee 1946) makes these suggestions for speakers on avocational or vocational topics:

Relate the talk closely to the audience. Discuss plans in advance with the person arranging the meeting.

If the group is under 75 in number it is advisable to try to make the meeting more of a discussion than is possible in a large group.

Use some illustrative material if possible.

Show interest in your subject. Sufficient zest to create immediate interest and to hold attention is important.

Express some humor.

Allow a few minutes for questions from the audience.

A young group of junior high school age requires a shorter talk than an older group. The interests and general mentality should be considered in planning time.

A copy of the talk should be left with the group if possible.

Ten minutes is usually long enough for a talk to seventh grade students. When the talk is illustrated by sketching, sculpturing, or other activities, the time may be extended without loss of interest. One speaker is usually sufficient for one assembly period if other items are on the program.

Information well presented on leisure time activities and individual hobbies naturally interests students and enriches the assemblies.

Speakers on local leisure time activities are frequently those already well known to the group. Students like to see their friend from the neighborhood center on the platform. They enjoy a talk from one they know. For a talk of this kind it is advisable to give the speaker an outline such as is suggested in the following form letter to a leisure time agency.

DEAR (name)

Some of our students inquired about your activities. We should like to have a member of your organization come and talk to our —— grade assembly of boys and/or girls on ——————— (date) at —————(hour). From ten to fifteen minutes are allotted for this part of the assembly program (or class program).

Our students would be glad to hear the speaker tell about the following:
Kinds of activities in your center for boys and girls
Days and hours of the activities
Fees and other membership requirements
Time students may apply for admission
Name of the person students may contact
Illustration or demonstration of any activities or hobbies featured in the center

We plan to invite students' parents to hear the speaker so that they may see their own responsibility in leisure time education.

Outline 32 of Chapter I is one example of correlation of leisure time activities with an assembly or classroom discussion.

Teachers may be persuaded to tell about and demonstrate their own most interesting hobbies and to show how students may begin stamp collecting, recipe collecting, dressmaking, art, nature lore, music, photography, or other hobbies teachers may have.

A talk by the principal on the use of leisure time always lends importance to the program. One principal gave a concise talk on his present and earlier hobbies which were inexpensive. Another principal talked on summer activities, suggesting a book, a good friend, and an interesting walk. Collecting recipes was the hobby of another principal who told her girls about her interest and what it has meant to her.

English and speech can tie closely with assemblies. Students may tell about neighborhood centers to which they belong. Those who have gathered local information for civics or other subjects may present it convincingly and from memory in an assembly so that other students will want to visit community centers. Students may also tell about their hobbies or sights they have enjoyed in their leisure.

In Junior High School 172, Manhattan, students tie up their leisure time interests, visits, and class talks with assemblies and the school newspaper. A small group was taken to see the annual hobby exhibition at a department store. The students enjoyed the display and especially one of an old seaman who showed samples of 500 different kinds of knots. The seaman told the students, "Today, boys learn only 17 different kinds of knots, but there are over 500." He showed designs made of knotted string. The students wrote up a few of their impressions for the school paper.

Displays

One teacher said, "The hobby display of my group is not very good. But it's their work. They like to see some of their own interests exhibited and it helps them to improve." After all, it is their own work and that of their friends that students are thrilled to see. Gradually we help them to improve their skills and to elevate their interests. The next display may be better but it must always be creative, not something beautifully improved by adults.

Students should prepare several weeks in advance so that they may have their displays ready on time. A committee of students may announce to the various classes that they are to bring to assemblies the articles which they make. Committees are usually fun for them. Musical, dramatic, and other talents should also be featured.

A student may be selected from the committee to announce the numbers on the program. Students who bring displays may tell briefly about their hobby, with such an outline as this in mind:

    Display of my hobby
    Brief description
    How I became interested in this hobby
    My satisfactions from this hobby
    Other interests that my hobby brought me
    How to begin this hobby: materials and expense
    The community centers that will give help

It may be desirable for some of the students to carry their hobby articles through the center of the assembly hall so that students may see them more closely. A similar program may be a part of a "hobby day" or "hobby week" program. One teacher in Junior High School 172, Manhattan, called her hobby program a "Show and Tell" program.

Mrs. Bertha H. Jones, a principal in Belmont, Illinois, reports, "Our area is quite rural. At our Community Fair we exhibit sewing, canning, art, collections and models. Prizes are given for garden products." Public School 30 in Indianapolis, Indiana, conducts similar displays and reports that: "Garden projects have been promoted through the school. Last year we had a Fair with displays of canned goods and vegetables. Ribbon prizes were awarded."

Plans for displays should be talked over with the principal, who will no doubt be glad to offer suggestions and, perhaps, participate in the program.

Outlines in Chapter I that may give further ideas on displays are 3, 4, and 23.

Visual Aids

Films are often available from neighborhood centers. The Scouts, Y's, museums, and colleges, for instance, sometimes have films, slides, and pictures that may be borrowed or rented.

Bulletin boards are a reflection of the life of the school. Announcements, pictures, displays, and other material on leisure time should be attractively placed or mounted on colored paper. Their placement where many students may see them is important whether they are in the corridor, classroom, or elsewhere. Students may be trained to keep the bulletin board appealing. They may make posters in art classes to illustrate notices.

Some of the materials that may be posted on the bulletin boards relate to the following:

Afterschool activities in the school building
Activities in settlement and neighborhood houses, clubs, Y's, libraries, music
    and art centers, museums, parks, educational centers
Things to do in the summer
Summer camping opportunities
Church clubs, activities, and religious education on released time
Sightseeing opportunities
Radio and motion picture programs recommended
Reading references on hobbies and talents
Clippings from the newspaper on the day's activities
Centers for adult members of the family.

Some schools make their bulletin boards of major importance by discussing in assemblies all notices placed on the bulletin boards in the corridors, guidance rooms, or classrooms, to develop students' awareness of opportunities. Students may be trained to replenish the bulletin boards and to announce the new materials and their importance.

These references are suggested for teachers planning bulletin board and poster displays:

Gertrude Forrester, *Methods of Vocational Guidance*, Ch. IV, "The Use of Graphic Materials."

B. J. R. Stolper, "The Bulletin Board as a Teaching Device."

Radio

The radio is an excellent means for cultivating appreciation for music, dramatics, speech, and other school subjects. Class discussions of radio programs help students to discriminate between worth-while and inferior programs. Schools are beginning to suggest to students some desirable radio programs. Better still would be letting students discuss the programs with the view of making recommendations to the school, with the guidance of the teacher. Each week a student could mention a few programs to watch for during the week.

In a survey[13] which was made to determine how youth obtained most of their news information, it was found that the radio was the chief source. Because of this fact youth need suggestions on the most reliable radio news programs.

Outline 9 of Chapter I discusses radio programs.

BIBLIOGRAPHY

Auditorium Activities: Elementary and Junior High School Grades, Austin Public Schools, Texas.

BELL, ENID. *Tin-craft as a Hobby.*

BOYCE, GEORGE A. AND WILLARD W. *Mathematics of Everyday Life*, Leisure Unit.

Community Life; A Suggested Unit Organization for the Seventh Grade Program in Social Studies, Division of Secondary Education, New York State Department of Education, Albany, N.Y.

The Condensed Butterick Sewing and Dressmaking Book.

DE LEMOS, PEDRO. *Creative Art Crafts.*

[13] *Fortune Magazine*, November, 1942.

DICKSON, SALLY, AND BLONDIN, FRANCES. *The New Encyclopedia of Modern Sewing.*

DOBBS, ELLA. *First Steps in Weaving.*

DOUGHERTY, JOHN W. *Pottery Made Easy.*

FRETWELL, ELBERT K. *Extra-curricular Activities in Secondary Schools.*

Good Reading, The National Council of Teachers of English.

HALTER, HELEN. *Society in Action;* a guide for the social studies.

HILDEBRAND, J. R. "The Geography of Games," *National Geographic Magazine, August,* 1919.

HOBBS, HARRY J. *Working with Tools.*

HUTCHINS, MABEL REAGH. *Creative Handicrafts.*

HUTCHINS, ROBERT MAYNARD. "The Value of the Museum," *Science*, October 15, 1943.

LEE, JOSEPH. "Play in Education," *Recreation*, December, 1942.

LEEMING, JOSEPH. *Fun with Leather.*

———, *Fun with Wood.*

MARTIN, LAURA K. *A Selected List of Magazines for High School Libraries.*

McKOWN, HARRY C. *Extra-curricular Activities.*

PARKHILL, MARTHA, AND SPAETH, DOROTHY. *It's Fun to Make Things.*

STIERI, EMANUELE. *Woodworking as a Hobby.*

STOLPER, B. J. R. "The Bulletin Board as a Teaching Device."

A Suggested Outline of Subjects to be Covered in Auditorium Periods, Medford Public Schools, Medford, Mass.

THOMPSON, BETTY LYND. *Fundamentals of Rhythm and Dance.*

Chapter III

HOBBIES AND TALENTS

"Recreation includes all the beautiful skills, crafts and hobbies that human beings can practice, on and up to the finest of the fine arts. I call this the Higher Recreation."

—LAWRENCE P. JACKS

TEACHERS and leaders of youth may find that some students like only physical activities and have nothing to do with music, art, or reading. The director of a large youth center said, "Let them have plenty of athletics and social activities. Start there. You can't interest some youngsters in the more mental and esthetic activities but you can work them up to appreciate higher and higher forms of enjoyment."

Many schools mimeograph or print lists throughout the year showing opportunities in the community for the development of hobbies and talents. Here are a few suggestions for lists that may be used in the class and posted on the bulletin boards:

What to Do and Where to Go
Reading about Hobbies and Talents
Radio Programs
Motion Picture Programs
Going Places and Seeing Things
Church Activities
Fun in Summer
Summer Camping
Centers for Adult Activities

These areas of information are briefly discussed in the following pages.

What to Do and Where to Go

Students like definite information about opportunities that may be offered in such places as the following:

The afterschool center in the school
Settlement and neighborhood houses
Clubs for youth
The Y's
Boy Scouts and Girl Scouts
Libraries: activities and collections, and reading lists on hobbies and talents
Churches: clubs, activities, religious education on released time
Music and art centers: class and individual instruction in art, music, sculpture, dramatics
Department of parks: athletic fields, play streets, swimming pools, bicycle paths, programs
Educational centers: evening schools, colleges, classes for adults

The kind of definite information that students like about these opportunities includes:

Name and address of the center
Name of the person whom students may contact
Kinds of activities offered for boys, and for girls: through the year, in summer
Day and hours of the activities
Ages required for membership
Fees, and plans for payment
Other requirements for membership
Special services offered: medical, dental, employment, home visiting, nursing, interviews about problems, other individual services
Circulars illustrating activities

Here is a sample of one item as it was mimeographed with others on a two-page list called, "What to Do and Where to Go":

Boys Club, 321 East 111th Street
Athletics, swimming, movies, library, boxing, softball leagues, dancing, track meets, Boy Scouts, dramatics, club groups.
Summer: roof playground, deck tennis, shuffleboard, ping-pong, checkers, baseball, free tickets for Yankees and Giants games, camping $6 for 2 weeks.

Regardless of whether the school or some local council of agencies draws up this information, it should be available every September to be of maximum use in class discussions through the school year. A school may wish to summarize this information in an alphabetical list of the activities and places where they are offered. Students may then easily find on the list the activities in which they are especially interested. Such remarks as these are heard: "That's what I want," "That's my Scout troop, number 546!" "We can swim in three places!" "Glee club this term!" "Trumpet club! That's where I'm going."

School clubs may be co-ordinated with community organizations. For example, South High School of Minneapolis, Minnesota, makes this report:

School Club	Community Organization
Blue Triangle, and Silver Triangle	Y. W. C. A.
Hi-Y	Y. M. C. A.
Seton Hi	Seton Guild
Red Cross	Red Cross Organization
Foreign Language Clubs	Norwegian and Swedish Societies

These service groups co-ordinate their activities with those in the community: Projection Crew, Stage Crew, Hall Guides. The Fellowship group co-operates with churches for the development of ideals and for church service. The Radio Club broadcasts for local stations. The results of club work are shown in the new hobbies and interests which students develop in South High School.

Reading about Hobbies and Talents

The local libraries are usually glad to compile a brief list of references on hobbies and talents of boys and girls. The list serves the purpose of inspiring students to explore their own interests further.

A class of ninth graders expressed their hobby interests, which were passed on to the local library with the result that some reading material was suggested in reference to those interests. The hobbies most mentioned were:

Baseball	Hiking
Birds	Orchestra
Cartooning	Softball
Carving	Stamps
Dramatics	Trumpet playing
Dress designing	

The list of hobbies and the references were then mimeographed and used by the adviser of the ninth grade. Subject teachers

Students of Junior High School 83 and 172, Manhattan, read about hobbies and vocations in Aguilar Branch Library

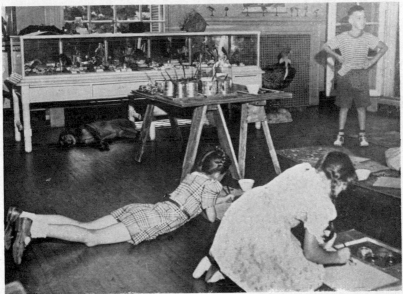

Photo by Jean Snow—Courtesy National Recreation Association

Corner of a paint class at Villa Rosa, a children's museum in Washington, D. C.

know many interesting books of pleasurable reading on their subjects, which they can recommend to students.

Magazines on mechanics, radio, aviation, science, music, needlework, art, sports, and other activities are popular reading material and should be mentioned, in a general way at least, when a list of reading references is compiled.

References on boys' and girls' interests are classified in the back of the book. The list of magazines which is also in the bibliography touches on many hobbies. These magazines seem to appeal to boys and girls and make a colorful display in the classroom.

Radio Programs

Parent associations are sometimes interested in compiling a list of recommended radio programs adapted to youth. It has been found desirable to have such a list compiled twice each year and sent to the schools. Some schools use these lists in English, speech, music, dramatics, and in individual guidance.

One parent association mimeographed a list showing the programs for youth 5 to 9, 9 to 12, and 12 to 16 years of age. The station and time were given. Whether the value was educational or entertainment was also noted after each program. Schools found this information helpful to the students.

Motion Picture Programs

Other suggestions that might be posted on the bulletin board, discussed in class and clubs, and reported upon by students are the current motion pictures that the school recommends. In one class the students evaluated the current pictures and pointed out the value and weakness from the standpoints of acting, education, moral influence, and entertainment.

Films on leisure time activities are frequently available through local settlements, Y's, Scouts, and boards of education. It is well for someone to see them before they are shown in the school to make sure whether they are up to date or too old and queer, and to determine their fitness for the group.

Going Places and Seeing Things

Guidebooks on sightseeing may be obtained from newsstands in large cities. Chambers of commerce and bureaus of information have interesting circulars and other suggestions. This material may be adapted to the class.

Sightseeing trips on school time are becoming a greater part of the curriculum. They offer excellent opportunities for co-ordination with the assemblies, school clubs and newspaper, and with all school subjects.

Information lists which suggest sightseeing possibilities should be obtained or compiled for class use and for the bulletin boards. The following is a sample of such a list as it was prepared for use in two schools[1] in New York. This list was called, "Going Places and Seeing Things."

Aquarium, Bronx Park
Fraunces' Tavern, Broad and Pearl Streets: relics of the Revolutionary War
Cunard Building, 25 Broadway: interesting interiors
Trinity Church, Broadway and Wall Street: built in 1696; site given by
  Queen Anne; Alexander Hamilton and Robert Fulton are buried there.
St. Patrick's Cathedral, Fifth Avenue
St. John the Divine, W. 110th St. and Amsterdam Avenue
Riverside Church, Riverside Drive and W. 122nd St.
City Hall, City Hall Park: The Governor's room contains many relics and
  paintings; built in 1812
Cleopatra's Needle (Obelisk), Central Park near the Metropolitan Museum
  of Art; brought from Egypt. It is 3500 years old
Columbia University, Broadway and W. 116-120th Streets
National Broadcasting Company, Rockefeller Plaza
Radio City, Sixth Avenue and 49th Street
Empire State Building, 34th Street and Fifth Avenue
Ellis Island, New York Harbor: pass for visit is obtainable at the Barge
  Office
Holland Tunnel, Canal Street to Jersey City under the Hudson River:
  length under water one mile; fresh air is provided by an enormous ven-
  tilating system
New York Public Library, Fifth Avenue and 42nd Street: the art galleries
  contain numerous paintings by masters
Bronx Zoological Park and Botanical Gardens, Bronx Park

Museums

American Museum of Natural History, West 77th Street and Columbus
  Avenue: a rich collection of birds, animals, reptiles, and other things of
  natural history
American Numismatic Society, Broadway and W. 156th Street: collection
  of coins, medals, and an extensive library

[1] Junior High Schools 83 and 172.

The Cloisters, end of Fort Washington Avenue: medieval art, tapestries, colonnades, natural settings with gardens

Dyckman House, Broadway and 204th Street: a farm house of Dutch Colonial times with a collection of historical relics of the period

Hayden Planetarium, West 81st Street and Central Park West

Metropolitan Museum of Art, Fifth Avenue and 82nd Street

Museum of the American Indian, Broadway and W. 155th Street

Museum of the City of New York, Fifth Avenue and 104th Street

Museum of Modern Art, 11 West 53rd Street

Museum of Science and Industry, 30 Rockefeller Plaza

New York Historical Society, 170 Central Park West

For other places of interest see: *The Red Book Information Guide to Manhattan* and other boroughs.

Church Activities

Some students do not realize the opportunities their own family church offers during the week, but students as well as their parents are usually glad to hear teachers include their family church in the suggestions for community activities. Teachers advise students to consult their parents for advice on church clubs, teams, discussion groups, choir, socials, book groups, and religious education. Many churches make a special effort to develop talents of youth through church activities. The Riverside Church, New York, is only one of many churches which tax their facilities to the maximum to serve youth in all kinds of activities. Recent members of church activities reported that brotherhood in action, prevails in all the craft groups and activities. The catholic youth organization, known as the C.Y.O., can supply information on their local clubs and activities for boys and girls. Synagogues also offer diversified programs after school.

A recent link between schools and churches is religious education on released time, a program that more and more states are adopting. A symposium of the work carried on by three faiths, "Released Time in New York City," written by Imogene M. McPherson and the presidents of associations of three denominations, was printed by the Greater New York Interfaith Committee. It indicates the increasing co-operation of principals who are releasing students punctually each week for these religious education classes in the community churches. It reports an improved attitude of students toward each other and toward religion. The Greater New York Interfaith Committee believes that schools today are trying to impart to the students a genuine conception and understanding of cultural and spiritual values as well as to train their minds. One student wrote, "I think I learned a lot in released time school. I want to act like what I learned about."

Just as students learn from the school about local Scouts, Y's, settlements, sports, libraries, and other centers, so can they learn whether there is a released time class in their own church. The decision is then up to the child and the parent. The parent may write a note to the teacher in the public school requesting that the child be released punctually to attend the weekly released time class in the family church once each week at 2:30 P.M. Although churches are trying to make their programs known in the neighborhoods there may be students who for some reason do not get the information.

Speakers from local churches address assemblies in most schools, but not as representatives of any one denomination. They give talks of a character-building nature that help students make better use of their social, educational, or leisure time opportunities. Whether the speakers are from Jewish, Protestant, or Catholic churches, the talks are, of course, nondenominational. Students have expressed to teachers their appreciation of these talks. One student asked his teacher for the address of the speaker, who was willing to talk to parents and students about any home or personal problem. Another proudly said he attended the activities to which the speaker referred.

Junior High School 83 in New York carefully selects speakers from the community to address various assemblies. As a result, students have received some helpful suggestions about exploration of interesting books, community opportunities, clean habits, sense of values, parent companionship, home relationships, occupations, preparation for a vocation, healthful and happy living, and what local agencies including churches offer in leisure time activities.

Fun in Summer

A list of summer opportunities is useful for class discussion the last few weeks of school.

Summer can be a boresome time for youth but the school can help classes and individuals find some interesting things to do in the community clubs, settlements, churches, and school play centers.

A mimeographed list of one or two pages with a heading something like "Fun in Summer" or "Things to Do This Summer" should be useful to all teachers and students. This information may be posted the last two weeks of school when summer activities are discussed.

The following statements indicate the ways some schools are helping students to plan their summer:

The biology teacher makes up a list of activities that would be interesting to children inclined to take walks or roam the mountains. This is done at the close of the year and reports are made on it when school reopens in the autumn.

Thurmont High School, Thurmont, Maryland

Our school is a consolidated rural elementary school. Most of the children are busy during the summer months with the many farm chores; however, the churches have daily vacation Bible schools, and the 4H Clubs are active.

Bellevue School, Alabama City, Alabama

For several years we have made a practice of having every child write a short essay just before the end of school on what he or she planned to do during the summer. Several class periods are used to discuss this material. When school opens in the fall the activities actually completed were discussed in class. This practice has been very beneficial in stimulating a worthwhile use of leisure time.

Sanford Grammar School, Sanford, Florida

The Floral Park-Bellerose School, Floral Park, New York, makes this report about summer activities:

There are two playgrounds open from May through September in Floral Park and Bellerose. The larger of these is also available for ice skating in the winter and is the home of a semiprofessional softball team, so that there are scheduled "double-header" games every Sunday throughout the spring and summer open to residents and friends free of charge.

In addition, the usual playground activities are carried on such as: small children storytelling, arts and crafts, volleyball and softball tournaments, tennis tournament, shuffleboard and horseshoe pitching, checkers, chess, and other games.

The boys' physical education teacher for both elementary schools in town is the director of the larger playground during the summer. The smaller playground is usually staffed by one or two of the regular teachers who are willing to be assigned to summer work.

In Washington, D. C., the third graders of the Buchanan School discovered ways of using their free time. Their teacher, Miss Grace V. Spencer, wrote in an article how more of her class became interested in the neighborhood Boys' Club. They saw boys with bath towels over their shoulders going for a swim and wanted to go too but learned that they could not go because they were not members. The teacher writes:

> The next morning quite a lively discussion was held on "What you can do at the Boys' Club." One of the nonmembers asked John if he could swim. "Of course, I can swim," replied John. "The instructor teaches you to swim. I can swim across the pool now!" Another boy told about swimming under water and how clear and clean the pool was. "You have to take a shower before you can go in, too," he said.
> Soon came the questions: "Who can join?" "How much does it cost?" When they were told it cost only 75 cents a year for Midgets and that any boy over seven years of age could be a member, a good many were sure they could belong.[2]

The children arranged to visit the Boys' Club and saw the game room, gymnasium, the ring where the boxing matches were held, the special exercise room, the library, the art room, and the swimming pool with its shower and lockers, the printing shop, the log-cabin room for the Cub Scouts and Boy Scouts, and last of all, the theater where the workers were putting the final touches to the stage.

"Before that week was up," the teacher said, "every boy in our room was a member! The girls were also interested and joined a dancing class held there on Saturday morning." That summer the Boys' Club filled the needs of these eager children.

One of the 5A classes in the same school in Washington, D. C. followed a regular plan for summer play. Miss Mary V. Willson, teacher, makes her plan clear in the following excerpts from her article:

[2] *The Pilot*, pamphlet for teachers, May, 1944, p. 2.

For the past several years my 5A class has been experimenting with vacation pastimes. We wished to budget our time to allow for play and learning experiences. Last year's plan worked with considerable success.

About the first of June we began planning neighborhood clubs. We found out what activities were offered by the Boys' Club, Friendship House, Christ Child Society and the Bible Schools in our churches. We also wanted to have things we could do when we were alone or in small groups. We discussed interesting things the children enjoyed doing. These were listed on the board and arranged in order of interests displayed.

The children attracted to a particular club would meet with the teacher to make plans. In this way each child made his choice of a club. Discussions followed and fifteen different kinds of clubs were organized.

. . . The "Help at Home Club" was organized to teach children that vacation time is learning time as well as play time. Every child was to help at home at least two hours a day. These two hours were divided in any way desired. Every week each child contracted to perform sixteen household tasks. Among these were: wash and dry dishes, set and clear table, dust and mop, run errands, and help make the beds, especially his own.[3]

The teacher of that project also reported a number of other efforts to tie up leisure time education with the home and the community. Children cooked, sewed on buttons, read many interesting books, and participated in a Visit Washington Club. Children who were out of the city in the summer carried plan books with them. When school resumed in the fall the children enjoyed hearing and seeing what various members had done to spend a happy and worth-while vacation.

Summer Camping

Whether children need a free camp or whether their parents can pay for a private camp, students usually welcome suggestions of camps which would suit their needs and the wishes of the parents.

A form may be devised and mimeographed ready for interested students to fill out about two months before the close of school so that there may be time to serve individual needs. Questions such as the following should be adapted to the situation at hand:

[3] *The Twenty-Fourth Yearbook of the National Elementary Principal*, N. E. A., Washington, D.C., September, 1945.

QUESTIONNNAIRE

SUMMER CAMPING AND ACTIVITIES

Name of student_____ Class_____ Date_____
1. Do you plan to go to a camp this summer? Yes___ How long___ No___
   If you went to camp last year, name the camp_____
2. Do you wish the school to help you find a camp this summer?

   Yes___ No___
3. Do you plan to go away to visit? Yes___ How long?___ No___
4. What do you plan to do while you are home this summer? (consult
   the school's list of summer activities)_____
Do not write below this line
_____

Teacher's suggestions and comments:

Directories for summer camping are usually available at some central welfare office or in the local community council office. This information on camping opportunities is essential for use in the individual interviews with students and parents seeking advice. Settlements and other social agencies can usually find free or inexpensive camping opportunities for boys and girls thirteen years of age or younger. Agencies have been known to reserve a certain number of camp places for one school. Older children may have to be sent to a camp requiring a charge which the parent must assume or which the school may be able to share.

It is advisable to have all the interviewing done before the first of June. By that time health defects should be corrected, otherwise registrations may not be accepted by the agencies. Interviews directly with the parent are advisable in order to make sure that the parent will take all the necessary steps such as having the child examined. Without the full co-operation of the parent the child may change his mind, decide to visit his uncle instead of going to camp, or get homesick in camp and have to return home in a few days. It is also advisable to try to give camp opportunities to those who most need them.

Centers for Adult Activities

A school may wish to make a separate list of centers for adult recreational and educational opportunities and to distribute this list through students to parents and other adult members of the family. Parent organizations should also find the information valuable. Classes for adults are frequently offered in schools, churches, libraries, the Y's, and other centers. The specific subjects taught in each center should be indicated in a list. Parents might like to assist in the preparation of this information, which should be ready for use in September.

Hobbies and talents of boys and girls can be developed somewhere in the community. It is a joy to all who work with youth to find the right opportunities for individuals and to see their satisfaction in creative activities.

BIBLIOGRAPHY

ARNOLD, ALFRED G. *Neighborhood Activities in Country Communities.*

DAKIN, W. S. "Summary of Reports on Programs for Guidance of Children's Time During Summer Vacations," State Department of Education, Hartford, Conn.

DIMOCK, HEDLEY S., AND HENDRY, CHARLES E. *Camping and Character.*

MANLY, STACEY. *It's Fun to Make It Yourself*, The Journal of Living Publishing Corporation.

New York Handy Guide, a sample of sightseeing guides available at newsstands or chambers of commerce.

PANGBURN, WEAVER WEDDELL. *Adventures in Recreation.*

PARTRIDGE, E. DE ALTON, AND MOONEY, CATHERINE. *Time Out for Living.*

SEYFERT, W. C. "New Interest in Religious Education," *School Review*, June, 1945.

∽ Chapter IV ∽

THE CREATIVE SCHOOL AFTER 3 O'CLOCK

"Life, life more abundant is the impulse of our time."
—MAX C. OTTO

LET'S keep the school door open after 3 o'clock for some of the things boys and girls like to do.

If the afterschool program is to be a welcome one to teachers, careful planning for any extra assignments in leadership and supervision is important. Otherwise schools may defeat their purpose by inadequate planning. Each activity should be carefully mapped out so that teachers and other leaders have a sense of organization and specific responsibilities. Thus the teachers' interest may be obtained. Once it is obtained it needs to be sustained, otherwise the spirit that is the vital factor in leisure time education is lost. Only as fast as those concerned follow with enthusiasm can a school move ahead on the afterschool activity program.

A music teacher volunteered to train a small group of music lovers after 3 o'clock weekly. Before long she had an orchestra of which any school could be proud. Another teacher formed a group of enthusiasts in photography. She led them in experiments for an hour each week and took them to a photographic exhibition in the local library.

These activities were successfully carried out because the principal had discussed and planned them with the teachers, and assigned activities according to the teachers' special interests. Necessary materials were planned for and a clear schedule was made out.

One teacher who volunteered to conduct an art group after school was assigned for one afternoon each week. The mother of a student in that group came to express her gratitude for the extra help in art which her son was receiving. She was glad when the teacher invited her to sit down with the group and do anything she wished in art or crafts. "May I try to design a dress?

You see I used to do dressmaking in a factory," she said. Costume designing became her hobby and joy. The students showed that they were proud to have her there with them.

Group Leadership

Teachers frequently give extra time to afterschool activities. Interschool and intergrade activities under teacher supervision are common. For instance, Public School 33 of Indianapolis, Indiana, arranges intergrade contests in baseball among the boys. In Arcadia, Louisiana, the coach and music teacher assist in leisure time activities. Follow-up of students' activities becomes natural and easy if the teacher was the play leader the day before. Students who enjoy this afterschool relationship are better for it and are easier to live with in school. They see the teacher in a new light because they have played with him.

Although schools depend largely upon volunteer leadership, some schools have found it desirable to pay for these extra services. For example, physical education teachers of the Morcy Junior High School in Denver, Colorado, receive extra pay for conducting evening activities in the gymnasium.

The school board leads the way in furnishing leadership for many schools. Some of the activities provided by the school board leaders usually are: basketball, handball, softball, ping-pong, games, crafts, music, art, stories, sewing, and games for small children. Indoor and outdoor yards are commonly used. These activities are usually open to all boys and girls in the community.

The Division of Recreational and Community Activities of the Board of Education in New York has made some commendable demonstrations. There is a need for their services to continue and to expand. As is true of many other worthy demonstrations the problem of an inadequate staff curtails their standards and extent of service. This Division had a well-organized program in a Manhattan school where close co-ordination had developed between the Division and the principal. Even some of the "problem" students were beginning to benefit from the activities. After three months the Division lost some of the staff, activities diminished, students dropped out, until all that remained was ping-pong and outdoor play. The board has plans for staffing the units of activities with more permanent personnel because the Division under the leadership of Mr. Mark A. McCloskey has already proved their value.

Where leadership can be provided for an afterschool program, it will usually be found that students like activities in their school building. They can start them as soon as school is dismissed and not have to walk a long distance first. Then too, they know each other and feel at home at once. Therefore, group leadership is justifiable for the afterschool program that meets students' needs and that provides interesting variety.

In Monterey, California, the school board is operating and directing the municipal recreation program with good results. School instructors receive extra pay for their recreational work. Some of the activities are baseball, football, swimming, archery, ping-pong, nature walks, softball, bicycling, sewing, wood and other art crafts, dancing lessons, and a variety of games suitable to the various age groups.

Whether the group leadership comes from the board of education or from outside organizations, permanent leadership is essential for the proper development and success of any afterschool program in the school.

Local organizations frequently lead school groups. Leaders from the Scouts, the Y's, the neighborhood house, or the churches are usually well trained for group leadership. These organizations might be prevailed upon to start a new group in the school. Other interested and qualified volunteer workers might also serve school groups commendably. Parent-teacher organizations may be appealed to. A teacher in Memorial Junior High School, Orlando, Florida, said: "Last winter our parent-teacher association was instrumental in starting a recreational center for the senior high students. In my own school the parent-teacher association sponsors a dance or party in our school gymnasium every two weeks."

An interesting and worth-while afterschool program for young children is described in *Play Centers for School Children*, by Adele Franklin and Agnes E. Benedict.

Financial aid through philanthropy may be the means of carrying on activities in certain areas. Some schools are fortunate enough to receive a large sum of money from some organization to carry on a program of activities during or after school for a few years. The Mott Foundation has assisted the Central High School in Flint, Michigan. The New York Foundation co-operated with the Board of Education and benefited the students of Junior High School 101 in New York, which makes this report:

Junior High School 101 Manhattan is one of the three schools carrying on an experiment in socialized activities under the joint auspices of the Board of Education and the New York Foundation. As part of the experiment there has been established in Junior High School 101 a program of afterschool activities, directed in part toward the worthy use of leisure time. In the short time we have carried on the program, much progress has been made in service to these girls. The afterschool activities include the following:

Athletics, games
Needle-work, sewing, novelties
Arts and crafts: weaving, clay modeling, block printing, painting, design
Music, dancing, dramatics
Marionettes
Swimming
Home nursing
The lounge: games, discussions
English for Spanish-speaking adults

The Easter vacation plans included: Treasure Hunt, skating party, hiking, Chinatown, movies—"Song of Russia," swimming.

Teachers and principals frequently appear in afterschool groups just to look on a moment. This pleases boys and girls more than we may realize. Any evidence of interest on the part of the school staff kindles friendly relationships between students and their teachers and subjects. Students then feel the teachers' interest and are not afraid to talk to them in class about the tournament, the dance of next week, or the raffia mat for the classroom window sill.

Kinds of Afterschool Programs

The Hawthorne School in Helena, Montana, has a commendable Crafters' Club, as these reports show:

The Crafters' Club developed in response to a need for leisure time activities for a rather large class of junior high school students of more than average mental ability, but extremely wanting in manual dexterity and skills. A sixth-grade unit on Days and Ways of the Guilds gave a good point of departure for a class activity based on pupil organization. Rules adopted permitted students to transfer to other guilds at six-weeks intervals. Each guild arranged for necessary materials and tools. Typical crafts engaged in were: model building (airplanes and boats), string-craft, woodworking, puppetry, knitting and weaving, whittling and carving.

Outcomes were very satisfactory. Every student had mastered at least one craft. Reports and exhibits as well as demonstrations of work greatly increased interest and research. Every member was pledged to teach his craft to at least one person.

What other schools are doing in providing leisure time activities for their students is indicated by these sample reports:

The physical education teacher for girls gives extra time outside school hours to groups of girls who enjoy sports, games and dancing in leisure time. Our teacher of physical education for boys gives two nights each week to boys interested in games held in the school gymnasium during winter months. In summer the instructor is in charge of swimming at Isaac Walton Lake near the city.

                    Woodrow Wilson Junior High School, Terre Haute, Indiana

In addition to our physical education program we have boys' and girls' athletic "turn-out" twice a week after school. Points are given for participation and for personal hygiene. Letters are presented in assembly at the end of the year.   Lewiston Junior High School, Lewiston, Idaho

The Ebert School in Denver, Colorado, supervises its own playgrounds until nine in the evening.

The kinds of activities for any afterschool program are best determined through a survey of students' interests. However, there may be occasional need for interpreting to the students certain desirable club opportunities. For instance, one school had an opportunity to get a community leader who was skillful in making miniature boats. As soon as this opportunity was revealed there were more students who wanted to enter the club than could be accommodated.

One leader who held her weekly Scout meeting in the gymnasium of Junior High School 81, Manhattan, opened her session with some discussion which interested the group. This discussion was of a character-building nature. Then came a period of physical exercise followed by crafts, music, or art. Hikes and sightseeing trips were also in the term's schedule.

This leader often remarked about the convenience of the first-floor gymnasium for her troop work. The outdoor playground was also available to her when she needed it but the indoor space suited her needs for all sorts of weather.

Afterschool activities that may be carried over into the home life or community life of the students are of special constructive value. This carry-over idea is expressed in the following words of the district superintendent, Mr. Stuart Mitchell, of Westwood Junior-Senior High School in Westwood, California, who says:

> Our emphasis has recently been changed after consultation with some leading college professors. We now stress carry-over sports and activities. For example, hunting, skiing, and ski mountaineering are strong in this particular community; fly-tying, fishing, fishing lore, golf, tennis, basketball, softball and kindred activities take precedence over football and track. Archery seems to be a coming sport here.
>
> We have six men in the Mountain Regiment. Our Ski Patrol sleeps in snow caves, takes four-day trips, carrying all equipment. We have a school holiday on opening of fishing season, duck season, and deer season. There is an apparent need for more social activities in small groups. Possibly a recreational hall will be constructed.

Another carry-over activity is music. In the Deming Public Schools, Deming, New Mexico, the school employs a year-around director. They recently began a year-around music program.

Schools seem to offer leisure time opportunities after 3 o'clock in line with their facilities and the voluntary or paid personnel which can be obtained. The need is for permanent personnel to plan and carry on the afterschool program over a long period without interruption.

Are afterschool activities in the school preferred to community activities? Both are essential services for boys and girls. The school can make its facilities serve as an end in themselves or as means for adjusting individuals to community activities which they may continue long after they leave the school.

A boy joined the Y. M. C. A. while in a junior high school. He continued to enjoy dramatics, printing, and games after he graduated from senior high school. At Christmas time when the usual party and play were given he brought his mother and younger brother, who also became a member. The Y was an essential source of self-development and community contact for the boy.

Teen-Age Mixers and Canteens

The heyday of snacks, cokes, and the juke box has come to the old lodge hall, the vacant store around the corner, the school gym just off the street, the settlement, and the neighborhood center. Some place to go, someone to chat and joke with—that's what youth like, and adults are helping them get it.

In its pamphlet on "Teen Trouble," the National Recreation Association says that a place where boys and girls may chat and have fun together without self-consciousness has an advantage in providing a wholesome setting not only for the boy-crazy girl or the girl-crazy boy, but also for the group that does not get very much publicity. This latter group has never had very much chance to meet youngsters of the opposite sex in pleasant social ways. These boys and girls are often neglected or have not had proper training to help them adjust easily to social situations.

In New Philadelphia, Ohio, the Kiwanis, Rotary, and Lions Clubs and the Ministerial Association developed the Community Youth Recreational Center with the co-operation of the park's playground committee. The Seattle Park Board of Washington co-operated with the Roosevelt High School in arranging a mixer called the Romix, with funds from the Landham Act. The Romix was successful in interesting young people and in maintaining its standards.

Oceanside, New York, began plans for a youth center. Miss Anna D. Haertter reported:

The situation which called for consideration was the large number of very young as well as older children on the streets up to ten or eleven o'clock each night. Our superintendent of schools called a meeting of the ministers and priests of the various churches, the heads of the civic associations, the school attorney (who is also president of the business men's association), and the junior and senior high school principals. The pupils represented stated that the reason that boys and girls gather at a tavern after school games was not that they enjoyed going to such a place particularly, but that none other was available. Our report to village organizations recommending a youth center is only a preliminary step toward community coordination.[1]

The Benjamin Franklin High School in New York planned two teen canteens through the co-operation of the 23rd Precinct Co-ordinating Council, churches, city police, patrol corps, community agencies, and parents. The steering committee of young people participated in the operation of the canteens and shared their responsibilities well.

Another activity in that school was the gala fiesta in November, 1944, arranged through the co-operation of students of that high school and Junior High School 172 which is in the same building. The two principals, Dr. Leonard Covello and Dr. Joseph O. Loretan, succeeded in making the fiesta a delightful occasion. After a fiesta the joyous atmosphere lingers in the great halls, making conversation easy for students and staff alike, and promoting understanding between the parents and the school.

Parents of Manhasset, Long Island, participate in a teen-age canteen organized with help from Professor Frederic M. Thrasher of New York University. Some parent is always there to open and lock the door and to stand by with her knitting enjoying the fun from the side lines. Professor Thrasher made this informal report:

As a result of seeing the new March of Time film, Youth in Crisis, 22 young people in a Long Island community formed a Youth Council for the Prevention of Delinquency. These are high school young people, 14 to 18 years of age. They have a committee to develop a more interesting and more varied program of wholesome spare time activities for young people, a committee to work on the problem of hoodlumism in the motion picture theaters, and another committee to take up the question of enforcing the laws with regard to the sale of liquor to minors. The Youth Council includes Protestants, Jews, Catholics, colored and white, and representatives of all youth groups in the local community. I think this plan might be applicable to young people of high school age in or around New York if adapted to meet the needs of local communities.

[1] *Rho Journal*, March, 1944, p. 56.

High school boys in Kalamazoo, Michigan, gathered their own facts and presented them to the Council of Social Agencies to prove their needs. They checked court records of juvenile delinquency and teen-age patronage of bars, and surveyed youth programs in their vicinity. The result was valuable information used in establishing activities such as were needed there. They proved themselves capable of running their own activity. Today, they have a center of their own, self-supported, self-governed, and highly popular.

Ventures in mixers and canteens have proved outstandingly popular and successful in many cities. Some of these places where the idea has been successful are: Seattle, Washington; Kalamazoo, Michigan; University School of Indiana University; New Philadelphia, Ohio; Benjamin Franklin High School in New York City; and Summit, New Jersey. Schools in the South have also made a beginning as reported by Dr. Harold D. Meyer, executive director of the North Carolina Recreation Committee in Chapel Hill, North Carolina. More and more schools in North Carolina are adopting the idea.

The do's and don'ts of the club. Mixers and canteens should be governed by certain standards and rules. A club constitution may result from discussions of such matters as: name, objects, eligibility of members, officers, and adult council (nominations, elections, duties), meetings, responsibilities of members, committees, and hours.

Some of the teen-age groups are called by unique names such as: Co-op, Hangout, Romix, Teen-Canteen, Bombardier, Commando Club, Teen Town, Keen Teens, and The Deck. One community worker of Summit, New Jersey, said, "Call it what you may—it is a place where young people of all ages can come, and play, dance, and eat; in short, do whatever they would do elsewhere, but under proper supervision and in appropriate and wholesome surroundings."

Difficulty sometimes arises about who may go to the mixer or canteen. The Roosevelt High School of Seattle indicated that "The only friction of any kind at our first mixer was a misunderstanding about who could attend. Former pupils, friends of pupils, and pupils of other schools sought to get in but were informed that the party was for Roosevelt students only."

The University School of Indiana University, Bloomington, decided that "Afternoon sessions should be limited to University School students but the evening sessions should include their invited guests." They arrange to have one faculty member present at each session to identify students and to be responsible for the building and equipment used. A sufficient number of parents is designated to serve as chaperons each session.

A creed often works as a guiding influence in social conduct if the boys and girls make it up themselves. In the Co-op of the Summit High School of New Jersey, this creed was drawn up:

I Want to Co-operate

1. With other members: in making and keeping our headquarters a place to be proud of.
2. With my family: in helping them adjust home living to present needs.
3. With my town: in respecting its property and the will of the community of which I am a part.
4. With my country: in giving some of my free time to patriotic service.

Some common features. Get-togethers are popular whether they are dances, parties, stunt nights, snack bars, game rooms, or athletics. Some clubs provide a "hang-out room." The National Recreation Association claims that closely tied up with social recreation is the necessity for providing specific space in which these boys and girls can meet each other in informal and attractive surroundings. The teen age is the age in which boys and girls are gradually becoming weaned away from family dependency and are growing more and more interested in being one of a large group of their own age. Young people of this age like an opportunity for meeting, laughing, talking, and having a good time all by themselves. Communities are competing with the corner drugstore and the candy store more and more.

Dancing, cards, ping-pong, a soft-drink bar, and a juke box are provided in the Summit Co-op. The Junior Board arranges for the door, bar, game room, and publicity committees. The young people of Summit feel that they have solved their problem well.

Some schools make their cafeteria the social headquarters, as does the University School in Bloomington. A member of that staff states that "The students' need is not for formally planned entertainment, but rather for a place to meet, a 'hang-out' where they may make their own good times in acceptable surroundings and with proper supervision. On this theory, the committees arrange little in the way of a formal program."

Are snacks enough? The teen-age club movement has flourished as an easy way out. Dr. Harold D. Meyer of the North Carolina Recreation Committee thinks that the situation calls for a very realistic view and a practical administration of the setup. He says:

Let no community be led to believe that by establishing such a club the problems of youth are all settled. Far from it. The scene calls for multiple action. A mobilization of the entire resources of the community all working together and each doing a special job, the sum total of which brings positive and wholesome results, is the desired aim. The teen-age club movement is but *one* force on the whole front. It has a definite contribution to make. It can fill a need and be most constructive in community well being.

Dr. Meyer's pamphlet on "Youth Recreation" and other material may be obtained from his office in Chapel Hill.

Some of the interesting conclusions made after canteen efforts in the Benjamin Franklin High School in New York are:

The canteen appealed to youth in the school area.
Young people liked the canteen and expressed the hope that a similar program would be carried through the fall and winter.
If the young people came once they usually returned.
A small fee seemed desirable for records and equipment.
Youth committees proved capable and should be continued.
Adequate support and protection by the city police and patrol corps are necessary.
The right kind of leaders and supervisors cannot be overemphasized.

Leadership of good quality is one of the great needs in any community recreation program including the teen-age canteen and mixers. There may be responsible people, parents or others, in the community who feel the needs of youth strongly enough to sacrifice an evening a week to supervise teen-age activities.

Volunteers are valuable in the canteen or mixers whether they are professional people, business people, athletes, artists, home-makers, or farm people. An enlightening pamphlet on "Volunteers in Recreation" is published by the Office of Civilian Defense, Washington, D.C. It contains suggestions on types of volunteers and what specific services they can render.

The National Recreation Association in its pamphlet, "Teen Trouble," says, "This leadership training can be most profitable if given in co-operation with as many as possible existing agencies like the parent-teacher association, Federation of Churches, council of social agencies and the like."

Friendliness is the keynote in dealing with youth and their interests whether we contact them in the home, school, church, or in the community recreation program. It takes patience and understanding for adults to work successfully with youth, to give them responsibility and to help them carry it without domination.

Tomorrow more schools will help to develop aptitudes and hobbies and to stimulate participation in the community, church, and home. More students will grow in inner resources like Marshall, a Negro boy who plays the bass viol in the school orchestra, sings in a church choir, and enjoys concerts at the Manhattan School of Music with complimentary tickets the school provides. The school counselor is helping him and his mother plan for a high school course with music. Marshall is a radiant, well-adjusted adolescent in school, in the community, and in his home.

The pattern of the world of tomorrow can reflect the strength of character, courage, and intelligence that youth develop in creative school activities and wholesome community environment, under leadership that inspires worthy character.

Trends in the Open School

Are dramatics, glee clubs, and orchestras important enough to youth to be included in the curriculum? One author says:

It may be that in time in all schools such activities as debating, dramatics, school publications, glee clubs, orchestras, and athletics will become curricular. The trend is in that direction.[2]

[2] Fretwell, *op. cit.*, p. 262.

This practice has already come to pass in many schools which include in the curriculum such activities as dramatics and journalism for school publications. A report from the Phoenix Union High School of Phoenix, Arizona, says, "We offer intramural athletic contests during school hours with all students present. The R. O. T. C. Reviews are arranged in a similar manner."

Another author expresses the following ideas on extracurricular activities:

Why should we go on speaking of extracurricular activities as if they were hung way off on the tail end of the curriculum, with the lurking implication that possibly they are not educative and simply must be tolerated? If some are not educative, drop them. But they can be made so, and when they are why not draw them right into the main tent and make the most of their possibilities? More than that: why have them a thing apart at all? Why not so change our whole point of view of how to educate the whole man, change our very philosophy of education, our spirit and techniques?

. . . Quite definitely in a number of schools the afterschool activities are regarded as an extension of the school's educational functions. They take up the free time for one thing and thus keep the boys and girls from possible harmful associations and doings.[3]

The school holds a unique place in community organization because it serves all children, and all races, nationalities, religions, the rich and poor. Since financial support comes from the people the school must give equal opportunities to all. The school needs to be cognizant of the good services available in all the leisure time agencies of the community whether they serve all, or mainly a racial or denominational group. Therefore, the school gives to students information about all opportunities in the community, and specific suggestions to meet individual needs.

A friend of the community, the school offers to all the leisure time agencies increasing opportunity to work with the students in the school after 3 P.M. The school might have leaders from the settlement house, Y's, or Scouts, for groups which could be graduated into the centers at any time. Surely the students would benefit by this unity of purpose and effort.

[3] Eugene T. Lies, *The New Leisure Challenges the Schools*, p. 147.

Another trend is indicated by the fact that boys and girls are meeting each other through planned groups. They have always wanted to meet each other one way or another. They have wanted to meet in little groups of their own sex and age, and to talk, laugh, and relate the daily funny experiences of the classroom, office, or plant. Some of their social needs are emergencies due to present conditions but some have always existed and are more pronounced today.

Some schools actively recognize the problem especially among students whose parents do not provide wholesome social outlets. Those who most need more wholesome social outlets are frequently boys and girls of these conditions:

Employed mothers
Disinterested parents
Crowded quarters or congested areas
Mentally and physically handicapped
Economic need

Delinquent youth may find enough social gratification at a canteen to be diverted from antisocial ways, but some may be so constantly exposed to harmful influences in the home and community that the influence of the school's activities has little effect on their behavior. Since causes of delinquency are so numerous and complex, the school cannot expect its activities to be a "cure-all" until the home, church, and community agencies work together to improve conditions and relationships.

One trend today is the training of co-ordinators, selected from the school staff or the community. Other titles used are director, assistant director, or supervisor. A co-ordinator usually assists with the afterschool activities as the following statements indicate.

We have a full time recreational director who co-ordinates this work with the community.
Brownsville Junior High School, Brownsville, Penn.

The Director of Recreation is not attached to this particular school, but serves this whole system. He directs the use of the school buildings and grounds, employs assistants, provides equipment and organizes the program of recreation for children and adults. A few activities include badminton, basketball and bridge instruction; Saturday and vacation baseball clinics, swimming lessons, dancing lessons for school children, music appreciation classes for adults, assistance with organization of picnics and parties, and other activities.

Monticello Junior High School, Cleveland Heights, Ohio

An area co-ordinator works with all schools on a community recreation program. Our Vice Principal and Council co-ordinate this program to encourage community recreation.

Montgomery Hill Junior High School, Silver Spring, Maryland

The Leland Junior High School of Chevy Chase, Maryland, has a recreational co-ordinator. It is also reported that the principal of the McKinley Junior High School in Middletown, Ohio, heads a Youth Welfare Education Committee which has sponsored a community recreation plan with a paid supervisor.

In the Royal Oak Junior High School, Michigan, the physical education teachers co-ordinate the city recreation program with the school program. Similar plans are carried on in Kalamazoo:

The local Board of Education and City Commission jointly sponsor a city-wide recreational program. A full-time director and two full-time assistant directors are employed. Many members of the school staff are employed during the summer months to assist with this program. The activities of the program are organized basketball, soft-ball, women's volley-ball, women's bowling, badminton, crafts for girls, dramatics and story-telling. Through the joint efforts of the American Legion and the Recreation Commission, the Legion Junior Baseball leagues are conducted.

Director of Research and Guidance, Kalamazoo Public Schools, Mich.

The Board of Education assigns one co-ordinator for each area. The co-ordinator in our area serves three schools. Duties of this person are:
To unify the recreation program.
To help the school and the community to plan for the best possible program.
To guide individuals in planning their program.
To keep students well informed as to possibilities available to them.
To assist in carrying out the program.
To train other teachers and citizens to take part in the programs.

Leland Junior High School, Chevy Chase, Maryland

The City employs an afterschool playground supervisor.

Childs Park School, St. Petersburg, Florida

Teachers who assist with afterschool groups can keep the school liaison person informed about changes in activities and about need for more members. These statements show how some teachers are lending a hand in afterschool activities:

Several instructors assist in the Boy Scout program.
> Lewiston Junior High School, Lewiston, Idaho

Regular elementary teachers are Scout leaders; a man for boys and a woman for girls.
> Thurmont High School, Thurmont, Maryland

Our school co-operates with the Y. M. C. A. and Y. W. C. A. in operating Day Camps for boys and girls for six weeks during the summer. The hours are nine to four. Some of our teachers were employed by these organizations. The facilities of the school were used to carry on the day camping activities such as crafts, gymnasium, and playgrounds. The attendance was between 50 and 60 per day for the six weeks period.
> Murphy Junior High School, Atlanta, Georgia

Various members of the staff assist with clubs in the high school gymnasium, in co-ordination with community clubs for boys and girls.
> Fair Lawn High School, New Jersey

We have several teachers serving in our Day Care Center, which operates from 6 A.M. to 6 P.M.
> School #33, Indianapolis, Indiana

The co-ordinators or leaders of any afterschool activities may find it helpful to keep a waiting list for replacement of members who drop out. The school is in a position to replenish these groups whenever the leader voices that need. For instance, if the Scout leader can care for twenty members, the school can assist the Scout leader in keeping the group filled. If it is necessary to organize a second group the main office of the Scouts may be able to supply another leader.

The following paragraphs indicate a national trend in afterschool activities:

The time may not be long in coming when public educational authorities will offer a program encompassing academic, vocational and leisure time activities for persons of all ages who may wish to participate. This will involve extension of the common school program both above and below its present limits to include kindergartens and nursery schools for young children and a broad program adapted to the needs and interests of older youth and adults. It will involve close co-ordination of school, library and recreation services under qualified and responsible leadership. It will require careful planning of the location and construction of educational facilities. The buildings will be adapted to the varied educational needs of the whole population. They will be situated in administrative units large enough to provide adequate tax support.[4]

The Educational Policies Commission foresees the ultimate unification of all public educational activities in communities or areas of appropriate size under the leadership of a public education authority. . . . Its functions will include the provision of a broad educational and leisure time program for persons of all ages.[5]

The school has taken on new responsibilities and come to grips with realities outside its gates. It wants to serve the social needs of young people. More school doors are open after three o'clock and more school windows are lighted for clubs, athletics, community services, and parent education. Current articles show that boys and girls are enjoying the new programs.

The afterschool program costs money! But if our purpose is to adjust youth *now* we must convince those who hold the money bag that the present cost cannot be compared with the immeasurable cost of training schools, prisons, and mental institutions that care for those we neglect.

BIBLIOGRAPHY

ADLER, L. AND .J. "Recreation Glamourized! Juvenile House Canteen," *Recreation*, January, 1945.

BREEN, MARY J. *Partners in Play.*

FRANKLIN, ADELE, AND BENEDICT, AGNES E. *Play Centers for Children.*

LAKE, E. "Younger Set; Youth Centers are the Kids' Own Ideas," *Reader's Digest*, September, 1944.

LAMBERT, CLARA, AND THE PLAY SCHOOL ASSOCIATION, *School's Out.*

LIES, EUGENE T. *The New Leisure Challenges the Schools.*

MASON, B. S., AND MITCHELL, E. D. *Social Games for Recreation.*

MEYER, HAROLD D. *Youth Recreation*, North Carolina Recreation Committee, Chapel Hill, N.C.

SHREFFLER, MARGARET, AND CORWIN, GEORGE B. *Boys and Girls Together.*

Teen-age Centers, National Recreation Association.

[4] *Social Services and the Schools*, N. E. A., p. 19.
[5] *Ibid.*, p. 54.

Magazines for leaders of youth
  The American Artist
  The Camping Magazine
  Country Dancer
  Folk Dancer
  Hobbies
  Junior Arts and Activities
  The Journal of Health and Physical Education
  Magazine of Art
  Nature Magazine
  Occupations
  The Parents' Magazine
  Parks and Recreation
  Plays
  Popular Mechanics
  Popular Science
  Reader's Digest
  Recreation
  Research Quarterly
  School Activities
  School Arts Magazine

~~ Chapter V ~~

CO-ORDINATION OF LEISURE TIME EDUCATION
WITH THE COMMUNITY

"Leisure is an indispensable part both of economics and of social existence—it is the greatest of all the challenges to the leaders of civilization."

—ARTHUR NEWTON PACK

HERE are a few suggestions which may be useful as a check list of possible sources of leisure time information. Such sources fully approved by the school should be contacted once a year to keep the information up to date.

Afterschool activities in the school building: sponsored by the school, a neighboring school, or some organization
Settlement and neighborhood houses
Clubs for boys and girls
The Y's: Y. M. C. A., Y. W. C. A., Y. M. H. A., Y. W. H. A.
Boy Scouts, and Girl Scouts
Libraries: for reference lists of books and magazines on hobbies and talents, and for information on any activities and collections in the libraries
Churches: clubs, activities, religious educational classes, and devotional services
Music and art centers: class and individual instructions in art, music, sculpturing, dramatics
Department of parks: athletic fields, play streets, swimming pools, and bicycle paths, programs
Educational centers: evening schools, colleges, classes for adults
Radio programs recommended by the school
Motion pictures recommended by the school
Commercialized programs of importance
Sightseeing opportunities recommended by the school: historic sights, collections, exhibitions, civic interests, colleges, stores, broadcasting stations, parks, museums, libraries, public buildings. Sightseeing booklets, maps, and pictures may be obtained from the newsstand or the chamber of commerce.
Summer programs, compiled in May

Information from Leisure Time Agencies

Essential information gathered from leisure time agencies should not be elaborate but it should be sufficient to give students a good idea of the offerings. The following form used by some schools in Manhattan show items which have been found useful in gathering information on leisure time activities:

Please return this blank
to (name of school)

LEISURE TIME ACTIVITIES

Date _____

Organization_____ Address_____ Phone_____
Person whom students may contact_____

Activities offered	*Ages*	*Boys*	*Girls*	*Day*	*Hour*

Annual fees_____ Installment payment permitted?_____
Other requirements for membership_____
Additional information_____
Summer program (use separate blank if necessary)_____

Name of the liaison person the school may contact for any
   further information_____
(Attach two circulars of information or other
   illustrative material if possible.)

Just as important as information gathered for students are facts obtained from close observation of each agency's organization. For instance, the school needs to know the answers to such questions as these:

Is there trained leadership in the leisure time agency?
   Do the leaders set worthy examples before boys and girls?
   Do leaders have personal acquaintance with members of their group?
   Do leaders show an interest in each member?
Are activities adequately supervised?
Will the agency direct individuals to some other source when students' interests and needs cannot be met there?

Does the agency have afternoon activities for students below senior high
    school age, or are most of the activities in the evening?
Can the agency offer group membership at reduced rates, or is any other
    provision made for students who have inadequate funds?
Is there a liaison person who co-ordinates the activities of the leisure time
    agency and of the school?
  Will this person speak in the school assembly or classroom?
  Will this person keep the school informed about activities and how the
    school can co-operate in using facilities to the maximum?
Can the agency give special attention to students in need of individual
    adjustment (neglected or of delinquent tendencies)?
If co-ordination between a leisure time agency and the school is difficult
    what is the obstacle that seems to hinder co-ordination?
  Is it personnel, space, equipment, distance, or relationships?
  Should there be a further conference for developing better co-ordination?

Full information should be given students before they are referred to a neighborhood house or a club like the Scouts. If a
student goes to a leisure time agency and finds that the activity
he wants is for little children, if the distance is greater than the
student thought, or if the agency says the fees are higher than the
family can pay, then the interest toward all neighborhood centers
may be lost.

Some agencies offer leisure time opportunities to boys only or
to girls only, but surveys show that there are about equal opportunities for both boys and girls.

An occasional leisure time agency serves one culture group
more than another because of the area in which the agency is
located. In some cases the financial support by a certain culture or
religious group determines what group will be served mainly.

It is well for the school to note the fact if a certain group
predominates in one recreational center. Knowledge of this fact
by the individual student may help him make a satisfactory social
adjustment for himself. Of course, schools with a mixed population make no distinction and emphasize most the opportunities
which are open to all.

Activities such as those operated by the city are usually free.
Some city swimming pools, however, ask a small operating
charge. Small fees of about five cents each week are commonly
charged by leisure time agencies. Installment payments of fees

can often be arranged as can also payment for uniforms and materials. It is frequently possible for the school to obtain a group rate, which further reduces the fees. Small fees do not often cover the cost of activities or of individual service.

Experienced leaders in leisure time agencies agree that when boys and girls pay at least a small fee for activities, they appreciate them more and attend more regularly. Appreciation of leisure time opportunities at little or no charge can be discussed in the leisure time education program so that students may understand and appreciate the services for which they pay only small fees.

Other requirements for membership, besides fees, should be made clear to students. The Sea Scouts, for instance, require that a boy be fifteen years of age and a First Class Boy Scout. For Camp Fire Girls also there are age requirements. Museums make requirements when they permit boys and girls to sketch there. But all requirements should be explained to the individual so that he will not try to join a group for which he does not qualify.

Circulars of information are usually available at the centers and can be informative to students if posted and discussed. Useful photographs of the activities sometimes appear in the circulars.

Free tickets for league ball games, theaters, exhibitions, and motion pictures are often available in the community. These tickets may be discussed and presented to interested students.

The local libraries have lists of reference books and magazines on hobbies and talents, which can be posted and otherwise used in the school. Sometimes these lists are in printed pamphlet form and are free or they may be obtained for a few cents.

The information gathered on leisure time opportunities can be used in class discussions. It can also serve as a factual guide in personal interviews with students.

Leisure time education findings in several junior high schools in Manhattan indicate the need for the school and leisure time agencies to work closely together to interpret and meet students' needs. The schools make these suggestions to the leisure time agencies even though many are already organized to serve in these ways:

To render individual attention to boys and girls in order to adjust them to leisure time activities according to their interests and needs.

To refer students to other good sources when their interests and needs cannot be met.

To maintain a liaison person to co-ordinate activities with the school.

To inform the school of any changes in their program of leisure time activities.

Larry was a boy who needed individual attention in the neighborhood center. He was not a social person and did not make an adjustment with any group. When the school counselor found that he belonged to no organized play group, she contacted the boy's former club director. The boy was sent there with a letter of introduction signed by the counselor and also by the parent. The boy talked over the matter of activities with the former director. Larry became interested in the game room. The director, who followed up on the boy until he had attended activities for several weeks, wrote this letter to the school:

Larry came in to see me with your letter. I agree with you, he is a fine boy. He has joined and I believe will take part in some activities here regularly. Thank you so much for referring him and for your co-operation.

Sometimes a student who participates in no activities and is always by himself may need to see the school doctor. Withdrawal tendencies noticed by teachers or group leaders, frequently require neurological or psychiatric treatment for a long period of time. Teddy, a boy thirteen years of age, had no friends with the exception of one who was equally unsocial. Morning and evening Teddy would wait for his teacher and walk with her to school and from school. It was impossible to get him to play with other boys. When the school nurse took an interest in the boy she visited the home and talked to the mother. At home the boy was helping his mother or just sitting doing nothing. After the school doctor examined the boy, he was referred to a neurological clinic for treatments. The nurse worked with the mother to gain her co-operation and understanding of the boy's needs. In this case the student needed treatments more than he needed an outside club.

Sarah expected to get into a dramatics group in a local center.

She was told that the dramatics group was for older girls who worked during the day and who came in the evening. It would have helped Sarah if the center had given her the name of another community center to go to for dramatics then while her interest was high.

Close contact between the school and the leisure time agencies helps the individual students to adjust immediately and easily. One method of close contact is through a liaison person in the leisure time agency, who confers often with the school liaison person.

A committee of two or more interested students may wish to visit some leisure time agencies with a letter of introduction from the school. They may observe activities in the game room, social groups, Scout troop, music, and other groups. A report may be given by one of the committee in the weekly assembly, classroom, or in the school newspaper. Different classes may form a small committee if more leisure time agencies are to be visited and reported upon.

How Some Schools and Leisure Time Agencies Co-ordinate

The following reports indicate how some schools co-ordinate their activities with those in many different community organizations:

We sponsor and hold night soft-ball games in co-operation with the Chamber of Commerce. A teen-age club is being planned jointly with the Kiwanis Club, Women's Club and Parent-Teachers Association. Its purpose is to provide wholesome recreation and dances in surroundings that will be beneficial to the moral welfare of the participants as well as provide much needed recreation during a time when travel is restricted.

                                    Pioneer School, Artesia, California

The school curriculum is fairly well integrated with the City Recreation Program. Many of the teachers assist in administration of the city program which is an elaborate year-round affair offering many opportunities for handicraft, swimming, games, and dramatics.

                                    Jefferson Junior High School, Dubuque, Iowa

Day Care Center projects include simple handcraft; building, painting, decorating, and furnishing a miniature house; some music and art work such as tonette band and crayon drawing; storytelling; outdoor and indoor games.

Public School #33, Indianapolis, Indiana

We have a summer playground program. Pupils play on city basketball teams, one business firm's team against another. Teachers assist in the program. Our coach happens to be the assistant to the City Director this summer. Many of the teachers act as supervisors of playground areas during the summer.

Memorial Junior High School, Orlando, Florida

The principal of the Hollenbeck Junior High School, Los Angeles, California, co-ordinates school activities with the Kiwanis Club program. He is vice president and program chairman of that organization.

In Houlton High School, Houlton, Maine, it is the director of Boys' Guidance who works in co-operation with service clubs like the Kiwanis, Rotary, and Lions.

In Monterey, California, the school department designs and programs all municipal recreation activities although the city hall retains general supervision. One of the chief virtues of the shift is that the recreation program, designed by the school department, is supervised exclusively by regular school instructors who receive extra pay for their recreational work.

That entire program is handled expeditiously by the regular school teachers because they know the personalities, the likes and dislikes of the school children and do not have to employ a trial and error method to learn what activities would or would not be of interest to them. Their activities are: baseball, basketball, swimming, archery, ping-pong, nature walks, softball, bicycling, sewing, wood and other art crafts, dancing lessons, and a variety of games suited to the various age groups.

Community leaders visit the school. The Grace Arents School of Richmond, Virginia, gives this account of their co-ordinating efforts:

Last fall under the guidance of our principal we gave a tea to which we invited all the social workers, representatives of community agencies, good-will centers, and also attendance officers, ministers and others interested in the welfare of our community. At that time we talked over some of the problems confronting us and offered suggestions for solution. It was agreed that a more advantageous expenditure of leisure time would be of inestimable value. Questionnaires were sent to the children of the two schools in the community to determine children's interests. When the findings were tabulated, action was taken to meet interest needs through community programs. The following is an announcement showing the variety of activities:

Have Fun   Join the Swing
                to the
St. Andrew's—William Byrd Playground
Linden and Cumberland Streets

Summer Program

open all summer
10 to 12 A.M.
6 to 8:30 P.M.

Play SOME—Play ALL of these activities

Soft-ball	Croquet	Storytelling
Volleyball	Crafts	Checkers
Kickball	Jump rope	Jack rocks
Dodgeball	Marbles	Dancing
Singing	Swinging	Sliding

Watch for these added attractions

Gypsy Day	Country Fair Days
Dude Ranch Day	Mexican Fair Days
May Day	Family Days
Pet Show	Doll Show
Trips around Richmond	Scavenger (treasure) Hunts

Selected Short Subjects for Pre-school Children

Nursery Corner with NEW Sandpile, storytelling, painting, drawing, singing, and games.

Family Get To-gethers

Adults and children are invited to come to the playground every Thursday evening after supper for special program and activities.

Neighborhood Clubs

Upon request or to meet a need:
Storytelling,
Amateur shows,
Crafts.
Give your suggestions.

One agency that is always ready to send a representative to talk in the school is the neighborhood library. The English class, group guidance period, or assembly period may be used for a discussion on interesting books. One grade adviser said that such a speaker got even the nonreaders into the library.

Public School #33, Indianapolis, Indiana, praises the co-operative efforts of the library in these remarks:

> Our nearby public library is perhaps our most co-operative leisure time agent. The librarian works with the teachers in organizing story hours and reading clubs for children's leisure time. These clubs are organized on different reading levels. An individual record is kept at the library of the books read and at given periods some award is given and a report is sent to school showing the reading done by each individual. The general reading has been increased in this way.

The Aguilar Branch Library in New York lends to local schools collections of books on hobbies, vocations, and biographies, for use in group guidance and for displays. Other libraries are always willing to do the same.

Leisure time agencies should feel free to contact the schools without a special invitation, and to send word to the schools when important changes occur in the leisure time program. A friendly exchange of visits once a year helps to maintain a good working relationship between the school and the local leisure time agencies.

The liaison person of a play center is usually a leader who has close contact with boys and girls and who is already a real friend of many of the students. When such a liaison person speaks in the school assembly the students' pleasure is evident as they see their friend on the platform.

Teachers and parents are commonly asked to conduct a community group for some agency so that more students may be served. Some of the finest leaders have been interested teachers and parents or volunteer college students who had much to give because of their personality, character, and sincere interest in youth. These personal qualities combined with training for group leadership are highly desirable.

What do youth like about their leaders? Boys and girls like a leader who calls members by name, visits their homes, recognizes and talks to them on the street, and knows how to conduct activities well. Leaders with these qualities are responsible for continued membership in a group because they make members feel at home and wanted. Leaders who do not appear before their groups regularly lose the interest of their members. We are dealing with youth. They have eagerness, feelings, responses, and spirit that challenge our personal leadership and skills. Leaders hold or lose the interest of their group largely by what they reflect in personal interest and other qualities which youth look for. Unlike adults, youth make no demands of their leaders. They only search elsewhere if they are not satisfied, or follow their buddies wherever they may lead.

As schools teach students to seek good leadership, and as leisure time agencies see that good leadership is expected, so may the quality of leadership gradually improve. It appears that leisure time agencies need more funds with which to maintain good leaders when they are assigned.

Co-ordination of the School with the Community Council

Local councils of social agencies and the schools can work together to use leisure time facilities to the maximum the year around. Are all leisure time centers for youth used to their maximum? We have been hearing that this is the case. But actual surveys show that almost every center has room for at least a few more youth in some activities. One center that was reported filled needed more members for the art and the music clubs. Another center needed some colored children to make a play group more mixed. One center had just started a new aviation crafts group and needed more members. It is common for a leisure time center to say, "If you have any special boy or girl in mind, telephone us. We can always fit in a few more." It has been generally found that leisure time centers are not used to full capacity.

Councils of social agencies are always glad to have members of the school staff contact them for information or advice. Schools are frequently represented in the community council by one or two staff members. There is often a recreation committee that may serve as one means of co-ordinating the leisure time agencies and the school. This committee often compiles a practical directory of leisure time opportunities for youth. An opportunity for committee participation awaits those who are willing to co-ordinate their efforts with those of others interested in similar problems.

Discussions which social agencies may find of common interest are suggested in the pamphlet, *Fundamentals in Community Recreation*, by the National Recreation Association. These fundamentals are:

1. That in nearly every community with a population of 8,000 or more there is need of a man or woman who shall give full time to thinking, planning and working for the best possible use of the leisure hours of men, women and children.
2. That community leisure time programs should continue throughout the entire twelve months of the year.
3. That it is the responsibility of the entire community to maintain recreation opportunity for all the citizens and that there ought, therefore, to be, as early as possible, support of the recreation program through public taxation under some department of the local government.
4. That there should be in every state a home rule bill which will permit the people of any city or town to make provision under local government for the administration of their community recreation.
5. That there is need in every community, even though the municipal recreation administrative body be most effective, for private organizations of citizens in their neighborhoods to make the fullest use of the facilities provided, to make sure that what is being done is meeting the deeper needs of the people of the neighborhood.
6. That the emphasis ought to be not only on maintaining certain activities on playgrounds and in recreation centers but also and definitely on the training of the entire people in leisure time activities, so that within the home, in the church and throughout all natural, human relationships there shall be the best opportunity for wholesome good times.
7. That the purposes in training children and young people in the right use of leisure ought not to be merely to fill up the idle hours but also to create an active, energetic, happy citizenship.
8. That even though the beginning of a city or town recreation program be children's playgrounds, other features ought to be added progressively from year to year until music, dramatic activities and discussion of public questions, training for more intellectual uses of spare time, and other valuable activities have been included, so that all ages and all kinds of people may find vital interest.
9. That every boy and every girl in America ought to be trained to know well a certain limited number of games for use outdoors and indoors,

so that there will never be occasion for any boy or any girl to say that he cannot think of anything to do.

10. That most boys and girls should be taught a few simple songs, so that, if they wish, they may sing as they work or play.

11. That all employed boys and girls should have opportunity in their free hours to enjoy companionship and wholesome social life.

12. That through the community recreation program every boy and girl should come to appreciate the beautiful in life.

13. That adults, through music, drama, games, athletics, social activities, community and special day celebrations, should find in their common interests the opportunity for a common community service.

14. That every new school built ought to have a certain minimum amount of space around it provided for the play of the children.

15. That nearly every new school building ought to have an auditorium preferably on the ground floor and should be so constructed that it is suited for community uses.

16. That if a suitable meeting place for community groups is not available in the schools or elsewhere, a community building should be provided through community effort.

17. That each child, under ten years of age, living in a city or town should be given an opportunity to play upon a public playground without going more than one-quarter mile from home.

18. That every community should provide space in sufficient area for the boys of the community to play baseball and football.

19. That every community should provide opportunity for the boys and girls to swim in summer, and as far as possible, to skate and coast in winter.

20. That every boy and every girl ought to have opportunity, either on his own home grounds or on land provided by the municipality, to have a small garden where he may watch the growth of plants, springing up from seeds which he has planted.

21. That in new real estate developments, a reasonable per cent of the area should be set aside to be used for play just as part of the land is used for streets.

The pamphlet stresses the fact that it is the privilege of community-minded men and women everywhere to work to restore and preserve for all the people of America their right to play and happiness.

Parent Associations

Co-ordination with parent associations helps the school to place the responsibility for the direction of a child's leisure where it rightfully belongs—with the parent.

Parents' associations are interested in receiving lists of local leisure time opportunities that the school or agencies may have compiled, and to discuss the information in their meetings. Some members of parents' associations have volunteered to assist schools by visiting other parents whose children need help in planning leisure time activities.

Films of leisure time activities may be recommended for parents' meetings. Leisure time agencies frequently have films that they are willing to show to parent groups.

It is highly desirable that parents visit individually or in groups the various leisure time agencies where their children participate or wish to participate in activities.

Some parent associations organize and supervise clubs for boys and girls in private homes for social enjoyment or training in sewing, cooking, photography, crafts, music, or art. Many parents are interested in the Scouts' Cubbing program for boys and the Brownie program for girls. One parent Cubmaster and Sunday school teacher of Michigan City, Indiana, says:

A group of interested people met several times to work on this new problem of Cubbing. After about two months the various officers were chosen—two den mothers, a committee of three men, and a cubmaster. We have had a committee meeting, including den mothers, once every month in one of our homes where we discuss various themes and projects for the Pack meeting of the following week. This Pack now has 32 Cubs.

One of the things to which we attribute most of our success is the fact that all meetings are planned in detail far enough in advance to give each person responsible for any part of the program sufficient time to be well prepared.

Handicraft holds a prominent part in our program. Each month one person is delegated to acquaint himself fully with the handicraft chosen for the following month. . . .

Sometimes materials can be used which do not need to be purchased. For instance, last month the boys made pictures using spices, seeds, graham cracker crumbs, cotton, toothpicks, matches, grain, sand, pencil shavings and cloth. The handcraft is started in the Den and then taken home where the boy's parents help him finish it. When gifts are made for the parents, they are completed in Den meetings.[1]

[1] John D. Nichols, "Cub Program," *Wisconsin State Journal*, Madison, Wis., August 16, 1945.

Programs similar to Cubbing and the Brownie program could be increased if more parents were willing to give time, effort, and leadership in such character-building work.

Warren T. Powell points out the parents' responsibility for leadership of youth in these lines:

> Many parents, when asked to give leadership to the activities of boys and girls, will attempt to excuse themselves by saying, "I have no time." This is a great mistake on their part. . . . Raising children will be no more successful without the expenditure of some time than would business under similar conditions.[2]

Problems in Co-ordination

Problems that leisure time agencies say they experience are: inadequate personnel, which is the greater problem; and inadequate space, which indicates a growing demand for leisure time activities.

Some areas improve their conditions through co-operative effort in their local council of agencies. It may be illuminating to school people to get a close view of the problems of neighborhood leisure time agencies. Perhaps the school and these agencies may develop better relationships by talking over their apparent limitations. A run-down club might be built up quickly with the school's co-operation. Perhaps the agency might be persuaded to use the school building for some activities. To work co-operatively, there should be a liaison person in the leisure time agency and one in the school. If an agency's personnel is limited, there may not be sufficient time provided for a liaison person to visit schools. But it would help if schools would voice the need for a liaison worker in each leisure time agency to contact schools at least once a year, personally, and to exchange ideas with the school liaison person. It is probable that this exchange of views will come about as schools invite the centers to send someone to the school each year for a conference or an assembly talk to students. In some schools in New York this practice is regularly carried out every term.

[2] *Recreation in Church and Community*, p. 118.

Sometimes a junior high or elementary school finds a scarcity of activities in the afternoon or early evening for students eleven to fourteen years of age. Most of the activities may be from 8 to 11 o'clock in the evening for senior high school students. In such a situation one school talked over the matter with a local recreational leader who said:

> Yes, my group, for instance, meets in the evening from eight to ten or later. I accept only senior high school boys because I don't want to be responsible for the younger boys being out of the home late at night. I am starting an afternoon club for younger boys of the seventh and eighth grades.

The leader and the school counselor co-operated in publicizing this necessary activity and filling the group with interested members.

The Trained Co-ordinator or Liaison Person

Adequate and trained leadership is even more important than equipment. A leader influences the habits and character of a child constructively or destructively. Leaders are usually carefully selected for their personal qualities and training, by the Scouts, the Y's, C.Y.O., churches, settlements, libraries, and school play centers.

Cities offer trained supervision in their park programs and play streets. Although the park activities are not always supervised, the environment and facilities are usually good.

Schools and leisure time agencies may need to urge students in some areas to see activities that are going on outside of their own community. Parents may be encouraged to escort their children. In large cities it may surprise leaders to find that many students about fourteen years of age are rarely escorted by their parents to interesting places, hobby exhibitions, beaches, museums, libraries with specialized collections, radio stations, concerts, educational movies, circuses, or displays of collections that boys and girls make. Neighborhood clubs may have a schedule of trips which students may join. University classes in sociology, recreation, or child study have furnished leaders for trips. Interested parents may be prevailed upon to assist with the plan.

The School

Leisure Time Education in the School

Through school subjects: English, Social Science, Music, Art, Library, Home Room Sessions, Health Education, Shops, Crafts, Home Economics.

Through school activities: Clubs, Dramatics, Speech, Assemblies, Speakers, Displays, Visual Aids, Bulletin Boards, Posters, Radio.

Through afterschool activities in the school building.

Aims: To habituate students to the worthy use of their leisure—the discovery of special interests, the development of skills for the enjoyment of leisure, the provision of opportunities for self-realization in the school and community, and follow-up.

The Trained Co-ordinator or Liaison Person of the School

The Leisure Time Agencies

Leisure Time Opportunities in the Community

Settlement and Neighborhood Houses
Clubs for Youth
Libraries
Churches
Music and Art Centers
Department of Parks
Radio
Motion Pictures
Other Commercialized Recreation
Sightseeing Opportunities
Adult Education Classes
Summer Recreational Opportunities
Character Building Organizations
Parents and Parent Associations

The accompanying chart indicates the place of the co-ordinator or liaison person in a program of leisure time education, and the kinds of agencies to be co-ordinated with the school.

Some of the opportunities offered by the leisure time agencies are:

Settlement and Neighborhood Houses
    Athletics
    Crafts
    Parties
    Family functions

Clubs for Youth
    Scouts
    The Y's
    Boys' Club, etc.

Libraries
    Books on special interests
    Clubs
    Collections
    Special programs

Churches
    Clubs
    Activities
    Religious education classes
    Devotional services
    Other youth programs

Music and Art Centers
    Music schools
    Centers for inexpensive lessons
    Museums
    Recitals and exhibitions

Department of Parks
    Athletic fields and activities
    Play streets
    Swimming pools
    Bicycle paths
    Programs for sports, music, and other interests

*Radio

*Motion Pictures

*Other Commercial Recreation

    * Programs recommended by the school.

Sightseeing Opportunities
  Historic sights
  Collections
  Exhibitions
  Civic interests
  Colleges
  Stores
  Broadcasting stations
  Parks
  Museums
  Libraries
  Public buildings
  The use of a sightseeing booklet

Adult Education Classes
  Evening schools
  Colleges
  Other adult classes

Summer Recreational Opportunities
  Information to be compiled each May

Character Building Organizations
  Churches
  Y's
  Big Brothers
  Big Sisters

Parents and Parent Associations
  It is possible that aid may be given in home visiting, listing of approved
  radio programs, distributing information on leisure time opportunities,
  and other valuable services.

Parents frequently show appreciation for what the schools are
doing to make valuable contacts for their children. This is
evidenced in appreciative notes from some of the parents when
the school arranges trips to exhibitions or play centers. However, teachers need help in leisure time guidance of students
whose parents show little or no ability to direct their children's
leisure time activities. A trained co-ordinator could give valuable
aid in such cases.

While agencies are endeavoring to solve their problems of
personnel, appropriate activities, space, and facilities, it is important that the schools co-operate toward the maximum use of

existing facilities, limited though they may seem. Churches and other community agencies are frequently taxing their facilities to the fullest. Combined and persistent efforts are necessary to meet problems of limitation. Desired results often take a long time to accomplish but sustained co-operative efforts finally bring some returns. The scene is more hopeful where there are trained co-ordinators.

BIBLIOGRAPHY

BUSCH, HENRY M. *Leadership in Group Work.*

ENGELHARDT, N. L., AND N. L., JR. *Planning the Community School.*

HADER, BERTA AND ELMER. *Little Town.*

HERRON, J. S. "Community School vs. Community Recreation," *Recreation*, October, 1944.

HURT, HUBER W. *The Influencing of Character.*

KEOHAVE, M. P. AND R. E. *Exploring Your Community.*

Know Your Community, National Recreation Association.

OVERSTREET, HARRY A. *A Guide to Civilized Leisure.*

SEYFERT, W. C. "New Interest in Religious Education," *School Review*, June, 1945.

Standards of Training, Experience and Compensation in Community Recreation Work, National Recreation Association.

SUTHERLAND, ROBERT L. *Color, Class and Personality.*

THRASHER, FREDERIC M. *The Gang.*

What About Us? Government Printing Office, Washington, D.C.

WYLAND, R. O. *Scouting in the Schools.*

Youth; Volunteers for Youth Recreation Programs, Government Printing Office.

∽ *Chapter VI* ∽

LEISURE TIME GUIDANCE

"He that will make a good use of any part of his life, must allow a large portion of it to recreation."

—LOCKE

INDIVIDUAL guidance should follow any group work done in leisure time education because students frequently need help in the selection of activities and centers. It may be more important to see the parents of some students so that the school's efforts may be more far-reaching than they would otherwise be. The individual counseling of students or parents is the most important part of any leisure time education program. For that reason the personnel for this phase should be trained and have a real interest in seeing boys and girls find interesting activities for self-development and creative living.

Some students may need more variety, sociability, or group play. Others may need suggestions for moderation, safety, and solitary activities. It is not uncommon to find students who never play outside or who have never learned to entertain themselves at home. The lonely child who has no one to go places with is the very one who should go. Perhaps such a timid child may be teamed with the enthusiastic or active child for activities in the school and outside.

Many other individual differences are necessary to consider as the following indicates:

For those pupils to whom esthetic recreations seem difficult, there should be provided such encouragement as is given by the band rather than the memorized drama. Similarly, in athletics we need many opportunities for the younger and weaker pupils on an appropriately lower level of skill. Craft work, too, requires encouragement, special equipment, and teaching, but no more useful recreation exists.[1]

[1] John M. Brewer, *Education as Guidance*, p. 390.

149

Studies carried on by the author in 1932-45 show that about one-half of the students who were interviewed were members of no clubs or recreational organizations. Schools that use community recreational facilities in their regular curriculum show a high club membership for those classes. Pupils who withdraw from the schools to work before graduation show a low percentage of members in outside clubs as compared with the regular student body of the eighth and ninth grades. There is a close correlation between persistence in school and continuance in outside clubs. It appears that some of the slow learners and over-aged students frequently need special help with their leisure time problems. Seventh grade boys generally show more readiness for participation in outside clubs and activities than do the older boys, who already have decided on their activities or who need to be appealed to individually. Older boys show more variety of club and organization contacts than do the seventh grade students because they frequently go some distance for their recreation while the younger students enter activities more in their immediate community. The average student attends the movies about twice a week.

Thomas O. Marshall made similar findings and states:

Factors which influence school persistence are also factors which have an influence on later group activity.[2]

... Many of the constructive activities begun in school are left off as soon as the pupils leave school. It is apparent that neither the school nor the adult organizations in local communities make any systematic effort to encourage out-of-school youth to continue activities begun in school.

... There are radio programs which might be considered highly educational but very few of the pupils who have been out of school less than a year number these programs among their favorites. Many pupils attend movies at least twice every week and indicate that they attend movies no matter what picture is shown. Such lack of discrimination probably indicates that the worst, as well as some of the best, films are seen.

Many pupils do not read books and magazines. Among those who do read, most of the pupils confine their reading to fiction, and much of this fiction is of an inferior sort. ... Neither the curriculum nor the extra-curriculum of most of these pupils has provided them with intellectual and

[2] *An Interview Study of the Adjustment and Withdrawals of New York State High Schools in Vocational, Citizenship and Leisure Time Activities,* p. 140.

emotional outlets. Not only do they lack deep-seated and important interests, but they do not even seem to know how to have fun. . . . In addition, consideration of the fact that so many of the pupils seem unready, even after graduation, for adult leisure time activities, leads to recommendations toward a program for out-of-school, as well as in-school, youth.[3]

Selection of Leisure Time Activities

Students may want to know how to go about joining a club and when activities are offered. Class discussions about a community crafts group, for instance, result in the question of how to join. The school should be prepared to give information about leisure time agencies which offer such opportunities and to help the students fill out such an application blank as the following:

APPLICATION FOR LEISURE TIME ACTIVITIES

Date_____

_____
Name of leisure time agency

_____   _____
    Person to Consult   Address

The activity I desire in your organization is_____
If fees are charged I am prepared to pay.

                 Student_____, Class_____

     Approval of parent_____.

     Home address_____

_____
Grade adviser

This form may also be used to refer students to the school orchestra and other school activities.

The choice of activity should be spontaneous and real. Sometimes these choices will seem strange or impossible, but as the teacher talks to students about their interests, some way is found for giving every student a sense of satisfaction in leisure time activities. When Doris said she would like to know more about the training of wild animals, contact was made with the lion-tamer in a large zoo. How could the trainer keep the lion from attacking? The story interested Doris. When the lion was very

[3] *Ibid.*, p. 164-165.

young and small the trainer observed that he assumed his best behavior when he heard the trainer's key in the lock because he was afraid of the whip which the trainer carried and occasionally had to use. Long after the lion surpassed the weight of the trainer, he feared the trainer. Now that the lion is full grown he is as easily controlled as when he was small. Doris became interested in the habits of animals and read about them in the local library.

Franz, who came from Europe, wanted to hear classical music. He objected to jazz music. Goldman's Band had just started to play on the Mall at Central Park. It pleased him to have tickets given him for the kind of concert he liked. His teacher encouraged him in his musical taste and opened the door to interesting leisure time enjoyment.

Some students will say they do not wish to join outside activities. The reason may be one of these:

Part-time job
Home duties
Time already filled with lessons in music, art, etc.
Parents' refusal of permission

These students may be glad to have the school suggest types of activities for whatever spare time they might have. Better service can be rendered if the parent is interviewed whenever this seems necessary.

Guidance by the Parent

The parent's written consent is important whenever the school refers any student to a community center. It is advisable that the student talk over at home the information about community activities that the teacher has given. In this way parents may be led to take more initiative in helping their children plan for leisure time activities. The school needs to encourage the parent's active interest whenever a student needs the parent's approval and support. This is best done by a personal interview. A student is often only too glad to bring his parent to talk about a hobby and a place to pursue it.

Some parents cannot pay large club fees for their children but installment payments can often be arranged. Fewer movies may provide enough money if students can be motivated to budget some of their movie money for club fees. However, a center requiring lower fees may be necessary for some students.

In Leland Junior High School of Chevy Chase, Maryland, students and parents work together. A student-parent social council plans school activities such as parties.

Parents' meetings offer an opportunity for furnishing parents with leisure time opportunities for their children. The importance of parent associations is discussed in Chapter V. One thought to impress upon a parent in connection with leisure time education is that the school encourages home and family recreation and is willing to help the home with any recreation problem.

Selection through Visits

Students should feel free to visit leisure time agencies individually or in groups to observe activities before making a definite selection. They will find it helpful to discuss the center first. Visual aids such as films, slides, posters, and pictures prepare students for visits. Discussions of visit reports of students who have already made a visit are also valuable sources of leisure time information for the class.

Two or more students may be sent together to leisure time agencies unless students are entirely willing and able to travel and visit alone. When groups of about ten are carefully selected and escorted or sent to some local leisure time agency of their choice, students are likely to find the experience appealing. They often need this help in getting started in a center where they will know someone, feel at home from the beginning, and join in the activities.

Students like to feel they are representatives of the school when they go to the Y, the Scouts, or to an exhibition, a conference, or a concert suggested by the school. They know they must make a report to the school or class. Contacts like this can be made an integral part of the student's school life. Class attention and participation should be noticeably increased as class work becomes more meaningful through such outside contacts. Visits to leisure time agencies are usually welcomed any afternoon after school. However, it is advisable to determine in advance which day an activity may be observed. September is usually the best time to join community activities. After October the groups may be filled and the membership closed.

Alvina, thirteen years of age, needed personal leadership which her working mother never gave. She had no father. After school each day she idled her time away walking around or listening to the juke box in the corner candy store and taking what amusement came her way until it was time for her mother to come home from work. When the counselor of the school spoke to her and her mother one day, it was agreed that the counselor would take her to activities which the mother did not know existed in the family church but which she highly approved. After the first visit to the church the girl went alone. She found new interests and satisfactions from the activities and from talking to the leader.

Students may not know activities are offered in their family church and may wish to investigate possibilities. The school furnishes a list of community activities in local churches and other centers, but the selection of the particular activity and center rests with the parent and the child. Church leaders are willing to see students, preferably with their parents, and to assist them with their leisure time or other problems.

Public libraries welcome students who wish to browse among the books and magazines on hobbies or other topics they enjoy, or to visit the story hour or club there. One school in East Harlem in New York arranged for a group of sixteen students to visit the local library, which had arranged a display of vocational and avocational literature. The students made posters on their vocational and avocational choices in their art class. These were then displayed in the library with some of the compositions done in their English classes.

Students should report back to the teacher any results of visits, the next day or as soon as possible, while interest is highest.

Students of Fort Wayne Public
Schools, Indiana

Burlingame Recreation Department,
Burlingame, California, presents Miniature Theater productions

Mural painting, Department of Recreation, Passaic, New Jersey

Problems in Leisure Time Guidance

Community opportunities do not always meet every individual's needs, but a school can render a real service to a student by telephoning some central source of information for the activity the student prefers most.

The student's interest may be so earnest that he will travel some distance to get what he wants. Other students may be satisfied to select another activity near home.

Youth's reasons for not participating in the afterschool programs may seem too childlike to the teacher but they should be considered seriously. Sometimes reasons such as the following indicate a need for social or psychological adjustment:

Shyness
Sensitiveness
Feeling of inferiority
Feeling of unpopularity
Fear of criticism
Lack of skill in any activity
Physical defect

Provision for individual adjustment is necessary for students in these situations, but should be carefully planned so that all who need the service may be assisted.

Olga recently moved into the community from the neighboring state where she was a Girl Scout. She felt strange and friendless. When she was told that there was a Scout troop two blocks from her home and that she could go with a girl in her class, she wanted to continue as a Scout. Henry was a highly sensitive boy from a disturbed home that was not guiding him in the use of his leisure. In a class talk on neighborhood opportunities the students wrote on slips of paper the activity they might like to consider. Henry wrote "pigeons." His teacher said, "He lives entirely to himself, is afraid to express himself. After school he flies pigeons on his roof." He was asked to join a group of boys who were going to visit a hobby show in a large store. That visit gave him new ideas and a tongue to express them in little group discussions in the guidance office. He joined an art club in the neighborhood and was proud when the school displayed one of his drawings.

Geraldine was not a very popular girl. She finally acted on her teacher's suggestion to join a settlement club and soon began to see her teacher and subjects in a new light. She began to co-operate in school, at home, and elsewhere. The process was a slow one but the teacher saw the gradual change in Geraldine's attitude in class. It was the teacher who opened the door and the girl found a new interest in her school, home, and community.

A student may change his mind about leisure time activities for a good reason, or it is probable he misinterpreted some facts about a leisure time agency. Perhaps he knew no one there. The parent may have objected to the distance or fees. In any case he should have a chance to talk over the matter with someone in the school, when another attempt for adjustment may be made. The second attempt may be a happy one for him.

Individual Counseling

How individual counseling is to be arranged depends upon the school and the principal. Whether the counseling is done by a trained counselor, the principal, or an interested teacher, the student should benefit from this individual service. Brewer agrees that leisure time guidance is important:

> Efficient guidance for leisure activities demands counseling as well as teaching skills and holding class discussions. This is to say, there must be one or more teachers in the school specially fitted to counsel on problems connected with leisure, and equipped with sufficient time and space to give the necessary attention to individual needs. They will usually combine counseling with class teaching. . . . But the provision for counseling should be definite, with no expectation that good work can be done unless proper recognition and encouragement are offered.[4]

The teacher establishes friendly relationships with students and shows concern over Mary's visit to the settlement clubs, or Tom's sketching class at the museum. One student said with delight to his teacher, "I went there!" The teacher could not recall at the moment where he had suggested the boy go, but answered with

---

[4] *Education as Guidance,* pp. 399-400.

interest, "How did you like it, John?" The boy then indicated where he had visited by saying, "They let me sketch there. Here is one sketch I made at the museum." The teacher praised him and the boy felt the friendly interest of his teacher. Then school became more interesting for John. Somebody had seen that he had some ability and was showing him a way to use it.

An eighth grade teacher of East Stanwood, Washington, was asked to give suggestions for dealing with difficult students. She suggested, "Love 'em." She started by giving students a sense of security and of belonging, as leaders in mental hygiene agree are most important to impart to students.

The school is also in a position to help individuals develop a sense of balance between work and play so that adult life as well as the present may not be all work and no play. In one of the country's finest sanitariums for the restoration of mental and emotional health patients made these statements about themselves or about others there:

1. One must be guided into hobbies when still in school to avoid overwork or boredom in adult life.
2. My illness has taught me that one must watch himself so as to discern that point or moment when rest and recreation are required. Do the schools try to teach this precaution?
3. One man here is a real estate man who has been keeping his nose to the grindstone too long. He belongs to several clubs but evidently developed no hobby with which to occupy his mind after business hours.
4. I have learned this: in sports one does not do well unless relaxed and with mind off other things. Any good hunter will tell you that only the hunter who is relaxed and "at ease" can hit anything. The spirit of recreation needs to be taught in school early.
5. Schools are inclined to stress high scholarship more than a balanced life with hobbies.

Leisure Time Guidance of Vulnerable Students

What do we mean by vulnerable? In a pamphlet outlining a program for New York State, a vulnerable or a vulnerable student is one with social behavior difficulties which may become serious. The observable symptoms of a vulnerable are listed as follows:

TEACHERS' CHECK LIST OF OBSERVABLE SYMPTOMS
OF POTENTIAL OR INCIPIENT DELINQUENCY

Extremely restless
Extremely excitable—lacks self-control
Extremely tense or inhibited
Often left out of play groups
Bullies other children
Is bullied by other children
Self-conscious over physical anomalies
Self-conscious because aware of socio-economic differentness
Resentful of criticism
Teases maliciously or with intent to hurt or annoy other children
Shows cruelty toward animals
Extremely self-important
Not a good sport
Cheats
Lies
Steals
Is frequently truant
Shows evidence of abnormal interest in sex
Unable to persevere in any mental effort
Mentally preoccupied—day dreams
Easily upset, depressed or angered by frustration
Wants constant reassurance
Not able to make decisions and stick to them
Afraid in many situations
Dogmatic: insists on having own way[5]

What can the school do about vulnerables? The pamphlet just mentioned discusses the need for trained personnel for these purposes:

Finding and routing vulnerable children
Adjustment of the school program to meet needs of vulnerables
Contacts with parents

The school cannot do much alone but contact with the home is a step in the right direction as the Educational Policies Commission suggests:

In thus serving the child, the school does not arrogate to itself any superiority over the home or other child-caring institutions or agencies.

[5] *Schools Against Delinquency*, The State Education Department, Albany, New York, p. 18.

It serves merely to co-ordinate public services on behalf of the child. Such a policy enlarges the responsibilities of school authorities but this consideration is more than offset by greater benefits from educational services through removal of handicaps to learning.[6]

Counseling and Records

Another step in the right direction is the use of a cumulative school record card for interviews, so that data like these may be carefully considered:

Age
Grade
Health
Teachers' comments
Personality: strong and weak traits
Home background
Interests
Attitudes

Interviewing of vulnerables should be carefully done and should always avoid prescription and control. The person prepared to do this may be the one who co-ordinates the leisure time education in the school. Time is necessary for this interviewing and should be planned for in advance. Knowledge of case work and techniques is essential in this phase of guidance. The cases are frequently already known to some specialist or bureau with whom the school may co-operate. If the school has a social worker, that person can help vulnerable students plan for some interesting leisure time activities.

Upon the skill of the interviewer depends the success or failure of the interview. The interviewer should have the ability to put the student at ease and to establish rapport. The student may be asked about his favorite games, sports, books, collections, or other activities. An informal friendly conversation usually brings out and stimulates his interests.

The skillful interviewer finds out the kind of influence a child's present friends have on him. Perhaps the school finds that it is the friend in another class who needs adjustment more than the student being interviewed. There may even be a so-called "gang"

[6] *Social Services and the Schools*, N. E. A., p. 24.

to study and to redirect. As the interview progresses there will be other questions to ask or problems to try to solve.

If the *case study method* is used, the cumulative record card information is a starting point. Further information may be obtained on the following:

Home Background

Number of brothers and sisters: older, younger
Parents or guardians living
Parents' attitude toward the child's use of his leisure
Economic status, ability to pay fees in a play center
Supervision given by parents outside of school hours
Influence of the neighborhood on the child

Interests of the Child

Leisure time activities, hobbies, talents
Special aptitudes: avocational, vocational
Present membership in outside clubs and activities
Participation in school activities
Study habits and achievements
Kinds of friends and their interests
Educational and vocational plans
Available spare time

Attitudes of the Child, toward

Family members
Classmates
Teachers
Church
Leisure time activities and groups

The needs of the case may be physical, emotional, social, personality, or other needs that may be met through planning with the student. Individuals' interests and needs can be met in some leisure time agencies that have the personnel for personal interviews, medical, dental, and nursing services, home visits, parent consultation, and other individual services. Sometimes a student needs special programming in school for more crafts, art, shop, or music, adapted to his interests and performance ability.

Schools are using their curriculum for student adjustment as these quotations indicate:

Problem students are given individual attention in an effort to interest them in group projects of recreational nature. Sometimes it works.

Woodrow Wilson Junior High School, Terre Haute, Indiana

Handwork in crafts to produce something worth-while has proved a most valuable means of social rehabilitation.

Hawthorne School, Helena, Montana

Shop is one of our solutions.

Memorial Junior High School, Orlando, Florida

Skills in hobbies are developed through shops.

South High School, Minneapolis, Minnesota

Our unit curriculum includes excursions, arts and crafts, and novelty instruction.

Junior High School 159, New York

The *group factor* plays an important part in the leisure time adjustment of vulnerable students. That is why it is necessary sometimes to improve a student's relationship to the school, family, neighborhood, church, and play groups. If, for instance, a vulnerable student is a member of a gang, the school may obtain information on the aims and activities of that gang. The inadequacy of our official machinery for handling delinquents is often due to a failure to recognize the group factor in delinquency.

The case method, if properly used, enables an investigator to make a thorough study of an individual and the situation in which he lives. One of the essential factors in the situation is the home. The degree to which parents will or can co-operate should be determined early.

Redirection of the Vulnerable Students

Any attempt to redirect the energies of vulnerable youth requires a genuinely friendly attitude such as professional case workers are trained to use. The method is that of indirect inducement, in which the individual is given every opportunity to express his attitude toward any possible plan for a solution.

These difficult cases need sympathetic treatment and leadership. Gradually they may become interested in new clubs and assisted in new adjustments. In this way new interests are substituted for the gang's activities. Each case requires different treatment according to its special needs.

Scouting may offer the adventure and excitement that problem students seek. Hiking may take the place of wandering. Boxing is a good substitute for fighting. Some police departments offer a variety of leisure time activities to youth and co-operate with schools regarding vulnerables. They are organized to help prevent and to solve problems of delinquency.

This intensive individual work should help students and parents plan activities, with the school's help. There was Margaret, for instance, whose home life was a constant chaos. She felt no companionship with her parents. When the school interested her in a neighborhood dramatic club she met girls who liked to do things. Margaret's spirit commenced to change. She always thought she would like to be in a play. She had a part to learn and a costume to plan. After the play was given she told about it in costume before her class. She had found a new interest. Her home adjustment improved at the same time, the mother said.

How some parents and schools work together to try to prevent delinquency is shown in these comments:

Home visits are made by regularly assigned teachers.
                    Phoenix Union High School, Phoenix, Arizona

We recommend parent-school planning.
                    Leland Junior High School, Chevy Chase, Maryland

Conferences with parents effect the home program.
                    Parke School, Oakland, California

Some of the schools in the county have recreation centers sponsored by the Parent-Teachers Association. We hope to have more centers established. We are sure they are helping to check the increase in juvenile delinquency.
                    Bellevue School, Alabama City, Alabama

The school is in a position to assist parents to redirect their children's leisure time activities if help is needed. Parents should not expect the school to take more interest in the welfare of their children than they do themselves. But the school stands ready to help the parent to guide youth in the pursuit of worthy leisure time activities in the home and in the community.

Adjustment and School Conduct

A vulnerable student who adjusts in leisure time activities through the help of the school often reflects improved class conduct, attendance, punctuality, and work. Students of this kind have been known to bring up their conduct mark from "D" to "A" in two weeks. Thomas was such a boy in former Junior High School 184, Manhattan. Praise from teachers and the principal, Mr. David Goldwasser, made him feel a sense of achievement.

One boy, Rocco, changed his school conduct because his teacher showed a real interest in his outside activities and talked frequently to his father, who seemed inadequate in guiding the boy. Since the mother died the boy and his father had lived together and prepared their meals, irregular as they were. The pet show and contest in the Boys' Club was about to occur. Was the teacher going, Rocco wondered. "Of course, I'm going! I wouldn't miss that for anything!" she told the boy. This delighted him. On the night of the show the judges solemnly witnessed the display of dogs and cats. Rocco took his cat, a beautiful white-breasted one that the store lady gave him a year ago. "And what is your cat's name?" asked one of the judges. "I call her Katy the lady cat," Rocco proudly answered. Rocco walked his cat down the aisle so that all could see and judge its worth. "This is Katy, the lady cat!" announced the judge. As Rocco's letter shows, Katy won a prize:

Dear————

Well there was a pet show at the boys club and I figured I go, and maybe I had a chance to win. We had prizes for the biggest dog—the smallest dog and the cutest dog. Then we had the biggest cat—the smallest cat—the cutest cat.—So I won with the cutest cat.

Yours truly
Rocco

P. S. My cats name is Katy and Mrs. Burton says its the cutest cat she ever saw. The cat eats anything we eat and I hope you like just by hearing about it.

The father of Rocco was so pleased with the teacher's interest in his boy that he has invited her to dinner at the restaurant where he is a waiter, when her son returns from service.

Mary's mother came to talk over a problem, saying that the girl walked the streets and did not enjoy doing anything in the home. The mother was skilled in fancy needlework, crocheting, and tatting. The teacher praised the mother's skill before the girl, who seemed to view her mother's abilities with surprise. One day Mary was asked to bring in a lace collar when the mother finished it. This was displayed in Mary's classroom. Then Mary wanted to make something to display and was encouraged to copy the collar or the beret. She learned from her mother to make articles which were always shown to different teachers and the principal, all of whom knew Mary's problem. Later the mother was called in to see the annual hobby show of Mary's grade. She was proud to see several of the girl's articles in prominent display. "She stays home a lot more now. She's changed. Thanks to the teachers," reported the mother.

Teachers deserve credit for encouraging students who are beginning to change to a more wholesome way of living. Praise from the teacher speeds a student's good intentions to accomplishments, while a word of discouragement may impede his progress along the new road.

Changing the Gang

Students often give up inferior clubs and activities for those attractively presented by the school. Careful interviewing and continuous follow-up help to habituate youth to wholesome activities. Sometimes just a friendly chat with the student reveals the quality of his club. One cannot tell by the name what kind of club it is. For instance, a club may be either desirable or undesirable and have a name similar to these: The Green Aces, Variety Girls, Hornets, Debutantes, Panthers, and Black Daggers.

Destructive gangs have been transformed into civic-minded groups. Instances of this are described by Frederic M. Thrasher in his book, *The Gang*.

One way the school can dissolve private clubs of deteriorating influence is by assisting the individual members into other clubs and activities that they may like. If the entire club is willing to be sponsored by organizations such as the Scouts or Y's, this method is likely to correct the conduct and aim of the group. If schools cannot dissolve or correct such clubs which may be serious influences, they should be reported to some council of social agencies or to the police department.

The subject of inferior private clubs may be discussed in the seventh grade for preventive purposes.

These agencies may be contacted for help in dealing with students who seem vulnerables.

> The home
> Parent organizations
> Community recreational centers
> Churches
> Police leagues and crime prevention organizations
> Juvenile court

As schools educate students in the selection of worthy activities, they look less to the court and police for help and more to leisure time agencies. Examples of co-ordination between the school staff and community leaders appear below:

Older boys who are members of the Hi-Y Club take a young delinquent as a "Pal" and try to guide him.

Houlton High School, Houlton, Maine

We have just finished our Junior Baseball schedule carried on by fifty per cent of the faculty but sponsored by the Lion's Club.

Sanford Grammar School, Sanford, Florida

We are centering our efforts at the present time on a community-wide program, under the sponsorship and direction of the schools, to teach young people the worthy use of leisure time. This program is in the nature of a youth planning program to prevent delinquency and is arranged by the Youth Planning Commission.

Brownsville Borough School District,
Brownsville, Pennsylvania

Harold E. Davis, supervisor of education in Clinton Prison, Dannemora, New York, said:

A leisure time education program is a preventive measure. We who are engaged in the prison educational field receive many of our students from the failures of the public school system, many of whom never would have reached us had they been fortunate enough to have been advised and guided into worth-while leisure activities while in school.

If this job of educating for the worthy use of leisure is to be performed properly the school needs adequate facilities and personnel. Even then there will still be some students with such unfortunate home influence that the school cannot help much. The friendly, understanding teacher is frequently the school's only hope of holding the student from the hands of the court, from the reform school, and from—we know not what else.

Changing the Community

It is not only the gang that needs changing; it may also be the entire community. Concerted effort for crime prevention through community organization may be necessary because a gang is usually a symptom of community disorganization. Community councils are doing constructive work throughout the country in striking at the roots, rotten as they may be, and making a more wholesome community environment for youth. This often means breaking down barriers between agencies and uniting community efforts for planning such environment.

Personnel for Guiding the Vulnerables

Schools use special workers, as these quotations show:

We make use of guidance teachers, psychiatrist, psychologist, social worker assigned to the school, and referral to the after school program.
                                                    Junior High School 101, New York

Our method is the use of counselors, Y. M. C. A., Scouts, Associated Aid, and other social services.
                        Camp Curtin Junior High School, Harrisburg, Pennsylvania

At Gordon, we have an adjustment committee which deals with attendance, health and delinquent problems.
                                Gordon Junior High School, Washington, D.C.

Cases are referred by teachers to our local Children's Center which recommends various types of methods in the field of leisure time activities. Diagnosis, treatment and follow-up are given.

Kalamazoo Public Schools, Kalamazoo, Michigan

Schools in difficult areas commonly cry out for help in contacting the home for the improvement of a child's health or behavior. The following quotation shows the importance of this service:

More and more attention is being given to health and the experiences of children in their homes and neighborhoods. This requires a new relationship between the home and the school, and the vital factor in bridging this gap is the visiting teacher. It surely can be no mere coincidence that the attitude of the visiting teacher toward the maladjusted and the delinquent child is quite in line with that of the enlightened probation officer.[7]

Child guidance bureaus and social services are gradually increasing but the pressure upon them precludes prompt service to many vulnerables. Schools would be more likely to impress their budget committees if they could show by the result of studies that they needed in certain proportions some of these specialized workers:

> School counselors
> Visiting teachers
> Psychologists
> Psychiatrists
> Social case workers

One school estimated its needs after making a two-year study in which vulnerables received special guidance by staff members. The recommendations were for these minimum essentials for their school of 900 students in a difficult area.

> One full-time licensed counselor
> One visiting teacher or a school social case worker
> A psychologist two days per week
> A psychiatrist in the school on prompt call

[7] Pauline Young, *Social Treatment in Probation and Delinquency*, p. 531.

With the proper clinical and probational staffs it would be possible for a school to handle more of its cases outside of the juvenile court. Problems could then be located, diagnosed, and solved without any court connection.

Vulnerables need leisure time guidance but they need this through case study, which requires trained personnel who can gradually educate youth in better choices and behavior. Thus the inspiration and development of a generous array of interests and hobbies of a sane and useful type may offer the finest corrective to misuse of leisure. John Ruskin said:

Education does not mean teaching people what they do not know. It means teaching them to behave as they do not behave. . . . It is a painful, continual and difficult work to be done by kindness, by watching, by warning, by precept and by praise, but above all—by example.

Unusual patience and courage are essential in leisure time guidance of vulnerables, otherwise one becomes completely discouraged with what seem meager results of strenuous efforts. The patient and courageous press on as though guided by the ancient Confucius proverb, "It is better to light one small candle than to curse the darkness."

BIBLIOGRAPHY

(Similar information as contained in the *Directory of Social Agencies of the City of New York* may be obtained from local chambers of commerce and social agencies.)

HATCHER, O. LATHAM. *Guiding Rural Boys and Girls.*

LAMPLAND, RUTH, ed. *Hobbies for Everyone.*

MASON, B. S., AND MITCHELL, E. D. *Social Games for Recreation.*

NICHOLAS, F. F. "Hobbies in Miniature; Exhibition for Hospital Patients," *Hobbies*, December, 1944.

PENDRY, ELIZABETH, AND HARTSHORNE, HUGH. *Organizations for Youth: Leisure Time and Character Building Procedures.*

Recreation for Blind Children, Children's Bureau.

Schools Against Delinquency; A Guide for New York Schools, State Education Department, Albany, N.Y.

"We are the Youth," *Recreation*, December, 1943.

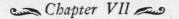

Chapter VII

ADMINISTERING LEISURE TIME EDUCATION FUNCTIONS

> "Boys and girls need to be instructed so that they can discriminate between the enjoyments that enrich and enlarge their lives and those which degrade and dissipate."
>
> —JOHN DEWEY

A. ORGANIZATION OF THE LEISURE TIME EDUCATION FUNCTIONS

Determining Objectives

THE objective of a leisure time education program is to educate students in the selection and pursuance of their leisure activities and to habituate them to the worthy use of their leisure through the presentation of leisure time opportunities. The application of thought to highly pleasurable and worthwhile activity is a prime necessity for all people; and it may never be learned if not taught in school.

This objective should be the means of character building, of maintaining good health, and of acquiring lasting satisfactions, through the wise use of leisure.

Some of these lasting satisfactions are:

> Personal satisfactions
> Loyalty to home, school, church, state
> Good citizenship
> Socialization and adaptability
> Wholesome health habits of body and mind

Happiness, joy, and a sense of freedom are some of the mental attitudes that naturally result from adjustment to wholesome leisure time activities. A leisure time education program that develops good character, sound bodies, and healthy minds is performing some of the highest functions of education.

The activities to which the school refers students should be participating activities in which one is doing something himself and not merely watching others. They should be challenging to the powers of the student and should be intensely interesting to him. Unless one is fundamentally interested in what he is doing, the activity will not be re-creative. There must also be real satisfaction in the activity, to the mind, emotions, and body. The choices open to a student should be broad enough so that he can find the thing in which he can participate, and which is for him creative. Through such activity students may satisfy also their needs for social contacts and growth. Stress should be made upon good selection and moderation.

Opportunities which such a program affords should be available to all secondary school students and not only to a selected few. The normal students should not be neglected for the vulnerable students. All need wholesome leisure time activities and assistance in selection. Pupils in the elementary grades often need help in selecting worthy activities.

Observing Students' Social Background

A knowledge of the home and community background of the school population is useful when the school is trying to develop activities to fit the needs and interests of all and the special needs of individuals. The principal may have this information available. If he has not, random samplings of about 100 school records of students should reveal at least a general background without burdening the busy school office with an extensive survey.

HOME BACKGROUND

How long has this student been in this school?

If the student turnover is great there is likely to be a need for helping students to adjust to the social life of the community. When students come from other communities there has been severance from the play groups. This situation may require the school's assistance in social readjustment.

What is the culture group of the student?

A knowledge of the kinds and general extent of groups helps the school to provide satisfactory leisure time opportunities for all. Students frequently prefer to be with others of the same group. Spanish children, for instance, like to be told about a coming "fiesta" in the community. However, the school also makes an effort to mix groups in many activities.

What is the economic status of the family?

Is the family well to do, average, or poor? The degree of unemployment in the families represented by the school population will indicate whether or not the average student can pay nominal dues in leisure time agencies or for any activities entailing expenses.

It is also desirable to know the degree of overcrowding in the homes to determine the apparent lack of opportunity for leisure time activities in the home.

Is the home broken?

A broken home may be thought of here as one in which one or more of the following conditions exist:

   Father or mother dead
   Parents separated
   Parents divorced
   Guardian
   Foster home
   Child living alone

Many students from broken homes are well adjusted emotionally, physically, mentally, and socially. However, the general opinion is that students from broken homes frequently need help in making friendly relationships such as with leisure time agencies.

Is the home supervision adequate?

If the student lacks home supervision the school has a difficult responsibility, especially if the parent will not come to school to discuss plans with the child and the teacher.

COMMUNITY BACKGROUND

Another social background of the students is the community with its organizations and social opportunities such as have been discussed in earlier chapters.

Information about the community background is available through many leisure time agencies and also through the local councils of social agencies. Recreation committees of councils frequently have lists of centers where students may enjoy leisure time activities. Most cities have directories of social agencies showing recreational centers.

The police department can give the school information on the degree of delinquency in the school area in comparison with other areas. Deteriorating influences such as undesirable private clubs without proper adult supervision, and places that impair the morals of youth, should be reported by the school and investigated by proper authorities.

Finding out Students' Interests

In junior high school the leisure time interests of boys and girls should be determined early in the first term. Many students would like to do some special thing in their leisure hours but do not know how to get started. One boy was shy in telling his real interest but finally confided that it was wood carving. He watched his neighbor carve but he had never thought of voicing his interest to anyone. The teacher showed him where to go in the neighborhood to do wood carving and told him where to buy tools and materials.

Some simple questionnaire may be used for finding out the leisure time interests of students. The questions may be written on the board or asked orally. Students may number their answers according to the number of the question asked. A suggestion for one kind of questionnaire is the following.

QUESTIONNAIRE ON LEISURE TIME INTERESTS

Name of Student_____ Class_____ Date_____
1. Name any organization or play group to which you belong_____
2. Is the activity supervised by a leader? Yes_____ No_____
3. Does the leader seem trained to conduct activities? Yes_____ No_____
4. Name one of your present leisure time activities_____
5. If you are not satisfied with your present activities, what would you like to do if you had the opportunity?_____
6. How many hours each week do you listen to the radio? _____hours.
7. How many hours each week do you attend motion picture theaters? _____hours.
8. How many hours each week do you spend on private instruction and practice (music, art, or other lessons)? _____hours.
9. How many hours each week do you spend on reading? _____ hours.
10. Check the kinds of reading you prefer (one or two choices).
    Adventure or travel _____
    Romance   _____

Mystery   ———
History   ———
Comics   ———
Other reading   ——————————

Teachers will find a summary of the responses for each class useful in pointing out general needs in leisure time education. Further summaries of the combined classes in the grade should be of practical value to principals. One principal spoke at length in a teachers' meeting about these responses and suggested steps that the school should take to meet the leisure time needs of students.

The summary sheet for the class and for the grade may look something like this:

SUMMARY SHEET ON LEISURE TIME INTERESTS
(for use with questionnaire)

Class ——————
Date ——————

1-3. Play groups to which the students belong:

Supervised play groups (name):	Number of students	Trained leadership	
		Yes	No
————————	————	————	————
————————	————	————	————
————————	————	————	————
————————	————	————	————

Apparently not well supervised:	Estimate of teacher or principal	
	Fair	Doubtful
————————	————	————
————————	————	————
————————	————	————
————————	————	————

4.

Present activities:	Number of students	Present activities:	Number of students
————————	————	————————	————
————————	————	————————	————
————————	————	————————	————
————————	————	————————	————
		No choice given	————

5. Activities desired by students not fully satisfied with their present activities:

Activities	Number of students	Activities	Number of students
_____	_____	_____	_____
_____	_____	_____	_____
_____	_____	_____	_____
_____	_____	_____	_____

6. Hours spent listening to the radio each week:

Number of hours	Number of students
0- 5 hours	_____
6-10 ”	_____
11-15 ”	_____
16-20 ”	_____
More than 20 hours	_____

7. Hours spent on motion pictures each week:

Number of hours	Number of students
0- 5 hours	_____
6-10 ”	_____
11-15 ”	_____
16-20 ”	_____

8. Hours spent on private instruction and practice:

Number of hours	Number of students
0- 5 hours	_____
6-10 ”	_____
11-15 ”	_____
16-20 ”	_____

Variety of subjects: _____ _____ _____

9. Hours spent on reading each week:

Number of hours	Number of students
0- 5 hours	_____
6-10 ”	_____
11-15 ”	_____
16-20 ”	

10. Kinds of reading preferred (one or two choices may be shown):

                                               Number of students

    Adventure or travel   _____

    Romance   _____

    Mystery   _____

    History   _____

    Comics   _____

    Other reading: _____

Signature _____

                 Person making summary sheet

Activities preferred. Boys and girls in the seventh and ninth grades in several Manhattan schools like these activities, which are arranged in the order of their choice:

Seventh Grade Girls	Seventh Grade Boys
Music	Outings
Outings, hikes	Crafts
Crafts	Model planes
Sports	Sports
Dancing	Collections
Art	Art (especially cartooning)
Dramatics	Dramatics
Collections	

Ninth Grade Girls	Ninth Grade Boys
Dancing	Sports
Sports and games	Outings
Music	Music
Crafts	Art
Outings and hikes	Collections
Dramatics	Dancing
Art	
Collections	

Whether students are slow, normal, or superior in intelligence they have shown about the same amount of interest in leisure time activities. However, their choices differ. Reading, music, and art are not ordinarily selected by slow students.

The seventh grade students seem to prefer the following organizations for activities:

Scouts
Y's
Settlements and neighborhood houses
Church clubs
Local library activities
Clubs in private homes
Afterschool clubs in the school
Museums

These organizations hold their members because of the variety of activities. The club spirit in these particular centers seems to be another force that holds the members. Students attend playgrounds with less regularity. When they must travel far to the play center their membership is likely to be of short duration. Interest and regularity of leaders seem to be essential factors in maintaining membership over three months.

These places seem to interest ninth grade students:

Outdoor play centers
      Desired more by boys than by girls
Athletic clubs
Clubs in private homes
Church clubs with physical activities
Y's, and C.Y.O.

Comparing the interests of ninth and eight grade students the ninth graders show more interest in athletics and reading.

Attendance at motion pictures was estimated as twice each week for junior high school students in six New York schools and twenty schools throughout the country. However, the students indicated that they would attend less if they could participate in hobbies that they would enjoy.

Students reported a preference for programs of travel, exploration, nature, science and fairy tales, to romance and tragedy. One is reminded that youth do not see the kind of motion pictures they prefer, but must take what the studios produce and what the movie houses show, be it tragedy, romance, or a melodrama of a questionable kind.

Another finding is that students are not fully aware of the variety of leisure time opportunities in and around their home

and school. This fact indicates the need for leisure time education in the schools.

Elementary school children in the sixth grade like to join
neighborhood play centers near their homes. Some of the activities and opportunities they prefer are games, reading, museums,
circus, zoo, crafts, bus riding, collections, art and dramatics.

Organizing Class Discussions

The presentation of leisure time information and experiences
to groups of students and to individuals is one of the major functions to be provided for in the organization of a leisure time education program. Plans for this should be made before the beginning of each new term. Unless a definite place is provided in the
curriculum for this function the entire program will appear in-
definite and spasmodic. It is recommended that a series of topics
be arranged for each grade and that one topic be discussed with
the class each week. Schools that co-ordinate leisure time activities with school subjects throughout the term may also arrange
days when hobbies and the worthy use of leisure are specially
featured through the school. For example, the Pioneer School
in Artesia, California, reports:

> We try to make the most of special occasions and days with parties and
> such events so that these may educate in manners and morals, and the social
> graces. Many of our pupils get relatively little of this outside of school.

If a school prefers to concentrate the discussions in one or
two grades, it has been found that the students need the discussions in the seventh grade in the elementary and junior high
schools. It is also desirable to conduct similar discussions in the
first term of the ninth grade in junior and senior high school.

Ungraded or adjustment classes profit by regular discussions
on leisure time activities with emphasis on demonstrations, pictures, films, dramatization, visits, and other means of student participation.

As previously stated, it is desirable that the program permeate
all subjects and activities in the school so that students may become more cognizant of the leisure time enjoyment that each

subject and activity of the school offers. For instance, the school club may be made a source of information concerning community opportunities for further pursuance of the child's school club activity. The music or science class may impart information on musicales or museum activities.

Whether leisure time education is presented mainly in group guidance, the home room, subject classes, school clubs, or in other periods, the personality and interest of the teacher are of basic importance. These are the essential factors in making leisure time education real and alive to the child. An author once said, "The teacher does not discuss with chalk and paper and pastels, but with his whole self, with what he is and what he lives by."

However energetic and efficient anyone in charge of the leisure time education functions may be, the program cannot realize its potentialities without the constant help of the teacher. Most of the leisure time instruction must be given by the teacher and much of the follow-up must be performed by him because others are not as much in touch with the class.

Where there is an interested teacher there is usually leisure time education, as this comment asserts:

Anything we may be doing is just happening because of the interest of the individual teacher who may deliberately, or by chance, direct her class's attention to the use of their leisure time. Many of our teachers are trying as individuals to help boys and girls with their own problems.
Harrisonburg High School, Harrisonburg, Virginia

Planning for Individual Interviewing

Similar organization for individual interviewing is necessary so that a student may be carefully adjusted through personal attention. He can then learn about the places where he may be taken by the parent or where he may go with his parent's consent. Recounseling is often necessary before a student finds leisure time activities or hobbies to his liking. Perhaps a student did not go to the activity he talked over with the teacher because it was too far, because his mother wants another activity for him, or because it rained.

The function of follow-up can often be done as the teacher happens to see the student whom he has advised about community activities. Frequently a student is so eager to report to the teacher the results of his visit that there is no need for any special follow-up. However, it should be of interest to the school to make some kind of follow-up of all students referred to community activities. Some definite plan may be made for obtaining this information in a simple way. For instance, there may be time in a weekly home room period when all such follow-up matters are attended to.

Personnel for special interviewing has been discussed in Chapter VI in which stress is placed on trained personnel for interviewing requiring case study such as vulnerable students need.

Students from college classes in guidance or sociology frequently seek opportunities for first-hand experience in interviewing vulnerables. Only those recommended by the college professor for their maturity and background of experience should be permitted to do interviewing and guidance. The immature and inexperienced college students would need more supervision than the principal, counselor, or other staff member in charge would have time to give. There is a point of diminishing returns which should be recognized. Otherwise, the principal finds that much is started by volunteers and nothing definite accomplished. It is estimated that volunteers take up almost as much of the principal's or counselor's time as the volunteer contributes. But the longer a volunteer remains the more likely will the school and students profit by his services.

In an experimental project[1] graduate students were selected by the professor and the school counselor and assigned to the guidance office for about two hours each week for five weeks. Plans were made in consideration of each volunteer's background and the short duration of the project. Emphasis was placed on service to the individual student. The graduate students who established the best rapport with the boys and girls were mature and experienced in one of these fields: nursing, psychiatric nursing,

[1] Arranged by Dr. Frederic M. Thrasher of New York University and Dr. Rufus M. Hartill, Asst. Supt., Districts 10 and 11, New York.

community recreation, teaching, mental hygiene, social work, or medical social work. The school was grateful to these college students who so earnestly and satisfactorily served individuals by adjusting them in leisure time activities, arranging for clinical appointments, taking them on trips, providing free tickets to entertainments, and giving them a sense of security and friendliness.

It is desirable that any volunteer workers remain from September through May to make their contribution most worth while to a school.

Centralizing the Program

It is recommended that some member of the staff have charge of centralizing the program of leisure time education in the school and of co-ordinating the program with leisure time programs in the community.

The person in charge of centralizing the program will find it advisable to co-ordinate the program with school subjects as suggested in Chapter II.

Some of the functions that may be performed logically within the school by the teacher in charge of the program are:

Studying the leisure time needs and interests of the school population
Formulating specific procedures
Compiling materials necessary for the program
   Information on community leisure time agencies and opportunities
   Discussion outlines for group guidance and subject classes
   Material for bulletin boards
Conferring with teachers
   To arrange for class discussions
   To help teachers meet the leisure time needs of any individual students
   To assist them in planning for assemblies, speakers, plays, and exhibits on leisure time activities
   To promote the leisure time enjoyment values of school subjects, through activities and reading
   To promote exploration in the school clubs
Getting the principal's approval on all steps in the program

Class discussion outlines need to be adequate and appropriate for the group and season. Information from local leisure time agencies needs to be current to be of real service to the student.

The various leisure time education functions are best shared by a group of teachers. A teachers' committee may share the responsibilities and promote the program. Pupils' committees are also satisfactory for participation in assembly programs and for reporting visits made to leisure time agencies. The students' committee may be directed by the teacher in charge of the program or by various teachers co-operating together.

Carrying out policies that seem desirable for the establishment of the program is not a one-man job. The interest and participation of all members of the school staff are required if the leisure time needs of students are to be adequately served.

Assigning a Liaison Person

To serve the student's leisure time needs is the purpose of co-ordination of the school's program with leisure time activities. This goal may be accomplished by:

1. Establishing a friendly working relation between the school and a community agency in the interest of the student
2. Obtaining for the school the necessary information on community leisure time agencies and activities, for use in discussions with the students
3. Promoting adequacy of and high standards in community leadership for youth
4. Affecting community planning for better leisure time opportunities for youth

The school person co-ordinating with leisure time agencies may be called a liaison person who establishes friendly relations with leisure time leaders in the community. When this liaison person makes the personal acquaintance of the leaders of community activities, the phone and mail contacts become more frequent and spontaneous. The student's present need is then more adequately served by the school and the leisure time agency.

In the plans for organization for leisure time education there should be provision for a liaison person in the school as emphasized by Brewer:

But the teachers are so busy teaching the so-called essentials that no effective liaison has been worked out. . . . Somewhere in the organization of the system we need a definite officer to make and maintain these outside connections.[2]

A teacher or another staff member may be this liaison person. This kind of co-ordination with the community includes these functions:

Visiting community leisure time agencies once each year
Telephoning and writing to community leisure time agencies
Representing the school on community recreational councils and committees
Contacting parent associations to interpret the program to them and furnishing them with a list of community leisure time activities. This list may be of value to parents who wish to advise other parents in the community of the leisure time opportunities for their boys and girls.

The liaison person of the school may find it necessary to search outside the immediate school area for certain desirable activities not offered in the neighborhood. Students are usually willing to walk as much as fifteen blocks if necessary, to some activity of special interest to them. The liaison person also works closely with leaders in the various leisure time agencies in the community and with recreational leaders of the afterschool programs on the school grounds. For instance, in the William P. Bancroft School of Wilmington, Delaware, the guidance counselor acts as co-ordinator with the Community Youth Council. In Northeast Junior High School, Kansas City, Missouri, "A co-ordinator of the district works with the schools of the district."

Teachers are always welcome to visit the local leisure time agencies to see for themselves what the community offers students of their class and school.

It is not uncommon to hear of teachers who assist with neighborhood programs in settlements, Y's, Scouts, and churches. In Lewiston, Idaho, several teachers of the junior high school assist in the Boy Scout program. Teachers help with summer clubs and activities as indicated by these comments from the La Porte High School, La Porte, Indiana:

Our school system has charge of summer playground work in the city. The staff is made up chiefly of teachers. Students who participate in the

[2] John M. Brewer, *Education as Guidance*, p. 407.

playground activities have opportunities not only in sports, athletics, and similar activities but also in music and art.

In cities where the programs of religious education on released time are carried on, questionnaires show that teachers frequently give their time to group work.

B. TRAINING, PLANNING, AND EVALUATING THE LEISURE TIME EDUCATION FUNCTIONS

In-Service Training

A series of lectures and demonstrations on leisure time education procedures may be offered to teachers. Discussions in teachers' meetings could bring out the personal, social, and mental hygiene value of creative arts, music, athletics, and hobbies. Other means for the development of teachers' knowledge and resources may be devised by the principal. Today, principals are placing more stress on the teacher as a human person having many interests which make him a resourceful teacher.

Another method is an in-service course planned by the school board for teachers. In such a course there should be a minimum of lecturing and a maximum of participation in the actual services that benefit the students: visiting leisure time agencies, compiling information on the community resources available to students, surveying classes for leisure time interests, making contacts for students, following up, and participating in other ways described in the previous chapters. Emphasis should be on actually assisting boys and girls and not on mere theory. Preparation for group leadership in afterschool activities may be another course.

The chapters in this book may be adapted for use in in-service training for leisure time education.

Community Planning

The purpose of participation in community planning by the school is to promote in the community social and recreational activities which will absorb the interests of the youth and others in the community and counteract the attraction of undesirable companionships and amusements.

There are but few communities in the United States where some integration of school and community life is not taking place. The question that each community should ask itself is whether the school can function more intimately in social recreation for the benefit of all of its citizens and how the community program can be best developed toward this end. Some authorities[3] state that the development of community schools in which adults as well as children frequently work side by side will help greatly in the advancement of American democratic living.

One of the best avenues for better community planning is the local welfare council of social agencies. Welfare and civic groups in the community welcome the co-operation of the school in planning for the maximum use of the existing facilities and for more adequate activities for youth. Through such a council the schools may voice the need for a new settlement house, a swimming pool, better leadership for youth, and other community needs. An interested leader in New Hyde Park, New York, says that local churches, schools and social agencies organized the Teen-towners and other activities through co-operative effort. Thus improved activities and leadership are provided youth.

If changes are to be permanent and far-reaching they must spring from the people and be at bottom an expression of the life of the people. It is necessary, therefore, that schools share in finding more and better ways of forming intelligent public opinion and of giving it effective expression.

It is difficult for any one agency to supply the necessary physical, social, and cultural opportunities, but through community organization the leisure time needs of youth can be met. A concerted community program of activities appropriately planned with a high standard of leadership develops wholesome personality and good citizenship on the part of members. By such co-operative thinking and acting conditions may be brought

[3] N. L. Engelhardt and N. L. Engelhardt, Jr., *Planning the Community School*, p. 170.

about by which each individual boy and girl may live and play safely, healthfully, and happily.

Three factors in community planning are emphasized in a report on the use of leisure: adequate facilities, information about opportunities, and leisure time education. These excerpts may provide discussion material for community planning:

Facilities to meet the varied interests of a heterogeneous population are needed. They should be equitably distributed throughout the community.

Knowledge of the existence of these facilities, and the manner in which they can be used, should be widespread in the community.

Training for the wise use of leisure is essential. This has been a recognized objective of education for many years, formally adopted as such by the National Education Association in 1918. Among other things, this means the development of skill in the leisure time activities in which one desires to participate.[4]

Dr. John J. Loftus wrote the following paragraph showing the significance of the school as a social center of the community.

In justifying the right of training for leisure to be a cardinal objective of education we are forced to take into account the growing conception of education which regards the public school not as an isolated institution, but as the social center of the community in which it is situated; which believes that the work and the conscious influence of a school must not be confined to the school day and the school premises, but must take the responsibility for redirecting and influencing as far as possible the attitudes, tastes, appreciations, and activities of public school children throughout their waking hours. There are principals who can never rise to this conception of a school, whose educational horizon is bounded by classrooms and blackboards and wardrobes; but to the principal who is an educational engineer, the problem of training for the desirable use of leisure time is indeed one of the cardinal objectives.[5]

Among other important community planning topics recommended for discussion in a community council, are the following:

[4] *Report of the New York Committee on the Use of Leisure Time*, National Recovery Administration, p. 52.

[5] "A Program for the Desirable Use of Leisure Time as a Cardinal Objective of the Public Elementary Schools," *Proceedings, Department of Elementary Schools*, N. E. A., 1928, pp. 390-394.

Leadership

Establishment of more definite standards for training and personality; making standards known in the community; emphasizing leadership as of first importance.

Activities

Adequate and fitting activities for all ages within walking distance; uninterrupted program; afternoon and early evening activities for elementary and junior high school students; promotion of necessary facilities such as a settlement house, swimming pool or better leaders; maximum use of facilities.

Information on community opportunities

Up-to-date information on activities for boys and girls of different ages gathered once each year and distributed widely; centralized places for further information.

Commercialized amusements

Standards of all local commercialized amusement centers to be determined; worthy amusements commended to youth; inferior amusement and places to be discussed in the council with the aim of improvement.

Liaisons for schools and agencies

Carefully selected and trained liaisons; emphasis on friendly relationship in the interest of individual boys and girls.

Friendly working relations

Open-mindedness, sincerity, listening to each other, giving and taking, neither dominating nor being dominated, mutual participation, and patience in what is sometimes a slow process of changing conditions.

Leisure time education

School and leisure time agency alike to realize their opportunity for training youth in the selection and pursuance of worthy activities; their programs and results to be reviewed so that all may understand what is being done and what is still possible to accomplish together.

How the training for the wise use of leisure and for social living is to affect our schools in the future is suggested in the following statements:

The time may not be long in coming when public educational authorities will offer a program encompassing academic, vocational and leisure time activities for persons of all ages who may wish to participate. This will involve extension of the common school program both above and below its present limits to include kindergartens and nursery schools for young children and a broad program adapted to the needs and interests of older youth and adults. It will involve close co-ordination of school, library and recreation services under qualified and responsible leadership. It will require careful planning of the location and construction of educational facilities. The buildings will be adapted to the varied educational needs of the whole population. They will be situated in administrative units large enough to provide adequate tax support.[6]

The Educational Policies Commission foresees the ultimate unification of all public educational activities in communities or areas of appropriate size under the leadership of a public education authority. . . . Its functions will include the provision of a broad educational and leisure time program for persons of all ages.[7]

Upholding Leadership Standards

The program of leisure time education will succeed or fail in proportion as the leader can learn about and draw out the varied interests of many individuals. Eugene T. Lies sums up the essential qualities of a good leader of youth in the following statement:

> To set a good example of conduct; to be able to instill in all his programs and activities and in all his workers and groups, the spiritual value of clean living, sportsmanship and citizenship; to be able to develop through his program and through his personal leadership the higher qualities of character; to be the embodiment of all that is best in the community recreation movement.[8]

Lawrence P. Jacks[9] says that we have too much leadership of the talking type and too little of the leadership that really leads. He says that what we need is pioneers for a new kind of leadership that will educate through activities. It is commonly agreed that proper leadership in leisure time activities for youth is more important than facilities. Trained leaders will procure necessary facilities but no amount of facilities can make up for an inadequate leader.

National viewpoints are expressed in the following comments which stress leadership:

[6] *Social Services and the Schools,* The Educational Policies Commission, N. E. A., p. 19.
[7] *Ibid.,* p. 54.
[8] Eugene T. Lies, *The New Leisure Challenges the Schools,* p. 302.
[9] *Education Through Recreation,* p. 24.

While professional associations of workers have definite views on placement of administrative responsibility for the social services, they all seem to agree on one essential; namely, that the conduct and administration of a particular service should be placed in the hands of properly trained and qualified persons. No form of "economy" in administration is more spurious and shortsighted than the employment of unqualified personnel.[10]

Recreation leadership demands persons of broad general training and special schooling in the philosophy and methods of organized recreation. . . . Good leadership is the very heart of successful community recreation.[11]

Personal qualities that the school looks for in community leaders of youth activities are:

Character
Energetic, wholesome, integrated, pleasing personality
Even temperament and disposition
Sense of humor
Good health
Ability to habituate youth to the selection and enjoyment of wholesome activities
Liking for the age group with whom they deal
Professional qualities including ability and training to perform their work
Ability to inspire good character qualities in others: honesty, cleanliness of body and mind

Leaders of these qualities will set a good example of conduct and instill in all their groups the real value of wholesome living.

Under the direction of a high type of leadership, community leisure time activities become educative. A leader influences youth by what he is, as James Russell Lowell brings out in his familiar lines:

> Be noble! and the nobleness that lies
> In other men, sleeping, but never dead,
> Will rise in majesty to meet thine own.

The vocation of a leisure time educator or adviser is sure to be emphasized in the future although the country is still stressing quantity of activities rather than quality of leadership. However, there are many leisure time organizations who employ only

---

[10] *Social Services and the Schools*, p. 106.
[11] *Recreation a Major Community Problem*, National Recreation Association, p. 20.

leaders of the highest qualities and of fitting training. The problem that such organizations are voicing today, according to a recent statement made by the National Recreation Association, is that of a limited budget that is making salaries too low to attract the best quality of leadership. When communities and cities work out that problem the vocation of leisure time leadership of youth will provide openings suited to those who cherish high ideals and possess fitting talents for leading the youth of our nation in the worthy use of their leisure and of their lives.

Whether the leadership would be better and more continuous if a city operated all of the large community recreational centers is a question. Such a plan has its advantages and yet it may mean the elimination of many small groups well organized in many places where the spirit of child welfare is high and relationships are warm and character-building. Regardless of what plan a city or community may adopt, co-ordination of efforts is necessary to give the best service to boys and girls.

The problem of adequately trained and interested leaders is such a serious one that co-operative effort on the part of schools and leisure time agencies is necessary. It is probable that every school has one or two teachers who are sufficiently interested in afterschool clubs to initiate and carry on some activity in the school building. Agencies seem to agree that it is difficult to find the recreational attitude among teachers because some may be inclined to carry over into the afterschool activity a certain academic atmosphere and method of conducting activities.

There is agreement, however, that teachers gifted to perform the duties of an afterschool club leader are highly desirable, and that they make for a closer tie between the school and outside clubs. The following quotation cautions schools about leadership:

Many [schools] have incorporated leisure time activities into the school curriculum in a perfunctory fashion without stopping to realize that values which are distinctively recreational may be destroyed by a traditional approach to learning. Some have opened school buildings and playgrounds under pressure from the community without making sure that both educational and recreational interests would be safeguarded by competent leadership.[12]

As a general rule, it is unwise to refer students to any leisure time agencies where the leadership is inadequate or untrained. It is well for schools to try to maintain standards as they present leisure time opportunities to youth. Standards of leadership are more important than equipment. What a leader is able to reflect to youth of the worth of his own character is of more value than a variety of games.

Leadership is the most important aspect in a youth program. Emphasis is made in a government pamphlet:

Leisure time agencies must have the kind of leaders who are not merely experts in physical culture, or dramatics, or arts and crafts. They must be sensitive to the needs of children and able to meet them. They must understand the implications of human behavior and be sufficiently trained to spot the child whose actions indicate some maladjustment as, for example, the child who always wants to be the "boss"; the child who always pursues his interests alone; the child who wanders around by himself and just "watches."[13]

Evaluating the Leisure Time Education Program

The following questions suggest criteria for the evaluation of a leisure time education program:

1. Have the leisure time needs of the school population been studied?
2. Has adequate information been compiled or otherwise obtained on community leisure time opportunities?
3. Have leisure time discussions and activities been presented so that students may learn how to use their leisure?
4. Has individual help been given students in the selection of community leisure time activities or hobbies?
5. Has co-ordination been worked out between the liaison persons in the school and in the community leisure time agencies?
6. Has the school increased the afterschool activities in the school building?
7. Has there been any follow-up?

One of the most important criteria of the success of a leisure time education program is: *Does the student now use his leisure*

---

[12] *Social Services and the Schools*, p. 47.
[13] *Understanding Juvenile Delinquency*, Publication 300, Children's Bureau, p. 34.

more wisely, healthfully, and enjoyably because of the school's efforts?

Criteria that may be used to measure the extent to which the school staff are promoting leisure time education are the following:

1. Do teachers consider leisure time education as worth while as arithmetic or geography?
2. Do teachers believe that students are better adjusted in their class work since they have had leisure time information, opportunities, guidance and follow-up?
3. Do teachers believe that students have improved their attitudes because of the program?
4. Do teachers believe that the program should continue?
5. Do teachers find that some students lost interest in inferior play and clubs in favor of activities offered by or through the school?
6. Are teachers willing to participate in the leisure time education program as far as time permits?

The following form is suggested for use in determining whether the school succeeded in improving the student's use of his leisure. Questions such as these have brought illuminating replies which have been helpful to schools.

FOLLOW-UP QUESTIONNAIRE
ON
LEISURE TIME ACTIVITIES

Name_____ Class_____ Date_____
Address_____

1. Did you join any outside club or activity that the
   school helped you contact?   Yes___ No___
   If you answered yes, answer also the following questions:
   Do you think your leader knows you well?   Yes___ No___
   Explain why you think he does or does not.
   _____
   Did you have an opportunity to make new friends? Yes___ No___
   If you are not attending there now, how long did
      you go there? _____years and _____months.
   Why did you leave? _____
2. Did you join activities elsewhere if you did not go
   where the school suggested? Yes___ No___ Where?
   _____

3. Has the school helped you to find at least one new hobby?   Yes___   No___
  If so, have your hobbies taught you new skills?   Yes___   No___
  Name the hobbies that the school has helped you to enjoy. _____

4. Do you think your study habits have improved since the school encouraged you to make a plan for your leisure time?   Yes___   No___

5. Which activities do you prefer? (check)
  Sports   _____
  Dramatics   _____
  Music   _____
  Dancing   _____
  Crafts   _____
  Art   _____
  Shop hobbies   _____
  Collections   _____
  Quiet games   _____
  Outings, hikes   _____
  Model building   _____
  Others (name them) _____
  _____   _____
  _____   _____

6. Do you wish the school to give you further information or advice about activities and hobbies?   Yes___   No___

Students frequently drop their selected activities for various reasons. The following are some of the reasons commonly given by boys and girls:

  Desired different or more activities
  Dissatisfied with the group
  Family moved far away
  Unable to pay dues any longer
  Wanted more social activities
  Wanted to meet more of the opposite sex
  Felt too young or too old for the group
  Found part-time employment

All of these reasons, except the last one, indicate that the students need to be interviewed again to see whether they desire any further suggestions from the school. The degree to which students pursue their home hobbies may also be followed up so that encouragement may be given.

When the students are reinterviewed it may be found that they need leisure time information to meet their changing needs. Some students may need a change of activity or of leisure time agency; some may wish to join their friends in another center; others may need to be informed about opportunities near their new home. Some students need activities on Saturdays since their part-time jobs may keep them busy through the week. Free activities may be obtained for those who cannot pay fees, or students may be shown how to economize on their spending money so that they may be able to pay small fees.

Students who belong to private clubs often enjoy sociability through meeting in each other's homes under a parent's supervision. Boys like to meet in athletic fields where they form a play group or club. Private clubs may be entirely wholesome or they may be found to have undesirable influences on boys and girls. These clubs frequently need to be investigated by the school or a social agency in order to determine the kind of influence they have on members. Parent organizations are usually glad to investigate any outside club to which their children belong.

Clubs in the home, supervised by interested parents, are perhaps more desirable to promote than any other kinds. The National Recreation Association has inexpensive booklets on all kinds of interesting home activities: music, art, crafts, orchestra, games, entertainment, and many other forms of recreation for the individual and a group.

Leisure time agencies may contribute to the school's follow-up findings. For instance, the leader of a student's outside club may become sufficiently interested in the need for adjusting each individual child who comes to him, to report results to the school.

A follow-up by the school for the purpose of obtaining parents' opinions on the value of the program for their children is also helpful in the evaluation of the leisure time education program.

The reports of specific cases serve as a means for gaining more co-operation from teachers, principals, superintendents, and parents. The few hours that any one person would need to spend on co-ordinating the program may be more readily granted if reports could substantiate the need for the service. It is therefore recommended that at least a few cases be written up in detail. Any direct or indirect benefit that the student received from the program should be included. Improvement in the student regarding any of the following factors should also be noted:

Health
Experiences
Skills
Personality
Social benefits
Creative hobbies
Attitudes toward school and general attitude
School conduct

Follow-up efforts need not be so extensive that they become a burden to the school staff. Some of the most valuable follow-up has been done informally through class discussions on leisure time. However, some schools may wish to make a scientific follow-up if they have the time and personnel.

The main concern in the evaluation of results is the individual's growth and improvement. How has the school developed and enriched the inner resources of youth for the enjoyment of their present leisure and adult life? In the final analysis the only values of leisure time education and the only ends humanly worth striving for are those of personal satisfaction which in the last resort are realized by and in individuals.

BIBLIOGRAPHY

BREWER, JOHN M. *Education as Guidance.*
BUSCH, HENRY M. *Leadership in Group Work.*
Creative Schools, Twenty-third Yearbook of the N. E. A.
DULLES, FOSTER RHEA. *America Learns to Play.*
ECKERT, RUTH E., AND MARSHALL, THOMAS O. *Report of the Regents' Inquiry.*
Education for the Recreational Use of Leisure through the Daily School Program, National Recreation Association.
ENGELHARDT, N. L. AND N. L., JR. *Planning the Community School.*
JACKS, LAWRENCE P. *Education Through Recreation.*
LEE, JOSEPH. "Play in Education," *Recreation,* December, 1942.

Lies, Eugene T. *The New Leisure Challenges the Schools.*

Loftus, John J. "A Program for the Desirable Use of Leisure Time as a Cardinal Objective of the Public Elementary Schools," *Proceedings, Department of Elementary Schools*, N. E. A.

Partridge, E. De Alton. "How a High School Trains for Leisure," *Recreation*, April, 1941.

The Purpose of Education in American Democracy, The Educational Policies Commission, N. E. A.

Recreation, September, 1940; issue on "Recreation and the School."

Social Services and the School, The Educational Policies Commission, N. E. A.

Standards of Training, Experience and Compensation in Community Recreation Work, National Recreation Association.

Youth; Volunteers for Youth Recreation Programs, Civilian Defense Office, Item 959.

BIBLIOGRAPHY

The classified bibliography is a ready reference for students, teachers, administrators, and group leaders. The references have been carefully selected by the author or recommended by reliable sources. Some of them are not annotated because the titles indicate clearly their content.

There is much more material which might be listed but space does not permit a more extensive bibliography.

The following is an outline of the bibliography:

I. HOBBIES AND ACTIVITIES FOR BOYS AND GIRLS

1. Art
2. Aviation
3. Beekeeping
4. Bicycling
5. Birds
6. Boatbuilding
7. Buttons
8. Camping
9. Circus
10. Collecting
11. Cooking
12. Crafts
13. Dancing and Drama
14. Dolls
15. Fishes
16. Fishing
17. Gardening
18. Gourds
19. Home Decorating
20. Home Hobbies
21. Indian Lore
22. Jiu-jutsu
23. Knitting
24. Magic
25. Minerals
26. Music
27. Nature
28. Outdoor Activities
29. Parties
30. Patchwork Quilts
31. Photography
32. Pottery
33. Quizzes
34. Radio
35. Science
36. Sewing
37. Sightseeing
38. Social Games
39. Sports
40. Stamps and Coins
41. Stars
42. Storytelling
43. Tool Hobbies
44. Toymaking
45. Whittling
46. Woodworking and Carving
47. General Hobbies

II. MAGAZINES FOR BOYS AND GIRLS

III. REFERENCES FOR TEACHERS AND GROUP LEADERS

1. Introduction to Leisure Time Education
2. School Subjects
3. Kinds of Leisure Time Activities
4. Safety in Play

BIBLIOGRAPHY

I. HOBBIES AND ACTIVITIES FOR BOYS AND GIRLS

1. *Art*

ALGER, JOSEPH. *Get in There and Paint!* New York: National Recreation Association, 315 Fourth Avenue. Pamphlet.
>If painting is your hobby or if you have the urge to paint just for fun this pamphlet is most stimulating.

ARNOLD, GRANT. *Creative Lithography and How to Do It.* New York: Harper & Brothers, 1941.
>An excellent handbook for beginners as well as those more advanced.

BIEGELEISEN, J. I. *The A B C of Lettering.* New York: Harper & Brothers, 1940.
>A complete introductory course in lettering with charts and illustrations.

BONE, CHARLOTTE D. *Linoleum Block Printing for Amateurs.* Boston: Beacon Press, Inc., 1936.

CARLSON, CHARLES X. *The Essentials of Pastel Painting.* New York: Melior Books, 1943.

CHANDLER, ANNA CURTIS. *A Voyage to Treasure Land.* New York: Harper & Brothers, 1929.
>Delightful stories about art in other lands.

————. *Story Lives of Master Artists.* New York: Frederick A. Stokes, 1933.
>This is interesting reading and useful for storytelling.

GREENE, FRANK F. *How to Create Cartoons.* New York: Harper & Brothers, 1941.
>Forty lessons for home study or class use.

GREENHOOD, DAVID. *Down to Earth Mapping for Everybody.* New York: Holiday House, 1944.

GUPTIL, ARTHUR L. *Freehand Drawing Self-Taught.* New York: Harper & Brothers, 1933.
>A compact guide for beginners.

LOOMIS, ANDREW. *Fun with a Pencil.* New York: The Viking Press, 1942.
>Simple lessons in drawing and cartooning.

PYLE, CLIFFORD. *Etching Principles and Methods.* New York: Harper & Brothers, 1941.
>This is a simple step-by-step manual.

THACII, STEPHEN D. *Painting as a Hobby.* New York: Harper & Brothers, 1940.
>To paint for fun is possible with such a manual as this.

THORNDIKE, CHUCK. *The Secrets of Cartooning*. New York: The House of Little Books, 1939.
. This is instructive and humorous.

ZAIDENBERG, ARTHUR. *Drawing the Human Figure*. Reading, Berkshire, England: Bradley & Son, Ltd. (Crown Press), 1944.
The book includes hundreds of helpful illustrations. Other books by the same author are available through the House of Little Books, 156 Fifth Avenue, New York.

ZUTTER, LA VADA. *Spatter Ink Techniques*. New York and Chicago: Sanford Ink Co., 1939.
Colored illustrations are numerous through this pamphlet.

2. *Aviation*

GRAHAM, F. P., AND CLEVELAND, R. M., EDITORS. *The Model Plane Annual 1942-43*. New York: Robert M. McBride & Co.

How Planes Fly. Prepared by the Aviation Research Associates. New York: Harper & Brothers, 1943.
Two other volumes of this series are: *Parts of Planes* and *Types of Planes*. They give direct and simple explanations for young readers.

3. *Beekeeping*

ONSTOTT, KYLE. *Beekeeping as a Hobby*. New York: Harper & Brothers, 1941.
The author encourages the novice with scant theoretical knowledge to learn the technique from keeping bees and following simple theories in this book. "Utterly to fail in the keeping of bees is difficult."

4. *Bicycling*

GEIST, ROLAND C. *Bicycling as a Hobby*. New York: Harper & Brothers, 1940.
Selection and care of a bicycle, safety, outings, racing, and clubs are discussed.

5. *Birds*

REED, CHESTER A. *The Bird Guide*. Garden City, New York: Doubleday, Doran & Co., 1943.

LINCOLN, FREDERICK C. *The Migration of American Birds*. New York: Doubleday, Doran & Co., 1939.

6. *Boatbuilding*

CROSBY, WILLIAM F. *Amateur Boat Building*. New York: The Rudder Publishing Co., 1941.
Steps in boatbuilding are given with many illustrations.

7. Buttons

ALBERT, LILLIAN. *A Button Collector's Journal*. Yardley, Penn.: The Cook Printers, 1941.

OLSON, LORRAINE. *Old Buttons and Their Values*. Chicago: Lightner Publishing Co., 1940.

8. Camping

BEARD, DAN. *Do It Yourself*. Philadelphia: J. B. Lippincott Co., 1934. This is descriptive and instructive material on many outdoor activities such as camping, fishing, boating, photography, nature study, and hiking.

MASON, BERNARD S. *Woodcraft*. New York: A. S. Barnes & Co., 1939.

9. Circus

HACKER, FRED A., AND EAMES, PRESCOTT W. *How to Put on an Amateur Circus*. Chicago: T. S. Denison & Co., 1923.

10. Collecting

BROOKS, WALTER. "The Shoestring Book Collector," *Reader's Digest*, June, 1932.

McMILLEN, WHEELER. *The Young Collector*. New York: D. Appleton-Century Co., 1928. Some of the collections discussed are: Indian relics, stamps, coins, geological specimens, shells, insects, flowers, dolls, photographs, scrapbook, and collections for very young children.

11. Cooking

MALTBY, LUCY. *It's Fun to Cook*. Philadelphia: John C. Winston Co., 1938. This is an aid for the aspiring young cook, giving good recipes and much practical advice about menus, table setting, and manners.

12. Crafts

BAXTER, WILLIAM T. *Jewelry Gem Cutting and Metalcraft*. New York: Whittlesey House, McGraw-Hill Book Co., 1942.

BELL, ENID. *Tin-craft as a Hobby*. New York: Harper & Brothers, 1935. A practical manual of specific directions for this useful and decorative hobby.

DE LEMOS, PEDRO. *Creative Art Crafts*. Worcester, Mass.: The Davis Press, 1944.

DENNISON-CRAFT BOOKS. Framingham, Mass. The books deal with crepe paper flower making, paper craft work, and party table decorations.

DOBBS, ELLA. *First Steps in Weaving*. New York: Macmillan Co., 1938.

The fundamental steps in weaving, and the tools, terms, and procedures are explained in simple language. For ages 14-16.

DODDS, ROBERT E. *Handicrafts as a Hobby*. New York: Harper & Brothers, 1939.

GABA, LESTER. *Soap Carving*. New York: The Studio Publications, Inc., 1944.

HUTCHINS, MABEL REAGH. *Creative Handicrafts*. New York: Sentinel Books, 1944.

ICKIS, MARGUERITE. *Crafts in Wartime*. New York: National Recreation Assn., 1942.

LEEMING, JOSEPH. *Fun with Leather*. New York: Frederick A. Stokes Co., 1941.
This book tells how to do decorative leatherwork of all kinds and how to make useful articles from leather. Illustrated.

MANLY, STACEY. *It's Fun to Make It Yourself*. New York: The Journal of Living Publishing Corp., 1944.

NEWKIRK, LOUIS V., AND ZUTTER, LA VADA. *You Can Make It—Things to Do With Scissors and Paste*. New York: Silver Burdett Co., 1944.
The book contains 214 illustrations.

PARKHILL, MARTHA, AND SPAETH, DOROTHY. *It's Fun to Make Things*. New York: A. S. Barnes & Co., 1941.

PERRY, EVADNA KRAUS. *Art Adventures with Discarded Materials*. New York: Noble & Noble, 1933.
Innumerable uses of old newspapers, magazines, rags, boxes, paper sacks, tin cans, spools, and stockings are interestingly described.

——. *Crafts for Fun*. New York: William Morrow & Co., 1940.
Some of the crafts described are: linoleum block-printing, spattering, bookmaking, clay modeling, pottery, weaving, knotting, embroidery, woodwork, modeling, and metal foil.

POWERS, MARGARET. *A Book of Little Crafts*. Peoria, Illinois: The Manuel Arts Press, 1940.
Ink-splotch designs, punched designs, finger painting, stencils, blueprints, stick printing, spatter, weaving, and experiments with color, design, shapes, sound, and dramatics are discussed in this book.

PYLE, CLIFFORD. *Leathercraft as a Hobby*. New York: Harper & Brothers, 1940.
Here is a uniquely practical manual for the beginner. It emphasizes facts essential to producing leather goods worthy of time, energy, and expense involved.

REYNOLDS, H. ATWOOD. *Low-cost Crafts for Everyone*. Garden City, New York: Blue Ribbon Books, 1943.
This is about crafts that are fun to use.

SHOEN, HARRIET H. *Let's Make a Book*. New York: Macmillan Co., 1934.

This small book of simple instructions is for rebuilding, stitching, and pasting books into the cover.

SOWERS, J. I. *Wood Carving Made Easy*. Milwaukee, Wis.: Bruce Pub. Co., 1936.

Square-knot Book. Brooklyn, New York: P. C. Herweg Co., 1926. A collection of illustrations and handsome designs with directions for working. Three parts.

TAYLOR, MARY PERKINS. *How to Make Hooked Rugs*. Philadelphia: David McKay Co., 1930.

The book is practical and well illustrated.

WHITE, MARY. *How to Make Baskets*. New York: Doubleday, Doran & Co., 1911.

WILLIAMSON, SCOTT GRAHAM. *The American Craftsman*. New York: Crown Publishers, 1940.

Hundreds of illustrations from photographs and contemporary prints are included. For adults.

ZWEYBRUCK, EMMY. *The Second Stencil Book*. Sandusky, Ohio: The American Crayon Co.

The same company also distributes materials on stitching, crocheting, hooked rugs, portfolios, and other crafts. Free catalogue.

13. *Dancing and Drama*

FORD, HENRY, AND MRS. FORD. *Good Morning*. Dearborn, Mich.: Dearborn Pub. Co., 1926.

Old-fashioned American quadrilles and contra dances, music, instructions, and a dictionary of dance terms are included.

MILLS, W. E., AND DUNN, L. M. *Shadow Plays and How to Produce Them*. New York: Doubleday, Doran & Co., 1938.

NATIONAL RECREATION ASSN.

An excellent source of literature on dancing and dramatic activities.

PAYANT, FELIX, ed. *A Book of Puppetry*. Columbus, Ohio: Design Pub. Co., 1936.

SHAW, LLOYD. *Promenade*. New York: Woman's Home Companion Service Bureau.

SMITH, MILTON. *Guide to Play Selection*. New York: D. Appleton-Century Co., 1934.

This is primarily an index and description of full-length and one-act plays, but it includes practical references for young producers.

14. *Dolls*

GRANT, J. A. *The Doll's House*. New York: The Studio Pub. Co., 1934.

Hobbies Magazine. July, 1944, and November, 1944 (costumed dolls).

15. *Fishes*

MORGAN, ALFRED P. *Tropical Fishes and Home Aquaria.* New York: Charles Scribner's Sons, 1935.
This is an excellent book for beginners.

16. *Fishing*

BERGMAN, RAY. *Just Fishing.* New York: Outdoor Life, 1942.
Fishing Facts. New York: Outdoor Life, 1941.
How, when, and where to catch more fish are described.
RODMAN, OLIVER H. P. *A Handbook of Salt-water Fishing.* New York: Frederick A. Stokes Co., 1940.
Game fish, tackle to use, surf casting, trolling, and short casts are discussed and illustrated.
WULFF, LEE. *Let's Go Fishing.* New York: Frederick A. Stokes Co., 1939.
Without overloading in details, the book gives such explicit directions and so many of the tricks of the art that it will be popular with boys.

17. *Gardening*

HOTTES, ALFRED C. *Plant Propagation.* New York: A. T. De La Mare Co., 1934.
"Hydrophonic Gardening," *House & Garden Magazine*, November, 1938.
LUCAS, JANNETTE MAY. *Where Did Your Garden Grow?* Philadelphia: J. B. Lippincott Co., 1939.
By means of beautiful pictorial maps in color and historical text this book traces many of the familiar flowers to their native habitats.
McFARLAND, J. H., HATTON, R. M., AND FOLEY, D. J. *Garden Bulbs in Color.* New York: Macmillan Co., 1928.
McKENNY, MARGARET. *A Book of Garden Flowers.* New York: Macmillan Co., 1941.
Thirty-three of the flowers most often found in gardens are described, and interesting bits of legend and history are included.
MATLIN, D. R. *Growing Plants without Soil.* New York: Chemical Pub. Co., 1939.
POST, KENNETH. *Plants and Flowers in the Home.* New York: Orange Judd Pub. Co., 1944.

18. *Gourds*

BAILEY, L. H. *The Garden of Gourds.* New York: Macmillan Co., 1938.
BEATTIE, W. R. *Useful and Ornamental Gourds.* U. S. Dept. of Agriculture, Farmers' Bulletin 1849. Washington, D. C.: Government Printing Office, 1940.

19. *Home Decorating*

"Landscaping the Farmstead." Office of Education; Vocational Division, Bulletin 189. Washington, D. C.: Government Printing Office, 1938.

Suggestions are offered on how to make the farm home grounds more attractive.

LEE, ELEANOR. *Practical Home Decorating.* New York: The House of Little Books, 1941.

TERHUNE, FLORENCE B. *Decorating for You.* New York: M. Barrows & Co., 1944.

VANDERWALKER, FRED N. *Interior Wall Decoration.* Chicago: Frederick J. Drake & Co., 1941.

Practical working methods for plain and decorative finishes, new and standard treatments, are described by this expert, who has written other books on house painting and wood finishing.

WAKEFIELD, LUCINA. *101 Home Furnishings and How to Make Them.* New York: Harper & Brothers, 1942.

This book is a stimulating guide.

20. *Home Hobbies*

Giant Home Workshop Manual. Prepared by the editorial staff of the *Popular Science Monthly.* New York: Popular Science Pub. Co., 1943.

Home and Workshop Index, issued by the Popular Science Pub. Co., New York.

This index covers about one year of articles in *Popular Science* on home workshops, gardening, and many other activities.

KELIHER, ALICE, ed. *Household Workers.* New York: Harper & Brothers, 1941.

The dignity and enjoyment of household work are discussed and illustrated with photographs.

LAWSON, ARTHUR. *Fun in the Backyard.* New York: Thomas Y. Crowell Co., 1938.

LEEMING, JOSEPH. *Games to Make and Play at Home.* New York: D. Appleton-Century Co., 1943.

Games for one, two, or more players, games for indoors and outdoors, and games with home-made cards.

MEYER, JEROME S. *Fun for the Family, 1000 Items to Amuse Everyone.* New York: Garden City Pub. Co.

This is designed to appeal to everyone in the family. It contains puzzles and problems that can be done alone as well as games and teasing questions for parties. Another book is: *More Fun for the Family.*

STARR, JULIAN, JR. *50 Things to Make for the Home.* New York: Whittlesey House, 1941.

STIERI, EMANUELE. *The Book of Indoor Hobbies*. New York: Mc-Graw-Hill Book Co., 1939.

> Hobbies for city apartments, the kitchen table, and workbench can be started with inexpensive tools purchased in five-and-ten-cent stores. Suggestions are given for home decoration.

ZARCHY, HARRY. *Let's Make Something*. New York: Alfred A. Knopf, Inc., 1941.

> This offers a wide range of ideas for the amateur craftsman. The necessary materials are easy to obtain. Directions are simple for making 67 different gifts from wood, clay, paper, glass, metal, textiles, and other materials. Illustrated.

21. *Indian Lore*

SOLOMON, J. H. *Indian Crafts and Indian Lore*. New York: Harper & Brothers, 1938.

WHEELWRIGHT, MARY. *Navajo Creation Myth*. Navajo Religion Series, Vol. I. Santa Fe: Museum of Navajo Ceremonial Art, 1942.

22. *Jiu-jutsu*

LOWELL, FREDERICK PAUL. *Jiu-Jutsu*. New York: A. S. Barnes & Co., 1942.

23. *Knitting*

THOMAS, MRS. MARY H. *Mary Thomas's Knitting Book*. New York: William Morrow & Co., 1938.

24. *Magic*

HUGARD, JEAN. *Modern Magic Manual*. New York: Harper & Brothers, 1939.

> This 345-page handbook by a famous magician reveals many professional magical tricks.

LEEMING, JOSEPH. *Magic for Everybody*. New York: Doubleday, Doran & Co., 1928.

> Cards, coins, rings, bottles, and other simple articles are the only paraphernalia necessary for performing these tricks which require little skill.

25. *Minerals*

FOSHAG, F. *Minerals from Earth and Sky*. Smithsonian Scientific Series, Vol. III, Part II. New York: Smithsonian Institute Series, Inc., 1934.

ZIM, HERBERT S., AND COOPER, E. K. *Minerals*. New York: Harcourt, Brace & Co., 1943.

26. *Music*

BARTON, FRED B. *Music as a Hobby*. New York: Harper & Brothers, 1941.

How to have fun with music as a performer and as a listener is told in an appealing manner.

An Index to Folk Dances and Singing Games, compiled by the staff of the music department of the Minneapolis Public Library. Chicago: American Library Assn., 1936.

Useful reference book on 100 collections of classic and folk dances and singing games.

MYTINGER, G. S. "Trying for Records," *Reader's Digest*, November, 1935.

The article suggests phonograph record collections.

NATIONAL RECREATION ASSOCIATION. This is an excellent source of literature on all kinds of music. One pamphlet, for instance, is *Starting and Maintaining a Community Orchestra*, 1940. Another is, *Starting and Developing a Rhythm Band*, 1937.

RANDOLPH, CARY. *The Cary Randolph Quick Method of Note Reading*. St. Louis, Mo.: Cary Randolph, 5330 Pershing Ave., 1944.

SPAETH, SIGMUND GOTTFRIED. *Music for Fun*. New York: McGraw-Hill Book Co., 1939.

This book tries to stimulate a normal enthusiasm for music. It suggests ways of getting started, for adults and children alike.

27. *Nature*

BROOKS, C. F. *Why the Weather?* New York: Harcourt, Brace & Co., 1942.

PARKER, BERTHA M. (Laboratory Schools, University of Chicago). *Living Things, The Basic Science Education Series*. New York: Row, Peterson & Co., 1941.

This booklet has colorful pictures of animals, flowers, and sea life, for use in the intermediate grades. Other booklets are available on clouds, rain and snow, solar system, and animal life.

PRICE, BETTY. *Adventuring in Nature*. New York: Association Press, 1939.

28. *Outdoor Activities*

BEARD, JAMES. *Cook It Outdoors*. New York: M. Barrows & Co., 1941.

CURTIS, CAPT. PAUL A. *Guns and Gunning*. New York: Outdoor Life, 1941.

McCORMICK, OLIVE. *Water Pageants—Games and Stunts*. New York: A. S. Barnes & Co., 1933.

The author has presented in a step-by-step sequence the most successful methods of producing any type of water pageant. Seven complete pageants are described and illustrated.

MARTIN, G. W. *Come and Get It*. New York: A. S. Barnes & Co., 1942.

OUTDOOR LIFE, New York. This is a source for literature.

Outdoors Indoors. New York: National Recreation Assn.

Other materials are also available on the subject.

29. *Parties*

> *Parties A to Z.* New York: National Recreation Assn., 1944.
> This booklet contains novel ideas for 26 parties.
> *Teen Parties*, Woman's Home Companion Service Bureau, New York.
> Six party plans with decorations, games, and favors are described.
> WHEELER, BLANCHE. *Party Plans.* Minneapolis, Minn.: Webb Book Pub. Co., 1939.
> This is a series of three booklets at 50 cents each on wedding anniversaries, showers, and delightful entertainments for children. Novel methods, gifts, and recipes are suggested.

30. *Patchwork Quilts*

> FINLEY, RUTH E. *Old Patchwork Quilts and the Women Who Made Them.* Philadelphia: J. B. Lippincott Co., 1928.
> This practical handbook includes a discussion of quilt making as an interpretation of its periods, and directions for making quilts. Illustrated.

31. *Photography*

> BARTON, FRED B. *Photography as a Hobby.* New York: Harper & Brothers, 1939.
> Here is something novel in amateur photography to help the beginner make pictures with the minimum of expense and equipment.
> DESCHIN, JACOB. *Tabletop Photography.* Chicago: Ziff-Davis Pub. Co., 1941.
> *How to Make Good Pictures.* Rochester, N. Y.: Eastman Kodak Co.
> *How to Make Your Own Photographic Equipment.* Prepared by the editorial staff of *Popular Science Monthly.* New York: Popular Science Pub. Co., 1941.
> The photographer who desires to make equipment for his darkroom and accessories for his camera will find this a practical handbook.
> KING, ELEANOR. *Make Your Own Movies.* New York: Coward-McCann, Inc., 1939.

32. *Pottery*

> CURTIS, EDMUND DE FOREST. *Pottery: Its Craftsmanship and Its Appreciation.* New York: Harper & Brothers, 1940.
> This is a systematic guide to the making of pottery, set against a background of masterpieces in this field.
> DOUGHERTY, JOHN W. *Pottery Made Easy.* Milwaukee: Bruce Pub. Co., 1939.

33. *Quizzes*

> FISHER, H. *Riddle-de-Quiz.* New York: Mills & Co., 1944.

HASKIN, FREDERIC J. *The American Quiz and Answer Book*. New York: Grosset & Dunlap, 1941.

34. Radio

Everybody's Radio Manual. Prepared by the editorial staff of *Popular Science Monthly*. New York: Popular Science Pub. Co., 1944.

KEITH, ALICE. *How to Speak and Write for Radio*. New York: Harper & Brothers, 1944.

This book is up to date and an excellent guide to anyone planning to broadcast. It contains methods, materials, scripts, and helpful suggestions concerning interviewing on the radio, advertising, and voice training. The author is connected with the National Academy of Broadcasting, Washington, D. C.

LEWIS, DOROTHY, AND MCFADDEN, DOROTHY L. *Program Patterns for Young Radio Listeners*. New York: National Assn. of Broadcasters, 1944.

35. Science

COLLINS, ARCHIE FREDERICK. *Inventing for Fun and Profit*. New York: Coward-McCann, Inc., 1943.

MORGAN, ALFRED P. *Simple Chemical Experiments; Things a Boy Can Do with Electrochemistry*. New York: D. Appleton-Century Co.

The contents include: your laboratory, experiments with sulphur, oxygen and gasses. The amateur scientist with limited equipment can perform most of the experiments described.

PARKER, BERTHA M. *Beyond the Solar System, The Basic Science Education Series*. New York: Row, Peterson & Co., 1941.

———. *Clouds, Rain, and Snow. Ibid.*, 1941.

Other booklets by the same author discuss birds, insects, living things, plants, animals, and balance in nature.

Wonders through the Microscope. Prepared by the editorial staff of *Popular Science Monthly*. New York: Popular Science Pub. Co., 1938.

36. Sewing

The Condensed Butterick Sewing and Dressmaking Book. Chicago: The Beckley-Ralston Co., 1944.

DICKSON, SALLY, AND BLONDIN, FRANCES. *The New Encyclopedia of Modern Sewing*. New York: National Needlecraft Bureau, 1943.

LENT, D. GENEVA. *Needlepoint as a Hobby*. New York: Harper & Brothers, 1942.

This unusual manual on the art of stitchery provides an interesting approach to the subject by linking each technique with the historic period in which it originated.

PICKEN, MARY BROOKS. *Sewing for Everybody*. Yonkers, New York: The World Book Co., 1944.

POWELL, VEE W. *How to Make and Trim Your Own Hats.* New York: Journal of Living Pub. Corp., 1944.

37. Sightseeing

New York Handy Guide. New York: Manhattan Post Card Pub. Co. and also Nesterman Pub. Co.

The Red Book Information Guide to Manhattan, and other boroughs. New York: Interstate Map Co.

These are samples of official information such as any city may have at newsstands. They list public buildings, parks, transportation lines, and sights worth seeing.

Chambers of commerce and newsstands have similar guides for any locality.

38. Social Games

MASON, B. S., AND MITCHELL, E. D. *Social Games for Recreation.* New York: A. S. Barnes & Co., 1935.

More than 1200 activities and games are described for use in the home, school, for a party, on the playground, in the clubroom, or at any social gathering. The volume is a veritable encyclopedia of social games and activities adaptable to whatever equipment is available.

39. Sports

Barnes Dollar Sports Library. New York: A. S. Barnes & Co., 1940. A series of 39 small books.

BONIFACE, J. J. *Riding.* New York: A. S. Barnes & Co., 1940.

This manual for beginners was written by a retired colonel of the U. S. Army. It is a part of the Barnes Dollar Sports Series.

GRAHAM, FRANK. *McGraw of the Giants.* New York: G. P. Putnam's Sons, 1944.

This is a biography of a great baseball figure. The author has written these books also: *The New York Yankees* and *Lou Gehrig.*

HENDERSON, EDWIN BANCROFT. *The Negro in the Sports.* Washington, D.C.: The Associated Publishers, 1939.

The book describes the achievements in the field of sports of many young Negro men and women.

HENIE, SONJA. *Wings on My Feet.* New York: Prentice-Hall, Inc., 1940.

HOLLIMAN, JENNIE. *American Sports, 1785-1835.* Durham, N.C.: The Seeman Press, 1931.

This is an interesting history of the beginnings of American sports and athletics.

MASON, B. S., AND MITCHELL, E. D. *Active Games and Contests.* New York: A. S. Barnes & Co., 1935.

PFEIFER, FRIEDL, ED. *The Sun Valley Ski Book*. New York: A. S. Barnes & Co., 1939.

> The author gives one an education in skiing by unusual and effective photographs with few words.

RICE, GRANTLAND, AND POWELL, HARFORD, EDITORS. *The Omnibus of Sport*. New York: Harper & Brothers, 1932.

> Short stories are told about football, baseball, golf, tennis, ancient pageant passes, combat, racing, hunting, and fishing.

TUNIS, JOHN R. *Sports for the Fun of It*. New York: A. S. Barnes & Co., 1940.

> This handbook tells about official rules for 20 sports including archery, badminton, bowling, croquet, deck tennis, fencing, golf, handball, horseshoes, paddle tennis, ping-pong, shuffleboard, skating, and other activities. Illustrated.

40. Stamps and Coins

KIMBLE, RALPH A. *How to Collect Stamps*. New York: Grosset & Dunlap, 1933.

Standard Postage Stamp Catalogue. New York: Scott Stamp & Coin Co. Published annually.

STILES, KENT B. *Stamps*. New York: Harper & Brothers, 1935.

United States Stamp Catalogue. New York: Scott Stamp & Coin Co. Published annually.

41. Stars

PROCTER, MARY. *Our Stars Month by Month*. New York: Frederick Warner & Co., 1937.

WILLIAMS, LOU. *A Dipper Full of Stars*. Chicago: Fallett Pub. Co., 1944.

42. Storytelling

BREEN, MARY J. *For the Storyteller*. New York: National Recreation Assn., 1943.

> The first steps in telling a story are explained. The book will give inspiration and courage to undiscovered storytellers.

CHANDLER, ANNA CURTIS. *Dragons on Guard*. New York: Frederick A. Stokes Co., 1944.

> These are colorful stories on the art and history of China, useful in the art or history class.

———. *Famous Mothers and Their Children. Ibid.*, 1938.

43. Tool Hobbies

BRITTON, KATHARINE. *What Makes It Tick?* Boston: Houghton Mifflin Co., 1943.

> Explanations are given about equipment in the home and on the farm, air conditioning, radio, furnace, gears, planting, harvesting, and the weather. Amusing illustrations.

BURKET, H. "We Plan Alterations: Game Room for the Keenans' Basement," *Woman's Home Companion*, January, 1945.

HOBBS, HARRY J. *Working with Tools*. New York: Sentinel Books, 1944.

This is a manual for the home workshop.

LA BERGE, ARMAND J. *Woodworking for Fun*. Peoria, Illinois: Manual Arts Press, 1941.

WAKELING, ARTHUR, ED. *Things to Make in Your Home Workshop*. New York: Grosset & Dunlap, 1939.

WELLS, JOHN AND ENID. *You Can Fix It*. Cleveland, Ohio: The World Pub. Co., 1944.

You Can Make It Series.

You Can Make It (out of wood).

You Can Make It for Camp and Cottage.

You Can Make It for Profit.

Washington, D.C.: Government Printing Office, 1929.

How to make wooden articles out of scrap material or second-hand boxes, how to build furniture, and many other interesting projects are explained.

44. *Toymaking*

FISH, H. D. *The Doll House Book*. New York: Frederick A. Stokes, 1940.

KLENKE, W. W. *Dolls Furniture*. Bloomington, Ill.: McKnight & McKnight, 1935.

MOCHRIE, E., AND ROSEMAN, I. P. *Felt Toys*. Peoria, Ill.: Manual Arts Press, 1943.

Model Railways. Prepared by the editorial staff of the *Popular Science Monthly*. New York: Popular Science Pub. Co., 1939.

The model railway builder will find this a handy guide for making, installing, and operating equipment and accessories.

MOODY, EDITH. *Dressed Soft Toys*. Peoria, Ill.: Manual Arts Press, 1943.

PLIMPTON, EDNA. *How to Make Toys*. New York: Macmillan Co., 1939.

The same author has a book on *Your Workshop*, also.

45. *Whittling*

HELLUM, AMANDA W., AND GOTTSHALL, FRANKLIN H. *You Can Whittle and Carve*. Milwaukee: Bruce Pub. Co., 1944.

Beginners will enjoy this illustrated book. It deals with shaping ordinary things into objects of interest and of value.

HUNT, BEN. *Ben Hunt's Whittling Book*. Milwaukee: Bruce Pub. Co., 1945.

LEEMING, JOSEPH. *Fun with Wood.* New York: Frederick A. Stokes Co., 1942.

Toys, puzzles, unusual figures, and decorative articles can be whittled. The same author has books on fun with leather, paper, string, boxes, and costumes.

46. *Woodworking and Carving*

BELL, ENID. *Practical Wood-carving Projects.* New York: Harper & Brothers, 1940.

Techniques are taught here through the making of useful articles. Useful items from a salad spoon to a door panel are described.

STIERI, EMANUELE. *Woodworking as a Hobby.* New York: Harper & Brothers, 1939.

This book for older boys deals with the home workshop, tools, machinery, design, furniture building, and the use of glue.

FAULKNER, HERBERT W. *Wood-carving as a Hobby.* New York: Harper & Brothers, 1934.

The author combines practical suggestions with his philosophy. He says, "You have to have a good disposition to work in wood. You have it or you get it for there is a tonic quality in the feel of chisel against block." This spare-time occupation is well described so that others may follow.

47. *General Hobbies*

CALKINS, ERNEST ELMO. *Care and Feeding of Hobby Horses.* New York: Sentinel Books.

Interesting hobbies are described in a series of booklets. Bibliography.

DUDLEY, L. "Can You Entertain Yourself?" N. E. A. *Journal,* November, 1943.

Many suggestions are offered on what to do by yourself to build up inner resources for pleasurable enjoyment.

LAMPLAND, RUTH, ED. *Hobbies for Everyone.* New York: Harper & Brothers, 1934.

Hobbies of noted persons are interestingly described. Some of these hobbies are: astronomy, beans, bridge, camping, chess, design, dogs, nature, and many others.

Modern Recreation Series. Chicago: Chicago Park District, Administration Building, Burnham Park.

Some of the activities covered in the booklets are: art, crafts, whittling, carving, puppetry and games.

Other sources of literature: (catalogues are available)

The American Crayon Co., Sandusky, Ohio.

A. S. Barnes & Co., 67 W. 44th St., New York.

Barnes & Noble, Fifth Ave. and 18th St., New York.

Boy Scouts of America, 2 Park Ave., New York.
The Bruce Pub. Co., 330 W. 42nd St., New York.
Co-operative Recreation Service, Delaware, Ohio.
Girl Scouts, 155 E. 44th St., New York.
Harper & Brothers, 49 E. 33rd St., New York.
National Recreation Assn., 315 Fourth Ave., New York.
The Ohio State University, Agricultural College Extension Service, Columbus 10, Ohio.
Sentinel Books, 112 E. 19th St., New York.
The Studio Books Publications, Inc., 381 Fourth Ave., New York.

II. MAGAZINES FOR BOYS AND GIRLS[1]

1. *The American Girl Magazine.* New York: 155 E. 44th St.
2. *Aviation.* New York 18: McGraw-Hill Pub. Co., 330 W. 42nd St.
3. *Boys' Life.* New York: Boy Scouts of America, 2 Park Ave.
   Official magazine of the Boy Scouts.
4. *Child Life.* Boston 6, Mass.: Child's Life, Inc., 729 Boyleston St.
   Stories and things to do.
5. *Flying.* Chicago, Illinois: Ziff-Davis Pub. Co., 540 N. Michigan Ave.
6. *Horn Book.* Boston 16, Mass.: 264 Boyleston St.
   For parents, teachers, and youth leaders as well as for boys and girls.
7. *The Junior Natural History Magazine.* New York: The American Museum of Natural History, Central Park West and 79th St.
8. *Junior Red Cross Journal.* Washington, D.C.: American Red Cross.
9. *Model Airplane News.* New York: 551 Fifth Ave.
10. *National Geographic Magazine.* Washington, D.C.: National Geographic Society.
11. *Natural History.* New York 24: American Museum of Natural History, Central Park West and 79th St.
12. *Nature Magazine.* Washington, D.C.: American Nature Assn.
13. *The Open Road for Boys.* Louisville 1, Ky.: The Open Road Pub. Co., 1100 West Broadway.
14. *Popular Mechanics Magazine.* Chicago 11, Ill.: Popular Mechanics Co., 200 E. Ontario St.
15. *Popular Science Magazine.* New York: Popular Science Pub. Co., 353 Fourth Ave.
16. *Radio-Craft and Popular Electronics.* New York 7: Radcraft Publications, Inc., 25 W. Broadway.
17. *Radio News Magazine.* New York: 350 Fifth Ave.
18. *Science News Letter.* Washington, D.C.: 1719 N Street N.W.
    Weekly summary of current science.

[1] Partial list; see the local public library for further suggestions.

19. *Senior Scholastic*. New York 17: 220 E. 42nd St.

20. *Seventeen*. Philadelphia, Penn.: Triangle Publications, Inc., 400 N. Broad St.

21. *Story Parade*. Richmond 19, Va.: Story Parade, Inc., 8 N. 6th St.
    For elementary school children.

22. *Young America*. New York 22: Eton Pub. Corp., 32 E. 57th St.

III. REFERENCES FOR TEACHERS AND GROUP LEADERS

1. *Introduction to Leisure Time Education*

Educational Activities Promoting the Worthy Use of Leisure Time, Los Angeles City Schools, California. Bulletin 89, Board of Education, Los Angeles.

Encyclopedia of the Social Sciences, Vol. IX. "Leisure." Pp. 402-406. New York: Macmillan Co., 1933.

LIES, EUGENE T. *How You Can Make Democracy Work.* New York: Association Press, 1942.
This is a handbook for community-minded teachers and community leaders. Chapter IX deals with "Leisure in Your Community."

MEARNS, HUGHES. *Creative Youth.* New York: Doubleday, Doran & Co., 1939.
The author shows how a school environment sets free the creative spirit through the classroom, literature, library, and creative poetry.

PACK, ARTHUR NEWTON. *The Challenge of Leisure.* New York: Macmillan Co., 1934.
This deals with the possibilities of the use of leisure in various fields such as sports, art, music, education, nature study, and human relationships.

WISWELL, T. "Contribution of Recreation to Morale," *Recreation*, August, 1944.

2. *School Subjects*

BOYCE, GEORGE A., AND BEATTY, WILLARD W. *Mathematics of Everyday Life; Leisure Unit*, The Economics of Leisure Activities. New York: Inor Pub. Co., 1939.
The problems bear upon students' experiences. For junior high school.

Community Life; A Suggested Unit Organization for the Seventh Grade Program in Social Studies. Bulletin III-7, New York State Dept. of Education, Albany, N. Y., October 15, 1941.

"Creating Vocational Interests," *Occupations Magazine*, May, 1942.

FORRESTER, GERTRUDE. *Methods of Vocational Guidance.* Chapter X,

"Broadening Occupational Horizons Through Avocational Pursuits."
New York: D. C. Heath & Co., 1944.

FRETWELL, ELBERT K. *Extra-curricular Activities in Secondary Schools.*
Boston: Houghton Mifflin Co., 1931.

Good Reading. Chicago, Ill.: The National Council of Teachers of
English, 211 W. 68th St., 1944.
For college students and adults.

HALTER, HELEN. *Society in Action*; a guide for the social studies.
New York: Inor Pub. Co., 1936.
This valuable book ties up all social studies for grades 7-11. The
50 units relate to self-development and personality, group living
including recreation in the immediate community, and group
living in the larger community. Bibliography.

HILDEBRAND, J. R. "The Geography of Games," *National Geographic
Magazine*, August, 1919.
The games and sports described here show how they form an
index of the habits and histories of peoples throughout the world.

MARTIN, LAURA K. *A Selected List of Magazines for High School
Libraries.* State Dept. of Education, Div. of School Libraries, Nashville, Tenn. Nashville: Tennessee Book Co., 172 Second Ave., North,
1943.
The suggestions are helpful to libraries and English classes.

MOORE, ANNE CARROLL. *The Choice of a Hobby.* Chicago, Ill.: F. E.
Compton & Co., 1935.
The extensive list of suggestions includes: ships and ship models,
sailing, aviation, stamps, games and sports, fishing, horses and
riding, pets, wild life, camping, photography, amateur science,
and others.

RAMSEY, ELOISE. *Reading for Fun.* Chicago, Ill.: The National Council
of Teachers of English, 211 W. 68th St.
This pamphlet is a bibliography for the elementary school on
travel, animals, hobbies, tales and brave deeds, magic, poetry, and
festivals.

YATES, RAYMOND FRANCIS. *Science Calls to Youth.* New York: D.
Appleton-Century Co., 1941.
This is a guide to career planning in the sciences.

3. *Kinds of Leisure Time Activities*

PANGBURN, WEAVER WEDDELL. *Adventures in Recreation.* New York:
A. S. Barnes & Co., 1936.
This book is useful as a text or for collateral reading in junior and
senior high school courses, in social sciences, physical education,
and guidance classes. What the average community can offer in
leisure activities is discussed interestingly.

PARTRIDGE, E. DE ALTON, AND MOONEY, CATHERINE. *Time Out for Living*. New York: American Book Co., 1941.
> A book which the teacher or leader can give to students to read. Explanations are given on how to pursue hobbies and activities of all kinds. Amusing illustrations.

4. Safety in Play

DOUGHERTY, THOMAS F., AND KEARNEY, PAUL W. *Fire*. New York: G. P. Putnam's Sons, 1931.
> Valuable information that everybody greatly needs is contained in this book.

JENKINS, A. "Drive Right!" *Reader's Digest*, August, 1934.

LEAF, MUNRO. *Safety Can Be Fun*. New York: Frederick A. Stokes Co., 1938.
> Adapted to lower grades. Clever drawings.

National Commission on Safety Education.
> N. E. A., 1201 Sixteenth St., Washington, D. C.

5. Leisure Time Opportunities in the Community

HADER, BERTA AND ELMER. *Little Town*. New York: Macmillan Co., 1941.
> This panorama of life in a small town is adapted to lower elementary school children.

HUTCHINS, ROBERT MAYNARD. "The Value of the Museum," *Science*, October 15, 1943.
> Dr. Hutchins, Chancellor, University of Chicago, says, "It is not education to make a living that we require, but education to make a life."

"Lively Games That Are Played All Over the World." *Compton's Pictured Encyclopedia*, Vol. II. Chicago, Ill.: F. E. Compton & Co., 1942.
> The illustrated article shows the mythological, religious, and legendary origin of a number of games.

Rho Journal, March, 1944. Pi Lambda Theta, New York University.
> Forty-two teachers tell about methods they have found successful in dealing with the community. This issue is entitled: "Coordination of School and Community."

6. Self-Improvement through Leisure Activities

ALLEN, B., AND BRIGGS, M. *Behave Yourself!* Philadelphia: J. B. Lippincott Co., 1937.
> Everyday social behavior for boys and girls 15-18 years of age.

BAKER, RAY STANNARD. *Under My Elm, Country Discoveries and Reflections*. Garden City, N.Y.: Doubleday, Doran & Co., 1942.
> The author wrote many other books on contentment, friendship,

solitude, understanding, as well as a biography of Woodrow Wilson. Some of his books are under the name of David Grayson.

BENNETT, MARGARET E., AND HAND, H. C. *Designs for Personality.* New York: McGraw-Hill Book Co., 1938.

This book is adapted to the older high school student.

BOYKIN, ELEANOR. *This Way, Please.* New York: Macmillan Co., 1940.

This informal and lively book treats the problem of correct manners for boys and girls in a friendly and amusing way.

CABOT, RICHARD. *What Men Live By.* Boston: Houghton Mifflin Co., 1914.

EMERSON, RALPH WALDO. *Essays.* London: Oxford Univ. Press., 1936.

Of special interest may be the essay on friendship, page 134.

FEDDER, RUTH. *A Girl Grows Up.* New York: McGraw-Hill Book Co., 1939.

GILES, NELL. *Susan Be Smooth.* Boston, Mass.: Hale, Cushman & Flint, 1940.

This gives a modern approach to the problem of good grooming for girls, with advice on the care of the hair, skin, diet, make-up, and clothes.

GREENBIE, SYDNEY. *Leisure for Living.* New York: George W. Stewart, 1940.

The young adult will enjoy this book on leisure for relaxation, for learning, for enrichment, and for reflection.

LLOYD-JONES, ESTHER, AND FEDDER, RUTH. *Coming of Age.* New York: McGraw-Hill Book Co. 1941.

The book is intended for the use of young people themselves. It discusses, in their own language problems which young people face in achieving emotional maturity, building relationships with their own and the opposite sex, striving for vocational adjustment, and evolving a scheme of values.

McKOWN, HARRY C., AND LE BRON, MARION. *A Boy Grows Up.* New York: McGraw-Hill Book Co., 1940.

This book is useful in guidance of boys in home, school, and social adjustment. The interests of boys are considered in a revealing manner on pages 111-130 and 217-273.

OVERSTREET, HARRY A. *A Guide to Civilized Leisure.* New York: W. W. Norton & Co., 1934.

A helpful guide in work with individual and community problems of social adjustment. For the young adult.

RYAN, MILDRED. *Cues for You.* New York: D. Appleton-Century Co., 1940.

The book endeavors to answer the questions of social behavior which perplex high school students and to provide them with a framework within which they can build a fruitful life.

VAN ARSDALE, MAY, AND LINGENFELTER, MARY. *Manners Now and Then*. New York: Harcourt, Brace & Co., 1940.

This book points out that such graciousness as we have is a heritage which we can weave into our personal lives.

7. *Planning the Use of Leisure*

Making the Most of One's Leisure: A Social Studies Unit. Tulsa, Okla.: Board of Education. Mimeographed.

RUCH, FLOYD L., MACKENZIE, GORDON N., AND McCLEAN, MARGARET. *People Are Important*. New York: Scott, Foresman & Co., 1941.

Suggestions are offered for personality development. The bibliography, pages 165-186, is on "Planning Your Playtime."

8. *Play for the Small Child*

DOBBS, ALMA A. *Teaching Wholesome Living*. New York: A. S. Barnes & Co., 1939.

This is a book for parents, principals, and teachers. It emphasizes a point of view rather than subject matter, and a method rather than material of instruction.

FALLIS, EDWINA. *The Child and Things*. Yonkers, N. Y.: World Book Co., 1940.

This is a complete guide and handbook of practical directions for constructive play and equipment for the young child. It provides experimential activities with inexpensive equipment, and is adapted for classroom work with wood, cloth, paper bags, cardboard, empty spools, camera reels, old inner tubes, cans, and clay. Fallis toys are manufactured by the Judy Co., Minneapolis.

Home Play and Play Equipment for the Pre-School Child. Children's Bureau, publication 238. Washington, D.C.: Government Printing Office, 1941.

JONES, JESSIE ORTON. *Small Rain*. New York: The Viking Press, 1943. Verses from the Bible are portrayed for little children in appealing pictures of everyday American boys and girls.

LEAF, MUNRO. *A War-time Handbook for Young Americans*. New York: Frederick A. Stokes, 1942.

The development of citizenship qualities of elementary school boys and girls is the aim of this book. It has large print and amusing drawings. Other books by this author are: *Manners Can Be Fun* and *Grammar Can Be Fun*.

PLAY SCHOOLS ASSOCIATION, 119 W. 57th St., New York.

A good source of literature on play for the younger child.

9. *School Activities and Visual Aids*

> *Auditorium Activities: Elementary and Junior High School Grades, Austin Public Schools.* Austin, Texas: Board of Education, 1935.
>> Outlines of auditorium activities are suggested for training students in efficient citizenship, social contacts, self-expression, and worthy use of leisure time.
>
> McKown, Harry C. *Extra-curricular Activities.* New York: Macmillan Co., 1938.
>> "The main purpose of these activities is to give the student opportunity for practice in social relationships."
>
> Stolper, B. J. R. *The Bulletin Board as a Teaching Device*, New York: Bureau of Publications, Teachers College, Columbia University, 1940.
>> This pamphlet contains helpful suggestions for making bulletin boards attractive and educative.
>
> *A Suggested Outline of Subjects to be Covered in Auditorium Periods.* Medford, Mass.: Board of Education, Medford Public Schools, 1934. Mimeographed.
>
> Thompson, Betty Lynd. *Fundamentals of Rhythm and Dance.* New York: A. S. Barnes & Co., 1933.
>> This is a complete presentation of the principles of teaching dancing, including rhythms, tap, clog, folk dancing, and plans for staging festivals.
>
> Trow, William C., Zapf, Rosalind M., and McKown, Harry C. *Recreation and Leisure.* New York: McGraw-Hill Book Co., 1940.
>> This pamphlet contains many interesting discussion lessons and suggestions for students. Spaces are provided for students' own statements of preferences and for short compositions. It may be used for individuals as well as for groups.

IV. REFERENCES FOR ADMINISTRATORS OF LEISURE TIME EDUCATION

1. *Significance of Leisure Time Education*

> Brewer, John M. *Education as Guidance.* New York: Macmillan Co., 1932. Chapter XII on leisure time.
>
> Dreer, Herman. "The Negro in the course of Study of the High School," *The Negro History Bulletin*, April, 1944. Washington, D.C.: The Association for the Study of Negro Life and History. Bibliography.
>
> Dulles, Foster Rhea. *America Learns to Play.* New York: D. Appleton-Century Co., 1940.
>> This is an interesting history of popular recreation, 1607-1940.

ECKERT, RUTH E., AND MARSHALL, THOMAS O. *Report of the Regents' Inquiry: When Youth Leave School.* New York: McGraw-Hill Book Co., 1938.

> Leisure time pursuits of pupils were found to indicate that many of the constructive activities begun in school are left off as soon as the pupils leave school. "It is apparent that neither the school nor the adult organizations in local communities make any systematic effort to encourage out-of-school youth to continue activities begun in school."

Education for the Recreational use of Leisure through the Daily School Program. New York: National Recreation Assn., Bulletin 712, April, 1939.

JACKS, LAWRENCE P. *Education of the Whole Man.* New York: Harper & Brothers, 1931.

———. *Education Through Recreation.* New York: Harper & Brothers, 1932.

> The author considers what it would mean to us if we, as a people, solved the common problem of leisure and education. He says, "Let us have more joy in life." Administrators will receive inspiration and direction from this stimulating book which gives the spirit of play.

JONES, ANNA MAY. "Education for Leisure Helps to Prevent Delinquency," *The Clearing House*, March, 1943.

KINNEMAN, JOHN A., AND ELLWOOD, ROBERT S. *Living With Others.* Boston: Houghton Mifflin Co., 1939.

> Pages 445-469 give an excellent discussion of leisure and its social value.

LEE, JOSEPH. "Play in Education," *Recreation*, December, 1942.

> The effect of play on the child's personality and character is emphasized.

LIES, EUGENE T. *The New Leisure Challenges the Schools.* New York: National Recreation Association, 1933.

LOFTUS, JOHN J. "A Program for the Desirable Use of Leisure Time as a Cardinal Objective of the Public Elementary Schools." *Proceedings, Department of Elementary Schools*, N. E. A., Washington, D.C., 1928.

MITCHELL, ELMER D., AND MASON, BERNARD S. *The Theory of Play.* New York: A. S. Barnes & Co., Inc., copyright 1934.

PARTRIDGE, E. DE ALTON. "How a High School Trains for Leisure," *Recreation*, April, 1941.

ROGERS, JAMES EDWARD. *The Child and Play.* New York: Century Company, 1932.

> Based on reports of the White House conference on child health and protection.

The Purpose of Education in American Democracy. The Educational Policies Commission, N. E. A., Washington, D.C., 1938.

Recreation, September, 1940.

This entire issue is devoted to "Recreation and the School."

Social Services and the Schools. The Educational Policies Commission, N. E. A., Washington, D.C., 1939. Chapter V.

2. *Co-ordination of Leisure Time Education with the Community*

Directory of Social Agencies of the City of New York. New York: Columbia Univ. Press.

This is a sample of directories which many cities print for practical reference. A section is devoted to recreational centers. Chambers of commerce supply local lists of leisure time agencies.

HERRON, J. S. "Community School vs. Community Recreation," *Recreation,* October, 1944.

KEOHAVE, M. P. AND R. E. *Exploring Your Community.* New York: Harcourt, Brace & Co., 1940.

Know Your Community. New York: National Recreation Assn.

SEYFERT, W. C. "New Interest in Religious Education," *School Review,* June, 1945.

WYLAND, R. O. *Scouting in the Schools.* New York: Columbia Univ. Press, 1934.

3. *Wider Use of Schools*

Creative Schools. Twenty-third Yearbook of the N. E. A. of the U. S., Washington, D.C., Dept. of Elementary School Principals, 1944.

ENGELHARDT, N. L. AND N. L., JR. *Planning The Community School.* New York: American Book Co., 1940.

The community school is considered in this guide as the setting for adult activities. Plans, equipment, surroundings, and administration are discussed by these authorities in relation to their use in a community school.

FRANKLIN, ADELE, AND BENEDICT, AGNES E. *Play Centers for Children; A Guide to their Establishment and Operation.* New York: William Morrow & Co., 1943.

An afterschool program was organized in lower Manhattan in P.S. 33. The report shows how children learned in an atmosphere of play.

LAMBERT, CLARA, AND THE PLAY SCHOOL ASSOCIATION. *School's Out.* New York: Harper & Brothers, 1944.

This book points out the plight of the school-age child whose parents work and cannot exercise normal control. Specific suggestions are offered for setting up play centers, selecting and training workers. Illustrated.

V. REFERENCES FOR COMMUNITY GROUP LEADERS

1. *Leadership*

BUSCH, HENRY M. *Leadership in Group Work.* New York: Association Press, 1934.

A bibliography on leadership, psychology, and clubs is included.

HURT, HUBER W. *The Influencing of Character.* Hollywood, Fla.: The College Blue Book Co., 1934.

This book is useful to teachers and leaders of youth and in leadership training.

Standards of Training, Experience and Compensation in Community Recreation Work. New York: National Recreation Association.

Youth; Volunteers for Youth Recreation Programs. Civilian Defense Office, Item 959. Washington, D.C.: Government Printing Office, March, 1944.

The pamphlet was prepared in co-operation with church groups, group work and recreational agencies, and federal agencies concerned with youth. Suggestions for joint recruiting and training are given with a list of references.

2. *Community Recreation and Programs*

Annual Reports; may be obtained free from the following places:

Dept. of Playgrounds and Recreation, City Hall, Los Angeles, Cal.

Extension Dept., Milwaukee Public Schools, 1111 North Tenth St., Milwaukee, Wis.

Park and Recreation Commission, City Hall, Austin, Texas.

Park and Shade Tree Commission, Millburn, N.J.

Recreation Commission, City Hall, Mt. Vernon, N.Y.

Recreation Commission, 328 City Hall, Cincinnati, Ohio.

Recreation Dept., Municipal Bldg., Room 4, Roanoke, Va.

Recreation Division, Park Commission, 325 City Hall, Minneapolis, Minn.

THE ASSOCIATION FOR FAMILY LIVING, 209 S. State St., Chicago, Ill.

Pamphlets including the following are available from this source.

Art in Child Life
Art in the Daily Life of the Child
The Art of Leadership
Co-operative Play Groups in Seattle
Developing Attitudes in Children
Growing Edges in Family Life Education
Handbook on Play Schools for Leaders and Teachers
Home Play and Play Equipment for the Pre-school Child
How Communities Influence their Children

How to Lead a Discussion
Individual Adjustment through Group Activity
Mental Hygiene in Group Work
On Forming a Group
Play: A Yardstick of Growth
Play Materials Made from Waste
Programs One Way and Another
Radio—Problem and Privilege
Recreation and Living in the Modern World
Toys Children Like
What Motion Picture Means to the Child

ATWELL, E. T. *Recreation for Colored Citizens in the New Democracy*. Reprinted from *Recreation*, January, 1937, by the National Recreation Assn., New York.

BACCHUS, IRVING, "Hobbies for Defense," *Recreation*, March, 1942.
The hobbyist will find here some suggestions for promoting community services.

BALLARD, ALLEN B. "Education in the Boys' Club," *Southern Workman*, October, 1936.
A club of Negro boys in Philadelphia is especially described for its library, citizenship class, sex education, vocational guidance, recreation, case work with problem boys, and discipline.

Boy Scout Handbook. New York: Boy Scouts of America, 2 Park Ave.

BUTLER, GEORGE D. *Introduction to Community Recreation*. Prepared for the National Recreation Assn. New York: McGraw-Hill Book Co., 1940.

CASETY, M. Z. "Post-college Recreation; Syracuse University has a New Approach to Physical Education," *Recreation*, November, 1944.

DU BOIS, RACHEL DAVIS. *Get Together Americans*. New York: Harper & Brothers, 1943.

GAUDETTE, MARIE E. *Leader's Nature Guide*. New York: Girl Scouts, 155 E. 44th St., 1942.
This guide is for collecting, making equipment, planting, walking, and the study of rocks and stars.

Girl Scout Handbook—for the Intermediate Program. New York: National Headquarters, Girl Scouts Federation of Greater New York, 670 Lexington Ave. 1933. Copies may be purchased from the National Equipment Service, 14 W. 49th St., New York. Catalogue #20-101.

Handbook for Recreation Leaders. Bulletin 231. Washington, D.C.: Government Printing Office.
This manual suggests appropriate recreational activities for different age groups, and is recommended by the Children's Bureau.

HOLBROOK, SABRA. *Children Object*. New York: The Viking Press, 1943.

Children like to learn by doing. They like to get out and play baseball and not just read about it, and they like to see things for themselves. They like to know reasons for conforming to rules. Teachers and group leaders will find this book a helpful source.

MARSHALL, THOMAS O. *An Interview Study of the Adjustment and Withdrawals of New York State High Schools in Vocational, Citizenship and Leisure Time Activities.* Ed. D. Thesis, Harvard University, 1941.

MULAC, MARGARET E. *The Playleader's Manual.* New York: Harper & Brothers, 1941.

Some of the activities discussed in the manual are: games, tournaments, folk dances, quiet games, music, storytelling, dramatics, first aid, nature, crafts, stunts, puzzles, and party programs.

NATIONAL RECREATION ASSOCIATION, New York. This is an excellent source for pamphlets including the following:

Fundamentals in Community Recreation
Nineteen Recreation Principles
Why Playgrounds?

PENDRY, ELIZABETH R., AND HARTSHORNE, HUGH. *Organizations for Youth: Leisure Time and Character Building Procedures.* New York: McGraw-Hill Book Co., 1935.

Character building programs, national in scope, are explained in purpose and organization. The book is helpful to those directing youth in the use of their leisure.

POWELL, WARREN T., ED. *Recreation in Church and Community.* New York: The Abingdon-Cokesbury Press, 1938.

Recreation a Major Community Problem. New York: National Recreation Assn.

Recreation for Young People. Washington, D.C.: Government Printing Office, 1943.

The pamphlet describes a community program.

A Survey of the Character Building Agencies of Rochester, New York. Conducted for the Survey Committee of the Rochester Community Chest by Arthur Swift and Isabelle Howard, October, 1938.

A. ACTIVITIES

BURCHENAL, ELIZABETH. *Folk Dances and Singing Games.* New York: G. Schirmer, Inc., 3 E. 43rd St., 1933. Three volumes.

These volumes contain the music and illustrated instructions for 26 folk dances from England, Ireland, Scotland, Sweden, Norway, Denmark, Russia, Hungary, Italy, Bohemia, and other countries. There are other books on dances by the same author.

Church Music and the New Leisure. New York: National Recreation Assn.

STAPLES, FRANK A. *Arts and Crafts for the Recreation Leader.* New York: National Recreation Assn., 1943.

The 36 projects described include: finger painting, clay modeling, sawdust modeling, bookmaking, bookbinding, magic, kites, rhythm band, and other activities.

B. MIXED GROUPS

ADLER, L. AND J. "Recreation Glamourized! Juvenile House Canteen, New York City," *Recreation*, January, 1945.

BREEN, MARY J. *Partners in Play.* New York: A. S. Barnes & Co., 1936. This book makes a plea for closer companionship between young men and young women. Topics such as these are developed: leadership for mixed groups, dances, games, stunts, parties, hikes, water sports, snow and ice sports, arts and crafts, music, drama, discussion groups, and study clubs. The book is useful to teachers, deans, and group leaders.

LAKE, E. "Younger Set; Youth Centers are the Kids' Own Idea," *Reader's Digest*, September, 1944.

MEYER, HAROLD D. *Youth Recreation.* Chapel Hill, N.C.: North Carolina Recreation Committee.

SHREFFLER, MARGARET, AND CORWIN, GEORGE B. *Boys and Girls Together.* New York: The Woman's Press, 1944.

This is a Y. M. C. A.–Y. W. C. A. manual for co-operative planning among teen-age groups.

Teen-age Centers. New York: National Recreation Assn., 1944.

C. CAMPING

DAKIN, W. S. *Summary of Reports on Programs for Guidance of Children's Time During Summer Vacations.* Hartford, Conn.: State Dept. of Education.

This report suggests ways in which the school, home, and community agencies can co-operate in planning programs for the use of children's leisure time during the summer.

DIMOCK, HEDLEY S., AND HENDRY, CHARLES E. *Camping and Character.* New York: Association Press, 1939.

The author tells of a camping experiment in character education.

D. RURAL PROGRAMS

ARNOLD, ALFRED G. *Neighborhood Activities in Country Communities.* Extension Service, North Dakota Agricultural College.

HATCHER, O. LATHAM. *Guiding Rural Boys and Girls.* New York: McGraw-Hill Book Co., 1930.

There are many practical suggestions which make this book valuable to rural leaders.

KELIHER, ALICE, ED. *Farm Workers.* New York: Harper & Brothers, 1940.
This book gives a brief description of the role of the farmer in American life. Pictorial charts and excellent photographs enhance the book's usefulness.

THE OHIO STATE UNIVERSITY, Agricultural College Extension Service, Columbus 10, Ohio. This is a source of helpful pamphlets including:
Learning to Live Through Play
Beautifying the Home Grounds
Recreation for 4-H Clubs and Other Groups
Basketry
Choosing Book Friends

E. CONVALESCENTS AND THE HANDICAPPED

ILLINOIS SOCIETY FOR MENTAL HYGIENE, Chicago, Ill. A bibliography is available from this source, on recreation as mental therapy.

NICHOLS, F. F. "Hobbies in Miniature; Exhibition for Hospital Patients," *Hobbies*, December, 1944.

Recreation for Blind Children. Washington, D.C.: Children's Bureau.

TROWBRIDGE, CORNELIA R. *Feeling Better? Amusements and Occupations for Convalescents.* New York: Dodd, Mead & Co., 1936.
Interesting suggestions for invalids are described. Bibliography.

3. *Sources for Materials and Advice*

The Associated Publishers, 1538 Ninth St., N.W., Washington, D.C. Books on the Negro for elementary and high school include: history, literature, art, biography, drama, music, poetry; and the *Journal of Negro History.*

Boy Scouts of America, 2 Park Avenue, New York
Camp Fire Girls, 88 Lexington Ave., New York
Colleges and universities
Girl Scouts of America, 14 W. 49th Street, New York
Local public libraries
Local offices of public and private recreational agencies
National Association of Broadcasters, 535 Fifth Ave., New York
National Catholic Youth Council, 1312 Massachusetts Ave., N.W., Washington, D.C.
National Federation of Settlements, 147 Avenue B, New York
National Jewish Welfare Board, 145 E. 32nd St., New York
National Recreation Association, 315 Fourth Ave., New York. Materials on all recreational topics, such as the following, may be obtained at little or no cost; lists are available.
Activities of every description
Church recreation
Contests

Facilities, layouts, and equipment
Family fun
Home-made play and apparatus
Leadership
Organization and administration
Our neighbors to the south
Parks
Philosophy of recreation
Play equipment
Rural recreation
Social recreation
Swimming pool
Youth and youth centers
National Vocational Guidance Assn., 82 Beaver St., New York
Office of Defense Health and Welfare Services, Recreation Section,
Federal Security Agency, Washington, D.C.
Play Schools Association, 119 W. 57th Street, New York
Public schools
U. S. Dept. of Agriculture, Extension Service, Washington, D.C.
U. S. Dept. of Labor, Children's Bureau, Washington, D.C.
Young Men's Christian Association, 347 Madison Ave., New York
Young Women's Christian Association, 600 Lexington Ave., New York
Young Men's and Young Women's Hebrew Associations, 145 East
32nd St., New York

VI. THE YOUTH PROBLEM

The Defense of Children Series.
  *Children Bear the Promise of a Better World; Through Play They
  Learn What Freedom Means.* Bulletin 8.
  Protect Them from Harmful Community Inflences. Bulletin 11.
  Children's Bureau. Washington, D.C.: Government Printing Office.
  12 different bulletins are available.
McGILL, NETTIE P., AND MATTHEWS, ELLEN N. *The Youth of New
  York City.* New York: Macmillan Co., 1940.
MELVIN, BRUCE L. *Youth—Millions Too Many?* Foreword by Eleanor
  Roosevelt. New York: Associated Press, 1940.
  What youth is thinking and doing, how they are working and
  playing, are reported.
SCOTT, WALTER L. "A Teen Age Recreation Survey in Long Beach,"
  Recreation, February, 1944.
SUTHERLAND, ROBERT L. *Color, Class and Personality.* Prepared for the
  American Youth Commission, American Council on Education,
  Washington, D.C., 1942.

Teen Trouble and What Recreation Can Do About It. New York: National Recreation Assn., 1943.

THRASHER, FREDERIC M. *The Gang.* Chicago: University of Chicago Press, 1936.

What About Us? Federal Security Agency, Recreational Division, Community War Services Offices. Washington, D.C.: Government Printing Office.

This is a report of community recreation for young people.

WRENN, C. GILBERT, AND HARLEY, D. L. *Time on Their Hands*; a Report on Leisure, Recreation, and Young People. Prepared for the American Youth Commission, American Council on Education, Washington, D.C., 1941.

VII. DELINQUENCY PREVENTION

BROWN, SPENCER. *They See for Themselves.* New York: Harper & Brothers, 1945.

This book shows how students have discovered intercultural facts about the communities in which they live. Findings are dramatized in plays or the "living newspapers."

CHATFIELD, GEORGE H. *Report and Recommendations of the Joint Committee on Maladjustment and Delinquency*, Part IV. New York: Board of Education, January 1938.

MARSHALL, JAMES, AND MCCOOEY, MARGARET. *Report and Recommendations of the Joint Committee on Maladjustment and Delinquency*, Part V. New York: Board of Education, January, 1938.

MULHOLLAND, JAMES V. "Juvenile Delinquency and the Wartime Recreation Budget," *Recreation*, December, 1942.

The author, director of recreation in New York City's park department, says, "If play and recreation are to be regarded as luxuries and non-essentials we are bound to have an increase in juvenile delinquency."

Schools Against Delinquency; A Guide for New York Schools. Albany: State Education Department, 1944.

In the foreword Dr. George D. Stoddard says, "As school people, we accept willingly the challenge to combat delinquency. The modern school emphasizes the individual pupil in his relation to home, school and community. But there is much to be done, for many boys and girls are deprived of counseling when it is most crucial to their adjustment. Parents, too, increasingly must understand and cooperate with their children. In all these endeavors we welcome the support of the various branches of the state government." This program is being tried out in many areas of the state including the upper East Side in Manhattan.

TAFT, DONALD R. *Criminology*. New York: Macmillan Co., 1942.
The prevention of crime is discussed in an up-to-date manner in pages 634-682.

Understanding Juvenile Delinquency. Publication 300, Children's Bureau, U. S. Dept. of Labor, Washington, D.C.

"We Are the Youth," *Recreation*, December, 1943.
These statements on juvenile delinquency were prepared by a group of young people from schools of East St. Louis, Illinois.

YOUNG, PAULINE. *Social Treatment in Probation and Delinquency*. New York: McGraw-Hill Book Co., Inc., 1937.
The book pools varied experiences and tested techniques found valuable in several large communities in this country.

VIII. MAGAZINES FOR GROUP LEADERS[2]

The American Artist. New York: 330 W. 42nd St.

The Camping Magazine. Chicago, Ill.: 343 S. Dearborn St.

Country Dancer. New York: 15 E. 40th St.

Folk Dancer. Long Island: Box 201, Flushing Station.

Hobbies. Chicago 16, Ill.: Society of Philatelic American, 2810 S. Michigan Ave.

Junior Arts and Activities. Chicago, Ill.: 740 Rush St.

The Journal of Health and Physical Education. Washington, D.C.: American Assn. for Health, Physical Education, and Recreation.
This is the basic magazine for the physical education teacher.

Magazine of Art. Washington, D.C.: Barr Building, Farragut Square.

MARTIN, LAURA K. *List of Magazines for High Schools*. New York: H. W. Wilson Co., 1941.

Nature Magazine. Washington, D.C.: 1214 16th St., N.W.

Occupations. New York 5: New York Vocational Guidance Assn., 82 Beaver Street, Room 510.

The Parents' Magazine. New York: 9 E. 40th St.

Parks and Recreation. Rockford, Ill.: American Institute of Park Executives.

Popular Mechanics. Chicago, Ill.: 200 E. Ontario St.

Popular Science. New York: 353 Fourth Ave.

Recreation. New York: 315 Fourth Ave. March issues have an index of all the articles for the previous year.

Research Quarterly. Washington, D.C.: 1201 16th St., N.W.

School Activities. Topeka, Kan.: 1515 Lane St.

School Arts Magazine. Worcester, Mass.: Printers Building.

[2] This is a partial list of magazines compiled with the co-operation of the National Recreation Association.

⚛ Index ⚛